NEUTRALISM AND DISENGAGEMENT

 SCRIBNER
RESEARCH
ANTHOLOGIES

Martin Steinmann, Jr., GENERAL EDITOR

PAUL F. POWER
University of Cincinnati

NEUTRALISM AND DISENGAGEMENT

SCRIBNER
RESEARCH
ANTHOLOGIES

CHARLES SCRIBNER'S SONS   New York

To L.A.H.P.

Preface

Each Scribner Research Anthology is a collection of written sources upon a single historical, political, literary, or scientific topic or problem—the Hungarian Revolt, Shakespeare's *Julius Cæsar,* or extrasensory perception, for example. In addition to these sources, it contains (1) "Guide to Research," an account of the rationale and the methods of research and of research-paper writing, (2) an introduction to the topic of the anthology, (3) suggested topics for controlled research, and (4) suggested sources and topics for library research.

Each anthology is designed to serve two purposes. First, each gives the student access to important sources—texts, documents, letters, diaries, essays, articles, reports, transcripts of hearings, for instance—on a given topic. Some of these sources are otherwise available in only a few libraries, some (manuscripts and historical and government documents) in only one. In any case, the collection as a whole is not otherwise available in one volume. Second, each anthology gives the student either all his sources for a controlled-research paper or some of them for a library-research paper. Each anthology can be valuable either for readings in courses in history, literature, science, or humanities or as the basis for a research paper in these or in other courses.

A controlled-research paper—a paper in which the student's search for sources is limited to, and in certain ways controlled by, those sources contained in one anthology—is not so noble an undertaking as a library-research paper. But it is often more successful—more rewarding for the student and easier for his instructor to teach effectively and judge fairly. Its advantages for both student and instructor are often considerable.

For the student, it sometimes provides sources unavailable in his school library. And it enables him to learn a good deal about research (selection, interpretation, and evaluation of sources; quotation and paraphrase; and documentation) without prior instruction in use of the library (and, incidentally, without overtaxing the facilities and the resources of his library and without loss of, or damage to, sources either irreplaceable or difficult and expensive to replace).

For the instructor, it permits focus of class discussion upon a limited set of topics. It enables him to track down the student's sources conveniently. And—perhaps the greatest advantage of all—it enables him to judge both conveniently and exactly how well the student has selected, interpreted, and evaluated his sources and how well he has quoted and paraphrased them.

In many schools, a controlled-research paper is either a preliminary to or a part of a library-research paper. A library-research paper is probably the most difficult paper that the student can be assigned to write. The problems that confront him are not simply those common to any paper—organization, paragraphing, and transitions, for instance—and those (already mentioned) common to all research papers. He has, in addition, the problem of using the library well—of, for example, using the card catalogue, periodical indexes, and other reference works. But, if the instructor assigns a controlled-research paper as a preliminary to or, as it were, an early part of a library-research paper, the student need not come to grips with all these problems at once.

Each Scribner Research Anthology is compiled according to the following editorial principles. Each source that is not anonymous is prefaced by a biographical note on its author. At the foot of the same page is a bibliographical note. Each source is reprinted exactly as it appears in the original except for (1) some typographical peculiarities, (2) explanatory notes, given in brackets, and (3) omissions, indicated by ellipses (". . ."). And, finally, for each source that has pagination in the original, page numbers are given in brackets within the source itself—thus: "[**320/321**]," where everything before the slash (and after the preceding slash, if any) is from page 320, and everything after the slash (and before the next slash, if any) is from page 321. For a source hitherto unpublished, no page numbers are given; and the student who uses it should cite the page numbers of the Scribner Research Anthology. Footnotes to a source are given as in the original. Where the original pagination of a footnote is not evident, its page number precedes it in brackets.

MARTIN STEINMANN, JR.

Bingham Bay
Lake Gogebic
August, 1960

Foreword

On first seeing the Scribner Research Anthologies prepared for use in English courses, I at once realized that here was a teaching device equally useful in political science courses. Consequently, I take satisfaction and pride in pointing out the virtues of these controlled-research books to other teachers of political science.

We who teach political science generally require students to do a paper involving research. To some degree, we are all, as Professor Steinmann suggests, confronted with the problems of limited library resources, with students who are unprepared for difficult research projects, and with the difficulty of fairly grading papers based upon sources not conveniently available.

My own experience suggests that, when we assign research papers, we spend an inordinate amount of time with individual students answering questions about methods of research and research writing at the expense of discussion of the subject. Here we can with confidence refer the student to the "Guide to Research" for brief and detailed instructions on research and on writing papers and thus redress the balance and use precious conference time for discussion of the subject.

These anthologies may be employed effectively in another way. As we sweep through the subject matter of the beginning courses, our students often become interested in specific problems which they would like to explore more fully. Not yet knowledgeable in the ways of exploring the pros and cons of an issue, it is common for them to go to one easily available source and assume that they are getting full coverage. These anthologies can be used to demonstrate how one must go about researching a problem so that a number of points of view are examined. Toward that end, students could be required to read an anthology without writing a paper. Student understanding could be developed by classroom discussion and tested by oral reports and written examinations.

Third, these anthologies can be used as can any other supplementary book of readings on important and timely subjects in political science. Each anthology presents a balanced variety of views and lets the students draw their own conclusions, while preparing them to do superior work in selected topics requiring greater sophistication in research.

Although the topic of each volume is in political science, no volume assumes that the student has specialized knowledge of this science; and each volume may, therefore, be used in other courses—freshman English, for example.

HAROLD W. CHASE

University of Minnesota

Contents

Introduction

The purpose of this anthology is to acquaint students with the concepts of neutralism and disengagement as defined and interpreted by leading political figures during the Cold War. The influence of these concepts either as an outward part of a nation's foreign policy or as an internal current of opinion cannot be dismissed in a world where nations are easily categorized as either "free" or "Communist," and all are "engaged" in some undertaking. To aid the student in his reading of the selections, a few basic definitions are offered here, and the plan of the anthology is described.

It has become common practice to categorize policies of nonalignment under the term "neutralism" and those who employ or advocate such policies, "neutralists." Simple categorizing, however, does not reveal the diversities of these policies and their advocates. It is significant that most leaders of nations that are generally considered to be following a policy of "neutralism" use other terms to describe their policy. For example, leaders in India speak of "nonalignment"; in Ghana and the United Arab Republic, "positive neutrality"; and in Yugoslavia, "active co-existence."

In a broad sense "neutralism" describes the ambition of men or states to seek by political means and, if successful, to maintain by any means, an international position equidistant in political and military terms from the great powers. The development of new power centers, especially in Paris and Peking, complicates the neutralist ambition, but to date this development does not make its attainment impossible. The ambition may be strong or weak varying with national ideologies or interests, the preferences of leaders, and shifting world developments. The object of the neutralist ambition may be one's own state or a foreign state. The ambition may or may not actually result in strict impartiality. For, the neutralist position is sought without prejudice to the power and the right of the neutralist country to judge a myriad of issues, opening the way to opinions and even policies which may deny impartiality in the Cold War. This possible denial of impartiality is distinguishable from coincidental agreement of a neutralist with a great power, for example, India with Russia on anti-colonialism.

Although the term "neutralism" is generally applied to the outward foreign policy of many former colonial (now developing) nations, it should be remembered that neutralism is also found in the developed countries. Here it does not directly affect foreign policy as it does in many nations of Africa and Asia. Neutralist currents have, however, influenced and continue to influence the governments of Canada, France, Italy, and Japan.

"Neutralism" has significant relationships with disengagement. The latter concept refers to a proposed or actual withdrawal of a state from a political and military commitment or involvement. In a historical setting "disengagement" often refers to proposals to reduce or eliminate foreign or indigenous military forces in Central and Eastern Europe. The expanded Rapacki Plan, included in this anthology, and Denis Healey's "A Neutral Belt in Europe?" are two such proposals. "Disengagement" may also refer to proposals for nuclear free zones that forbid the stationing or the use of nuclear weapons in Europe or elsewhere. Disengagement is seldom discussed apart from arms control and the political conditions making arms control possible or arising from it. Pursuit of disengagement may result in the adoption of a policy of neutralism. The neutralist country is likely to have achieved disengagement. Neutralism and disengagement feed each other, especially at psychological and intellectual levels.

Students may ask why selections on certain traditionally neutral nations are not included in this anthology. The answer is that the policy to which these nations are committed, called "legal neutrality," tends to be static and passive while neutralism tends to be dynamic and active. Legal neutrality often supports the international status quo; neutralism is revisionist. Legal neutrality makes an implicit or explicit promise to be nonbelligerent in wartime; neutralism makes no such promise. Because the concern of this anthology is with those nations whose expressions of neutralism are variable, it does not deal with the legal neutrality of Ireland, Sweden, and Switzerland; the Russian-imposed neutrality of Finland; the countries which were neutralized under great power sponsorship in the Cold War—Austria and Laos; or the efforts, for example, of Charles de Gaulle, to have the major states neutralize former French Indo-china.

The selections that follow are divided into four sections. The first two sections contain testimonies for neutralism; the last two, evaluations of it. Testimonies differ from evaluations in that the former, unlike the latter, present and describe current examples of neutralist policy as found in different countries.

The first section offers testimonies for neutralism and general aspirations, chiefly by spokesmen for the uncommitted states. This group of nations has received extensive publicity in recent years, as each year more developing nations become members of the United Nations. With increasing self-confidence and diplomatic experience, their total strength and influence in the international community increases. In what manner and to what degree this new influence will affect the balance of power in world politics is a provocative question.

The second section offers testimonies for neutralism and disengagement by commentators of the advanced nations, including Poland, France, Russia, Great Britain, the United States, Japan, and Communist China. These statements demonstrate a wide variety of meanings and interpretations of "neutralism" and "disengagement."

The third section offers evaluations of neutralism in the developing nations from commentators of the developing and developed nations. In some cases the selections focus on one particular geographical area, as in Arnold Rivkin's "A View of United States Policy in Africa." In other cases, as in "President Eisenhower's Views on Neutrality," they are broad commentaries on neutralism in the mid-twentieth century.

The fourth section offers evaluations of neutralism and disengagement in the developed nations by commentators of these nations. Among the selections are a comment on neutralist sentiments in Western Europe following the world wars, a statement on disengagement and NATO, and a declaration from members of the Warsaw Pact.

When reading the selections in this anthology, the student should be constantly aware of the diverse definitions accorded "neutralism" and "disengagement." It would be wise for him to refer to the basic definitions given earlier in this "Introduction."

In keeping with the purposes of the series to which this anthology belongs, the readings are offered without editorial interpretation, but with suggested topics for controlled and library research.

Helpful information on various points came from Margaret L. Bates, Howard L. Boorman, Robert V. Daniels, Dieter Dux, and Walter O. Filley, Jr. In securing materials and related matters, Jane Bertenshaw and Laszlo Velics aided in several ways. Two translations were made expressly for this book: Iliya F. Harik translated from the Arabic part of Clovis Maqsud, *The Meaning of Positive Neutrality*, and J.A.A. Stockwin translated from the Japanese portions of Sato Noboru, "Socialism and Neutrality."

PART ONE

TESTIMONY—NEUTRALISM IN THE DEVELOPING NATIONS

An Independent Policy*

JAWAHARLAL NEHRU (1889-1964) was prime minister and foreign minister of India from independence in 1947 until his death. Dedicated to Indian nationalism since the 1920's, he was influenced by liberal, Marxist, and Gandhian ideas. His power in India and his respected position among the emerging nations made him an international figure. This selection is based on a speech made in the Constituent Assembly on December 4, 1947.

. . . .
We have proclaimed during this past year that we will not attach ourselves to any particular group. That has nothing to do with neutrality or passivity or anything else. If there is a big war, there is no particular reason why we should jump into it. Nevertheless, it is a little difficult nowadays in world wars to be neutral. Any person with any knowledge of international affairs knows that. The point is not what will happen when there is a war. Are we going to proclaim to the world, taking the advice of Maulana Hasrat Mohani, that when war comes, we stand by Russia? Is that his idea of foreign policy or any policy? That shows to me an amazing ignorance of how foreign affairs can be conducted. We are not going to join a war if we can help it; and we are going to join the side which is to our interest when the time comes to make the choice. There the matter ends.

But talking about foreign policies, the House must remember that these are not just empty struggles on a chess-board. Behind them lie all manner of things. Ultimately, foreign policy is the outcome of economic policy, and until India has properly evolved her economic policy, her foreign policy will be rather vague, rather inchoate, and will be groping. It is well for us to say that we stand for peace and freedom and yet that does not convey much to anybody, except a pious hope. We do stand for peace and freedom. I think there is something to be said for it. There is some meaning when we say that we stand for the freedom of Asian countries and for the elimination of imperialistic control over them. There is some meaning in that. [24/25]

Undoubtedly it has some substance, but a vague statement that we stand for peace and freedom by itself has no particular meaning, because every country is prepared to say the same thing, whether it means it or not. What then do we stand for? Well, you have to develop this argument in the economic field. As it happens today, in spite of the fact that we have been for some time in authority as a government, I regret that we have not produced any constructive economic scheme or economic policy so far. Again my excuse is that we have been going through such amazing times which have taken up all our energy and attention that it was difficult to do so. Nevertheless, we shall have to do so and when we do so, that will govern our foreign policy more than all the speeches in this House.

We have sought to avoid foreign entanglements by not joining one bloc or

* Jawaharlal Nehru, from "An Independent Policy," India's Foreign Policy (New Delhi: Government of India, 1961), pp. 24-27.

5

the other. The natural result has been
that neither of these big blocs looks on
us with favour. They think that we are
undependable, because we cannot be
made to vote this way or that way.

Last year when our delegation went to
the United Nations, it was the first time
that a more or less independent delegation went from India. It was looked at
a little askance. They did not know what
it was going to do. When they found that
we acted according to our own will, they
did not like it. We were unpopular last
year at the United Nations. I do not mean
individually, but in regard to our policy.
They could not quite make out what we
were or what we were aiming at. There
was a suspicion in the minds of the first
group that we were really allied to the
other group in secret though we were
trying to hide the fact, and the other
group thought that we were allied to
the first group in secret though we were
trying to hide the fact.

This year there was a slight change in
this attitude. We did many things which
both the groups disliked, but the comprehension came to them that we were
not really allied to either group, that we
were trying to act according to our own
lights and according to the merits of the
dispute as they seemed to us. They did
not like that, of course, because the position today is that there is so much passion
and so much fear and suspicion of each
other between these great rival powers
and groups that anybody who is not with
them is considered against them. So they
did not like what we did in many in-
stances; nevertheless, they respected us
much more, because they realized that we
had an independent policy, that we were
not going to be dragooned this way or
that, that we might make a mistake just
like anyone else, nevertheless, we were
going to stick to our own policy and programme, so that while possibly we irri-
tated some of our friends even a little
more than last year, we got on **[25/26]**
much better with everybody, because they

understood that we did stand for something.

To give the House an instance of how
we acted, take the Palestine affair which
has given rise and will give rise to a great
deal of trouble. We took up a certain
attitude in regard to it which was roughly
a federal State with autonomous parts.
It was opposed to both the other attitudes
which were before the United Nations.
One was partition which has now been
adopted; the other was a unitary State.
We suggested a federal State with, naturally, an Arab majority in charge of the
federal State but with autonomy for the
other regions—Jewish regions.

After a great deal of thought we decided that this was not only a fair and
equitable solution of the problem, but
the only real solution of the problem.
Any other solution would have meant
fighting and conflict. Nevertheless, our
solution—which, as the House will remember, was the solution given in the
minority report of the Palestine Committee—did not find favour with most
people in the United Nations. Some of
the major powers were out for partition;
they, therefore, pressed for it and ultimately got it. Others were so keen on the
unitary State idea and were so sure of
preventing partition at any rate or preventing a two-thirds majority in favour
of partition that they did not accept our
suggestion.

When during the last few days somehow partition suddenly became inevitable
and votes veered round to it, owing to the
pressure of some of the great powers, it
was realized that the Indian solution was
probably the best and an attempt was
made in the last 48 hours to bring forward the Indian solution, not by us but
by those who had wanted a unitary State.
It was then too late. There were proce-
dural difficulties and many of the persons
who might have accepted this solution
had already pledged themselves to partition. And so ultimately partition was decided upon by a two-thirds majority, with

a large number abstaining from voting, with the result that there is trouble in the Middle East now and the possibility of a great deal of trouble in the future.

I point this out to the House as an instance, that in spite of considerable difficulty and being told by many of our friends on either side that we must line up this way or that, we refused to do so, and I have no doubt that the position we had taken was the right one and I still have no doubt that it would have brought about the best solution.

This applies to many other things. But inevitably it means that to some extent we have to plough a lonely furrow in the United Nations and at international conferences of this type. Nonetheless, that is the only honourable and right position for us to take and I am quite sure that by adopting that position, we shall ultimately [**26/27**] gain in national and international prestige, that is to say, when we take a long view of the situation, not a short view of getting immediately a vote here or there.

I have no doubt that fairly soon, in the course of two or three years, the world will find this attitude justified and that India will not only be respected by the major protagonists in the struggle for power, but a large number of the smaller nations which today are rather helpless will probably look to India more than to other countries for a lead in such matters.

. . . .

[The Five Principles of Peaceful Coexistence]*

> **PANCH SHILA** or the "Five Principles of Peaceful Coexistence" may be traced to the five principles of righteous living in Buddhism. The "co-existence" aspect of *Panch Shila* may be traced to Leninism. In the Cold War, however, the original source is the Tibetan trade pact of 1954 between China and India, excerpted below. In the same year the Indian historian K. M. Panikkar first called the principles "*Panch Shila.*" The principles subsequently found their way into declarations and treaties among nonaligned states and between them and Communist states.

The Government of the Republic of India and the Central People's Government of the People's Republic of China.

Being desirous of promoting trade and cultural intercourse between Tibet Region of China and India and of facilitating pilgrimage and travel by the peoples of China and India.

Have resolved to enter into the present Agreement based on the following principles:

(1) mutual respect for each other's territorial integrity and sovereignty,
(2) mutual non-aggression,
(3) mutual non-interference in each other's internal affairs,
(4) equality and mutual benefit, and
(5) peaceful co-existence. [98]

. . . .

* From "Agreement Between the Republic of India and the People's Republic of China on Trade and Intercourse Between Tibet Region of China and India," *Notes, Memoranda and Letters Exchanged and Agreements Signed Between the Governments of India and China: 1954-1959, White Paper* (New Delhi: Ministry of External Affairs, Government of India, 1960), p. 98.

Final Communique of Asian-African Conference*

THE ASIAN-AFRICAN CONFERENCE, convened by the Governments of Burma, Ceylon, India, Indonesia, and Pakistan, met in Bandung, Indonesia, April 18-24, 1955. In addition to the sponsoring countries, the following twenty-four nations participated in the conference: Afghanistan, Cambodia, People's Republic of China, Egypt, Ethiopia, the Gold Coast, Iran, Iraq, Japan, Jordan, Laos, Lebanon, Liberia, Libya, Nepal, the Philippines, Saudi Arabia, Sudan, Syria, Thailand, Turkey, the Democratic Republic of Vietnam, the State of Vietnam, and Yemen. The attendance of Chou En-lai, of Communist China, was a leading feature of the conference, which included committed as well as nonaligned states.

. . . .
The Asian-African conference considered the position of Asia and Africa and discussed ways and means by which their peoples could achieve the fullest economic[,] cultural and political cooperation.

A. ECONOMIC COOPERATION

1. The Asian-African conference recognized the urgency of promoting economic development in the Asian-African region. There was general desire for economic cooperation among the participating countries on the basis of mutual interest and respect for national sovereignty. The proposals with regard to economic cooperation within the participating countries do not preclude either the desirability or the need for cooperation with countries outside the region, including the investment of foreign capital. It was further recognized that assistance being received by certain participating countries from outside the region through international or under bilateral arrangements had made a valuable contribution to the implementation of their development programs.

2. The participating countries agree to provide technical assistance to one another, to the maximum extent practicable, in the form of:

Experts, trainees, pilot projects, and equipment for demonstration purposes;

Exchange of know-how, and establishment of national—and where possible—regional training and research institutes for imparting technical knowledge and skills in cooperation with the existing international agencies.

3. The Asian-African conference recommended:

The early establishment of a special United Nations fund for economic development;

The allocation by the International Bank for Reconstruction and Development of a greater part of its resources to Asian-African countries;

The early establishment of an international finance corporation, which should include in its activities the undertaking of equity investment; and

Encouragement of the promotion of joint ventures among Asian-African coun-

* From "Final Communique of Asian-African Conference," *Selected Documents of the Bandung Conference* (New York: Institute of Pacific Relations, 1955), pp. 29-30, 32-35. Reprinted with the permission of the Institute of Pacific Relations.

tries in so far as this will promote their common interest. **[29/30]**

4. The Asian-African conference recognized the vital need for stabilizing commodity trade in the region.

The principle of enlarging the scope of multilateral trade and payments was accepted. However, it was recognized that some countries would have to take recourse to bilateral trade arrangements in view of their prevailing economic conditions.

5. The Asian-African conference recommended that collective action be taken by participating countries for stabilizing international prices of and demand for primary commodities through bilateral and multilateral arrangements, and that as far as practical and desirable they should adopt a unified approach on the subject in the United Nations Permanent Advisory Commission on International Commodity Trade and other international forums.

6. The Asian-African conference further recommended:

Asian-African countries should diversify their export trade by processing their raw materials whenever economically feasible before export; intra-regional trade fairs should be promoted and encouragement be given to the exchange of trade delegations and groups of businessmen; exchange of information and of samples should be encouraged with a view to promoting intra-regional trade; and normal facilities should be provided for the transit trade of landlocked countries. **[30/32]**

. . . .

C. HUMAN RIGHTS AND SELF-DETERMINATION

1. The Asian-African conference declared its full support of the fundamental principles of human rights as set forth in the Charter of the United Nations and took note of the Universal Declaration of Human Rights as a common standard of achievement for all peoples and all nations.

The conference declared its full support of the principle of self-determination of peoples and nations as set forth in the Charter of the United Nations and took note of the United Nations resolutions on the right of peoples and nations to self-determination, which is a prerequisite of the full enjoyment of all fundamental human rights.

2. The Asian-African conference deplored the policies and practices of racial segregation and discrimination which form the basis of government and human relations in large regions of Africa and in other parts of the world.

Such conduct is not only a gross violation of human rights but also a denial of the fundamental values of civilization and the dignity of man. **[32/33]**

The conference extended its warm sympathy and support for the courageous stand taken by the victims of racial discrimination, especially by the peoples of African and Indian and Pakistani origin in South Africa; applauded all those who sustained their cause; reaffirmed the determination of Asian-African peoples to eradicate every trace of racialism that might exist in their own countries; and pledged to use its full moral influence to guard against the danger of falling victims of the same evil in their struggle to eradicate it.

3. In view of the existing tension in the Middle East caused by the situation in Palestine and the danger of that tension to world peace, the Asian-African conference declared its support of the rights of the Arab people of Palestine and called for the implementation of the United Nations resolutions on Palestine and of the peaceful settlement of the Palestine question.

D. PROBLEMS OF DEPENDENT PEOPLE

1. The Asian-African conference, in the context of its expressed attitude on the

abolition of colonialism, supported the position of Indonesia in the case of West Irian [Dutch New Guinea] on the relevant agreements between Indonesia and the Netherlands.

The Asian-African conference urged the Netherlands Government to reopen negotiations as soon as possible to implement their obligations under the abovementioned agreements and expressed the earnest hope that the United Nations could assist the parties concerned in finding a peaceful solution to the dispute.

2. In view of the unsettled situation in North Africa and of the persisting denial to the peoples of North Africa of their right to self-determination, the Asian-African conference declared its support of the rights of the people of Algeria, Morocco and Tunisia to self-determination and independence and urged the French Government to bring about a peaceful settlement of the issue without delay.

E. PROMOTION OF WORLD PEACE AND COOPERATION

1. The Asian-African conference, taking note of the fact that several states have still not been admitted to the United Nations, considered that for effective cooperation for world peace membership in the United Nations should be universal, called on the Security Council to support the admission of all those states which are qualified for membership in terms of the Charter.

In the opinion of the Asian-African conference the following countries which were represented in it—Cambodia, Ceylon, Japan, Jordan, Laos, Libya, Nepal and unified Vietnam—were so qualified.

The conference considered that the representation of the countries of the Asian-African region of the Security Council in relation to the principle of equitable geographical distribution was inadequate.

It expressed the view that as regards the distribution of the nonpermanent seats, the Asian-African countries which, under the arrangement arrived at in London in 1946, are precluded from being elected, should be enabled to serve on the Security Council so that they might make a more effective contribution to the maintenance of international peace and security. [33/34]

2. The Asian-African conference having considered the dangerous situation of international tension existing and the risks confronting the whole human race from the outbreak of global war in which the destructive power of all types of armaments including nuclear and thermonuclear weapons would be employed, invited the attention of all nations to the terrible consequences that would follow if such a war were to break out.

The conference considered that disarmament and the prohibition of production, experimentation and use of nuclear and thermonuclear weapons of war are imperative to save mankind and civilization [sic] from the fear and prospect of wholesale destruction.

It considered that the nations of Asia and Africa assembled here have a duty toward humanity and civilization to proclaim their support for the prohibition of these weapons and to appeal to nations principally concerned and to world opinion to bring about such disarmament and prohibition.

The conference considered that effective international control should be established and maintained to implement such prohibition and that speedy and determined efforts should be made to this end. Pending the total prohibition of the manufacture of nuclear and thermonuclear weapons, this conference appealed to all the powers concerned to reach agreement to suspend experiments with such weapons.

The conference declared that universal disarmament is an absolute necessity for the preservation of peace and requested the United Nations to continue its efforts and appealed to all concerned speedily to bring about the regulation, limitation, control and reduction of all armed forces and armaments including the prohibition of the production, experimentation and use of all weapons of mass destruction and to establish effective international control to this end.

3. The Asian-African conference supported the position of the Yemen in the case of Aden and the southern parts of Yemen known as the protectorates and urged the parties concerned to arrive at a peaceful settlement of the dispute.

F. DECLARATION OF PROBLEMS OF DEPENDENT PEOPLES

The Asian-African conference discussed the problems of dependent peoples and colonialism and the evils arising from the subject to what is stated in the following paragraph, the conference is agreed:

1. In declaring that colonialism in all its manifestations is an evil which should speedily be brought to an end;

2. In affirming that the subjection of peoples to alien subjugation, domination and exploitation constitute a denial of fundamental human rights is contrary to the Charter of the United Nations and is an impediment to the promotion of world peace and cooperation;

3. In declaring its support of the cause of freedom and independence for all such peoples; and

4. In calling upon the powers concerned to grant freedom and independence to such peoples.

G. DECLARATION OF PROMOTION OF WORLD PEACE AND COOPERATION

The Asian-African conference gave anxious thought to the question of world peace and cooperation. It viewed with deep concern the present state of international tension with its danger of an atomic world war. [**34/35**]

The problem of peace is correlative with the problem of international security. In this connection all states should cooperate especially through the United Nations in bringing about the reduction of armaments and the elimination of nuclear weapons under effective international control.

In this way international peace can be promoted and nuclear energy may be used exclusively for peaceful purposes. This would help answer the needs, particularly of Asia and Africa, for what they urgently require are social progress and better standards of life in larger freedom.

Freedom and peace are interdependent. The right of self-determination must be enjoyed by all peoples and freedom and independence must be granted with the least possible delay to those who are still dependent peoples.

Indeed all nations should have the right freely to choose their own political and economic systems and their own way of life in conformity with the purposes and principles of the Charter of the United Nations.

Free from distrust and fear and with confidence and good will toward each other, nations should practice tolerance and live together in peace with one another as good neighbors and develop friendly cooperation on the basis of the following principles:

1. Respect for the fundamental human rights and for the purposes and principles of the charter of the United Nations.

2. Respect for the sovereignty and territorial integrity of all nations.

3. Recognition of the equality of all races and of the equality of all nations, large and small.

4. Abstention from intervention or interference in the internal affairs of another country.

5. Respect for the right of each nation to defend itself singly or collectively in conformity with the charter of the United Nations.

6A. Abstention from the use of arrangements of collective defense to serve the particular interests of any of the big powers.

6B. Abstention by any country from exerting pressures on other countries.

7. Refraining from acts or threats of aggression or the use of force against the territorial integrity or political independence of any country.

8. Settlement of all international disputes by peaceful means such as negotiation, conciliation, arbitration or judicial settlement, as well as other peaceful means of the parties' own choice in conformity with the Charter of the United Nations.

9. Promotion of mutual interest and cooperation.

10. Respect for justice and international obligations.

The Asian-African conference declares its conviction that friendly cooperation in accordance with these principles would effectively contribute to the maintenance and promotion of international peace and security while cooperation in the economic, social and cultural fields would help bring about the common prosperity and well-being of all.

The Asian-African conference recommended that the five sponsoring countries should consider the next meeting of the conference in consultation with other countries concerned.

The Story of Arab Positive Neutralism*

CLOVIS MAQSUD (1926-   ) is the representative of the Arab League for India and Southeast Asia. A lawyer, born in Lebanon, he received his education in Beirut and the West. He is the author of several books on Arab socialism.

The realization of Arab nationalist goals like unity and freedom is firmly connected with reducing international tension and creating an atmosphere favorable for the progress of international relations in a natural and sound way. It is necessary, therefore, for the Arab nationalist movement to find a practical formula whereby it can participate seriously and effectively in international affairs. To be a realistic one, the required formula must be strongly related to the objective world and to the historical and political circumstances through which the Arab nation is now passing. It also has to take cognizance of the real demands and objectives which the people have been working for and are seeking to realize. [100/101]

. . . .

Nationalist objectives by themselves are not ultimate goals; they are rather preparatory means for strengthening the foundations of the new Arab society which is committed to happiness and equality in socialism. The formula which the Arab nationalist movement has discovered through serious search is positive neutralism.

Positive neutralism thus is the law directing the Arab nationalist movement in the international field so as to secure a favorable atmosphere for the realization of its national goals and aspirations. Here it becomes clear that positive neutralism is neither a principle nor an ideology, but a specific policy expressing a principle and a definite ideological commitment. Being no more than a particular policy, positive neutralism is therefore a passing phase which should last as long as do the facts of the international and Arab situations on which it rests. The fact that positive neutralism is only a passing phase does not mean that Arab nationalist commitment to it is temporary, but rather that any fundamental change in international relations should inevitably result in a basic change in our position toward these new international developments. This means that positive neutralism will not let our international policy remain inflexible within the grip of its frame. But in this momentous period through which the Arabs are passing, the policy of positive neutralism is the sound expression and the only salutary means to support our international position and international peace, conducive as it is to the good of our homeland and people. [101/102] The formula of positive neutralism did not, however, crystalize overnight. It was not attached to the goals of the national movement in a mechanical fashion, nor was it adopted spontaneously or improvisedly. The integration of the policy of positive neutralism into the nationalist movement has a long story of struggle and hardships.

* Clovis Maqsud, from "The Story of Arab Positive Neutralism," The Meaning of Positive Neutrality (Beirut: Dar al 'Illm lil-Malayin, 1960), pp. 100-112. This selection was translated from the Arabic especially for this anthology by Iliya F. Harik. Reprinted by permission of Clovis Maqsud.

The Arab fiasco in Palestine [Israel's 1948 defeat of Arab armies] was one of the main factors which hastened the process of bringing the Arab masses to realize the necessity of defining slogans clearly, instead of merely declaring these slogans without realizing what they mean. As the foundations for a wholesome popular leadership had not then been fully developed, the movement acquiesced to follow traditional leadership. Traditional leaders used slogans like unity and independence, for instance, without really believing in them or in their salutary consequences, and thus they misled the masses. One of the consequences of this deception was the great tragedy of Palestine. The Arab setback in Palestine was a turning point in our history and was followed by a period in which an urgent desire was manifested for revision of the nationalist movement platform, its leadership, organization and aspirations. The Palestine fiasco was sufficient to separate traditional leaders from the masses and to deprive them of the peoples' confidence, but it was not enough by itself to remove traditional leaders from the power positions they wielded, for the opposing popular [102/103] leadership had not itself been fully developed ideologically and organizationally. It was during this chasm between the traditional leaders and the people, on the one hand, and the ineptitude of the new leadership, on the other, that the military coups d'etat took place in Syria and Egypt, then in Iraq, in an attempt to fill the gap. Some of these coups found their way to success, others did not.

In this atmosphere of restlessness it was realized that the nationalist movement would have to deepen the understanding of its objectives and put the progressive elements at the head of the popular forces. As a result of this increasing consciousness, the true meaning of unity took a turn toward clarity in the nationalist movement. The concept of unity has ceased to stand for ostentatious signs of fraudulent Arab brotherhood and the

augmentations of inherent contradictions in Arab society. . . . It has come now to mean the unity of popular struggle for the unification of the divided nation in one national whole. This deeper sense of unity in turn has resulted in a new and dynamic meaning of independence. Independence is no longer limited to the legal status of sovereignty for an Arab state or for a special Arab region, but also the spirit of persistence to hold the right of initiative in making policy choices in the international field with complete freedom and in accordance with the interest of the Arab nation and international peace.

The Arab masses' increasing consciousness of their national goals strengthened the immunity of these masses against being swept away by opportunistic forces which utilize acceptable slogans without [103/104] being really committed to them. This immunity characterizing the Arab people was the great moral force that made of the policy of positive neutralism an original national reality and also an international fact, worthy of notice. The response of the Arab peoples to the general features of the plan of positive neutralism makes it necessary to define this policy, for it should not be understood that positive neutralism is just another slogan based on our firm desire for independence and sovereignty. It should rather be known to everybody that the policy of positive neutralism is well studied from all aspects and has its own bases, some of which are constant and others dynamic. It should also be understood that this policy is our means for realizing our aspiration as a people and a nation.

Certain Arab ideological groups started after 1948 to seek some solutions for the ills of their society and to search for a clear international policy which would speed up the process of putting these solutions into effect. It was clear to these ideological groups that salvation for the nation would not come through the capitalistic system or the imperialist bloc which rests on it, nor would it come through the opposite force, namely the communist bloc and its system. [104/105]

. . . .

But it was also clear that the decision to stand apart from both blocs is a negative attitude in itself, although it springs from positive values and commitments. The decision would also remain inadequate if it were not coupled with an effort to analyze the causes of our rejection of both systems and blocs, and with a clear statement of the formula which we would like to see. Although the positive aspects of any policy or philosophy cannot be put readily into relief, either briefly or in detail, their positive features nevertheless come out through the analysis of their negative form.

Much of the foundations of positive neutralism policy has become clear in the process of searching for the causes which made the Arab national movement reject the policy of alignment with both East and West. Arab rejection of alignment with the West was not at first due to a conscious grasp of the meaning of capitalism as a system of the cultural values of the West. It was rather spontaneous, constituting a natural reaction to the hegemony and imperialism which characterized Western relations with our part of the world. It was also a reaction against the exploitation of the Arab's potential to produce and grow, a policy which aimed at our impoverishment, in spite of the fact that it came with technical and financial assistance. . . . The new Arab leadership's rejection of the imperialistic West was the result of the direct clash, sometimes sanguine, between the Arab national movement and the West as a bloc. [105/106]

. . . .

Western attitudes in relation to Arab issues, in general, made clear to us that imperialistic policy in the West is not and cannot be completely separated from its socio-economic establishments and organizations in which lie the foundations of political hegemony and influence. With Arab awareness of the connections be-

tween imperialism and its main sources, the negative commitment toward capitalism and its ramifications took the form of a life commitment as well as an intellectual one.

Since the Soviet Union and its allies stood at the opposite pole from the West with respect to ideology and political organization, and because there was no direct or indirect clash between the Arabs and the Soviets, the latter posed as an attractive model for study and learning. It was inevitable also that the study should be brief due to the absence [106/107] of any research facilities for accurate and objective analysis. Our first serious interest as a movement—not as individuals—in the Soviet Union and in communism came at the era of complete Stalinist domination in international communism. The attitude of the Soviet Union in the United Nations toward the plan for the division of Palestine sowed the first seeds of disillusionment with the Soviet Union in the Arab nationalist movement. We also discovered that in Yugoslavia the desire of that young state to enjoy full independence was met by violent reaction from the Soviet Union, in spite of the fact that Yugoslavia had a communist system. This attitude of the Soviet Union clearly pointed out to us that the Soviets do not respect the independence of their allies and that they intend to deprive them of their rights of free policy choices in international issues. The interference of the Soviet troops in Berlin during a labor strike [sic] there, moved us further away from the Soviet Union on the international level. The validity of our decision to distinguish between cultivating friendly relations with the Soviet Union and having to become one with it was proved during consecutive events which took place in Hungary, Poland and Tibet. It became clear to us that the attitude of the Soviet Union toward its allies stems from the nature of the communist system which defines the kind of orientation given to the economic and political structure of the country. With the realization of this connection between the system and the policy, our stand in regard to communism as a social order took a form similar to that of our stand toward the Soviet Union. But this aloof attitude which developed into [107/108] one of rejection did not mean hostility to the Soviet Bloc or the communist order.

Were we to bow to the idea that the world is irretrievably divided into separate camps, the [Arab] nationalist movement's rejection of the policy of alignment would have led to an isolationist position. From this negative attitude a positive will was born, and took shape first in the formation of a third force or a third bloc, the purpose of which was to reject the existing division of the world in two competing camps. It was also meant to reject the necessity of such division and the inevitability of having to join one camp or the other. In groping through our state of restlessness for a positive policy, the concept of the third force emerged. Soon afterwards the Arabs discovered that the liberated Asian and African countries were, like them, committed to the same negative stand. They also discovered that the liberation of these countries from [the] Western yoke did not mean that they wanted to become Soviet satellites. The rejection of capitalism as well as communism . . . and the genuine desire to create a new society which would guarantee to the people the conditions of dignified life, made the nationalist movements in these countries move in the direction of socialist orientations, orientations which themselves differed markedly in their conceptions of socialism. It is our opinion that the logic of historical evolution in Afro-Asian countries and the objective conditions of their situations made the marriage between socialism and nationalism inevitable. The struggle for socialism led the nationalist movements [108/109] to try to isolate the political forces which were strongly tied to the international blocs in their orientations, namely the supporters of the West and the communist parties. For socialism to march to success

and self-realization after it joined forces with the nationalist forces, it was necessary for it to steer away from the negative attitude toward a positive one on the international level. Here the concept of positive neutralism emerged very clearly and powerfully as the formula for policy in international affairs.

It is important to point out here that there are several differences between the old concept of neutrality and that of positive neutralism. The concept of neutrality in the doctrine of positive neutralism is commensurate to a stand of non-commitment towards both camps. Neutrality thus amounts to a simple policy of rejection and consequently fails to represent fully the reality of the Arab nationalist movement and the reality of similar Afro-Asian movements. Neutrality shorn of a positive outlook, as we have seen in previous chapters, takes many forms none of which is consistent with the special interests of Arab nationalism, which is completely tied to international peace. We have previously seen that positive neutralism does not mean, for instance, "neutrality in wartime." This concept is no longer consistent with the kind of arms which can be used in a future war. For it is one of the characteristics of nuclear weapons that their effectiveness goes beyond national frontiers, a fact which makes such neutrality irrelevant. [109/110] Nor does positive neutralism mean withdrawal from international struggle. This would be an escapist attitude, harmful both to Arab interests and those of international peace. It is also an unrealistic stand, for the nature of international relations and the huge interests of the two blocs would make it impossible for other regions to stay neutral, even if they wish to stay out or withdraw from the conflict. Nor does positive neutralism mean perpetual neutrality, like that observed in Switzerland as a requisite for national existence. In spite of its potentialities for continuity and its positive contributions in humanistic fields, Swiss neutrality is consistent only with the interests of a small state which is unaffected by international tension and does not seek to introduce basic changes in its social order. Positive neutralism is not neutralization, namely the agreement of both blocs to keep a state neutral, as is, for instance, the case with Austria. Such a neutral status arrests all initiative in the neutralized state and deprives it of its natural effectiveness and independent power to make free policy changes. Besides, such neutrality is wholly dependent on the continuation of the neutrality pact between the powers which are parties to it. We have also indicated that this kind of neutrality may be suitable under special international conditions and might be preferred in greatly sensitive areas where a situation has reached a point of no return. A situation like this might develop in Germany in case an agreement should be reached between the two blocs. Then we explained that positive neutralism does not mean an equidistant position between the two blocs in the event of outbreak of hostilities, i.e. it does not mean [110/111] neutrality of the middle way, though a position like this has some advantages. For a state which adopts such a policy may be able to play the role of a mediator or arbitrator in times of crisis. But this policy of neutrality does not contribute positively in the vicissitudes of international conflict. It cannot prevent the generation of crisis or try to create an atmosphere more conducive to better and more wholesome international relations. It is an incomplete position, but as one aspect of policy, it is taken into account in the more comprehensive policy of positive neutralism. . . .

Positive neutralism is then the independent attitude which does not abstain from taking clear stands—unless abstention itself is a positive stand—and works with determination to play an effective role in international affairs. It is the policy which gives to international relations a blending from the Arab and Afro-Asian character. For it is the belief of these peoples that such a contribution as they can make strengthens the chances of peace and lessens tension in the world. It also weakens the policy of dividing regions into zones of influence, and it transforms the areas of crisis into areas of agreement and interaction. The positive aspect of neutralism is the policy of taking the initiative, and acting for the success of that policy, even if that should be contrary to the interest of one of the blocs. A stand based on positive neutralism might agree with the stand taken by one of the blocs, but such an agreement or convergence of views on policy takes off from different points of departure. A policy taken in this spirit in the final analysis forces each of the quarreling blocs to make its diplomatic and political record closer to the standards held by the positive [111/112] neutralists.

. . . .

An Address to the General Assembly of the United Nations, September 30, 1960*

SUKARNO (1901-   ) is the president of Indonesia. Trained as an engineer under Dutch rule, he entered nationalist politics and helped to establish the Indonesian National Party. In the Second World War he co-operated with the Japanese, who permitted him to further his career. Sukarno became president in 1949, and subsequently has balanced military, nationalist, Islamic, and Communist forces. In 1959 he ended parliamentary government and introduced "guided democracy."

13. Mr. Sukarno (President of the Republic of Indonesia): Today, in addressing this session of the United Nations General Assembly, I feel oppressed by a great sense of responsibility. I feel a humility in speaking to this august gathering of wise and experienced statesmen from east and west, from the north and from the south, from old nations and from young nations and from nations newly reawakened from a long sleep. I have prayed to the Almighty that my tongue will find those words which are adequate to express the feelings of my heart, and I have prayed also that these words will bring an echo from the hearts of those who listen.

. . . .

22. It is clear today that all major problems of our world are inter-connected. Colonialism is connected to security; security is connected to the question of peace and disarmament; disarmament is connected to the peaceful progress of the under-developed countries. Yes, all are connected and inter-connected. If we succeed in finally solving one problem, then the way to the solution of all the others will be open. If we succeed in solving, for example, the problem of disarmament, then the necessary funds will be available to assist those nations which so urgently need assistance. [278/281]

. . . .

56. Some months ago, just before the leaders of the great Powers met so briefly in Paris, Mr. Khrushchev was our guest in Indonesia. I made it very clear to him that we welcomed the Summit Conference, that we hoped for its success, but that we were sceptical. Those four great Powers alone cannot decide the questions of war and peace. More precisely, perhaps, they have the power to disrupt the peace, but they have no moral right to attempt, singly or together, to settle the future of the world.

57. For fifteen years now the West has known peace—or at least the absence of war. Of course there have been tensions. Yes, there has been danger. But the fact remains that in the midst of a revolution engulfing three-quarters of the world the West has been at peace. Both great blocs, in fact, have successfully practised coexistence for all these years, thus contradicting those who deny the possibility of coexistence. We of Asia have not known peace. After peace came to Europe we endured atomic bombs. We endured our own national revolution in Indonesia. We en-

* An Address to the General Assembly of the United Nations, September 30, 1960, U.N. General Assembly Official Records, 15th Session, Plenary 278, 281, 289 (A/PV. 880) (1960).

dured the torment of Viet-Nam. We suffered the torture of Korea. We still suffer the agony of Algeria. Is it now to be the turn of our African brothers? Are they to be tortured while our wounds are still unhealed?

58. And yet the West is still at peace. Do you wonder that we now demand—yes, demand—respite from our torment? Do you wonder that my voice is now raised in protest? We who were once voiceless have demands and requirements; we have the right to be heard. We are not subjects of barter but living and virile nations with a role to play in this world and a contribution to make.

59. I use strong words, and I use them deliberately, because I am speaking for my nation and because I am speaking before the leaders of nations. Furthermore, I know that my Asian and African brothers feel equally strongly, although I do not venture to speak on their behalf.

60. This session of the General Assembly is to be seized of many important matters. No matter, though, can be more important than that of peace. In this respect I am not at this moment speaking of issues arising between the great Powers of the world. Such issues are of vital concern to us, and I shall return to them later. But look around this world of ours. There are tensions and sources of potential conflict in many places. Look closer at those places and you will discover that, almost without exception, imperialism and colonialism in one of their many manifestations is at the root of the tension, of the conflict. Imperialism and colonialism and the continued forcible division of nations—I stress those words—is at the root of almost all international and threatening evil in this world of ours. Until those evils of a hated past are ended, there can be no rest or peace in all this world.

61. Imperialism—and the struggle to maintain it—is the greatest evil of our world. Many of you in this hall have never known imperialism. Many of you were born free and will die free. Some of you are born of those nations which have in-

flicted imperialism on others, but you have never suffered it yourselves. However, my brothers of Asia and Africa have known the scourges of imperialism. They have suffered it. They know its dangers, its cunning, its tenacity.

62. We of Indonesia know, too. We are experts on the subject. Out of that knowledge and out of that experience, I tell you that continued imperialism in any of its forms is a great and continuing danger.

63. Imperialism is not yet dead. People sometimes say that imperialism and colonialism are dead. No, imperialism is not yet dead. It is dying, yes. The tide of history is washing over its battlements and undermining its foundations. Yes, the victory of independence and nationalism is certain. Still—and mark my words well—the dying imperialism is dangerous, as dangerous as the wounded tiger in a tropical jungle.

64. I tell you this—and I am conscious of speaking now for my Asian and African brothers—the struggle for independence is always justified and always just. Those who resist that irresistible onward march of national independence and self-determination are blind; those who seek to reverse what is irreversible are dangers to themselves and to the world.

65. Until these facts—and they are facts—are recognized, there will be no peace in this world, and no release of tension. I appeal to you: place the authority and the moral power of this organization of States behind those who struggle for freedom. Do that clearly. Do that decisively. Do that now. Do that, and you will gain the full and whole-hearted support of all men of good will. Do that now, and future generations will applaud you. I appeal to you, to all Members of the United Nations: move with the tide of history; do not try to stem that tide.

66. The United Nations has today the opportunity of building for itself a great reputation and prestige. Those who struggle for freedom will seek support and allies where they can: how much better that they should turn to this body and to

our Charter rather than to any group or section of this body.

67. Remove the causes of war, and we shall be at peace. Remove the causes of tension, and we shall be at rest. Do not delay. Time is short. The danger is great.

68. Humanity the world over cries out for peace and rest, and those things are within our gift. Do not withhold them, lest this body be discredited and deserted. Our task is not to defend this world, but to build the world anew. The future—if there is to be a future—will judge us on the record of our success at this task.

69. Do not, I beg of you older established nations, underestimate the force of nationalism. If you doubt its force, look around this Chamber and compare it with San Francisco fifteen years ago. Nationalism—victorious, triumphant nationalism—has wrought this change, and it is good. Today, the world is enriched and ennobled by the wisdom of leaders of sovereign nations newly established. To mention but six examples out of many, there is a Norodom Sihanouk, a Nasser, a Nehru, a Sekou Touré, a Mao Tse Tung in Peiping, and a Nkrumah. **[281/289]**

. . . .

190. Since the Second World War, we have witnessed three great permanent phenomena. First is the rise of the socialist countries. That was not foreseen in 1945. Second is the great wave of national liberation and economic emancipation which has swept over Asia and Africa and over our brothers in Latin America. I think that only we who were directly involved anticipated that. Third is the great scientific advance, which at first dealt in weapons and war, but which is turning now to the barriers and frontiers of space. Who could have prophesied this?

191. It is true that our Charter can be revised. I am aware that there exists a procedure for doing so, and a time when it can be done. But this question is urgent. It may be a matter of life and death for the United Nations. No narrow legalistic thinking should prevent this being done at once.

192. Equally it is essential that the distribution of seats in the Security Council and the other bodies and agencies should be revised. I am not thinking in this matter in terms of bloc votes, but I am thinking of the urgency that the Charter of the United Nations, of the United Nations bodies, and its Secretariat should all reflect the true position of our present world.

193. We of Indonesia regard this body with great hope and yet with great fear. We regard it with great hope because it was useful to us in our struggle for national life. We regard it with great hope because we believe that only some such organization as this can provide the framework for the sane and secure world we crave. We regard it with great fear, because we have presented one great national issue, the issue of West Irian, before this Assembly, and no solution has been found. We regard it with fear because great Powers of the world have introduced their dangerous cold war game into its halls. We regard it with fear lest it should fail, and go the way of its predecessor, and thus remove from the eyes of man a vision of a secure and united future.

194. Let us face the fact that this Organization, in its present methods and by its present form, is a product of the Western State system. Pardon me, but I cannot regard that system with reverence. I cannot even regard it with very much affection, although I do respect it greatly.

195. Imperialism and colonialism were offspring of that Western State system, and in common with the vast majority of this Organization, I hate imperialism, I detest colonialism, and I fear the consequences of their last bitter struggle for life. Twice within my own lifetime the Western State system has torn itself to shreds, and once almost destroyed the world, in bitter conflict.

196. Can you wonder that so many of us look at this Organization, which is also a product of the Western State system, with a question in our eyes? Please, do not misunderstand me. We respect and admire

that system. We have been inspired by the words of Lincoln and of Lenin, by the deeds of Washington and by the deeds of Garibaldi. Even, perhaps, we look with envy upon some of the physical achievements of the West. But we are determined that our nations, and the world as a whole, shall not be the plaything of one small corner of the world.

197. We do not seek to defend the world we know: we seek to build a new, a better world! We seek to build a world sane and secure. We seek to build a world in which all may live in peace. We seek to build a world of justice and prosperity for all men. We seek to build a world in which humanity can achieve its full stature.

198. It has been said that we live in the midst of a revolution of rising expectations. It is not so. We live in the midst of a revolution of rising demands! Those who were previously without freedom now demand freedom. Those who were previously without a voice now demand that their voices be heard. Those who were previously hungry now demand rice, plentifully and every day. Those who were previously unlettered now demand education.

199. This whole world is a vast powerhouse of revolution, a vast revolutionary ammunition dump. No less than three-quarters of humanity is involved in this revolution of rising demands, and this is the greatest revolution since man first walked erect in a virgin and pleasant world. The success or failure of this Organization will be judged by its relationship to that revolution of rising demands. Future generations will praise us or condemn us in the light of our response to this challenge.

200. We dare not fail. We dare not turn our backs on history. If we do, then we are lost indeed. My nation is determined that we shall not fail. I do not speak to you from weakness; I speak to you from strength. I bring to you the greetings of ninety-two million people, and I bring to you the demand of that nation. We have now the opportunity of building together a better world, a more secure world. That opportunity may not come again. Grasp it, then, hold it tight, use it.

201. No man of good will and integrity will disagree with the hopes and beliefs I have expressed, on behalf of my nation, and indeed on behalf of all men. Let us then seek, immediately and with no further delay, the means of translating those hopes into realities.

202. As a practical step in this direction, it is my honour and my duty to submit a draft resolution to this General Assembly. On behalf of the delegations of Ghana, India, the United Arab Republic, Yugoslavia and Indonesia, I hereby submit the following draft resolution:

"*The General Assembly*,

"*Deeply concerned* with the recent deterioration in international relations which threatens the world with grave consequences,

"*Aware* of the great expectancy of the world that this Assembly will assist in helping to prepare the way for the easing of world tension,

"*Conscious* of the grave and urgent responsibility that rests on the United Nations to initiate helpful efforts,

"*Requests*, as a first urgent step, the President of the United States of America and the Chairman of the Council of Ministers of the Union of Soviet Socialist Republics to renew their contacts interrupted recently, so that their declared willingness to find solutions of the outstanding problems by negotiation may be progressively implemented."

203. May I request, on behalf of the delegations of the aforementioned five nations that this draft resolution receive your urgent consideration. . . .

.   .   .   .

An Address to the General Assembly of the United Nations, October 17, 1960*

V. K. KRISHNA MENON (1897-   ) is a former close advisor to Prime Minister Nehru of India and has frequently served his country as its vehement spokesman in the United Nations. Under domestic pressure Nehru dismissed Menon as minister of defense in November 1962, following the failure of India's policy of friendship with Communist China and the defeat of the Indian Army on the Sino-Indian borders. He continues as a demoted leader of the left-wing of the Congress party.

. . . .
99. Next, though it may seem somewhat removed from the United Nations, my delegation feels it necessary for my country, even if it may be regarded as, perhaps, special pleading, to give some exposition, some expression of view, as to our own approach in these matters. We are not a neutral country. We refuse to accept responsibility for the appellation "neutralist", which is purely a newspaper invention, originally produced as an epithet by people who did not like our policy. We are not neutral in regard to war or peace. We are not neutral in regard to domination by imperialist or other countries. We are not neutral with regard to ethical values. We are not neutral with regard to the greatest economic and social problems that may arise. Neutrality is a concept that arises only in war. If we are neutrals, the Soviet Union and the United States are belligerents—and I do not think they want to plead guilty to that! We are not neutral or neutralist, positive or otherwise. We would take part, we would participate, we would express our views. Even that expression "positive neutrality" is a contradiction in terms. There can no more be positive neutrality than there can be a vegetarian tiger.

100. Therefore, our position is that we are an unaligned and uncommitted nation in relation to the cold war. That is to say, in relation to the great international issues, we think it is good for sovereign nations, in conformity with international law and with their own historic backgrounds, to project into international relations their own internal policies in regard to toleration, democracy and neighbourliness. And the Charter provides the guide-lines that are required.

101. It is not necessary for us to belong to this school or to that school and to sacrifice our convictions, for it is our convictions that have led us to non-alignment in this way. Secondly, we believe that in the circumstances, where the balance of power in the world unfortunately rests on what Sir Winston Churchill called "the balance of horror", it is good for nations, and not only for the nations of Asia—and while I take up no position of telling other nations what to do, the greater the increase of the area of peace in the world, the greater the non-committedness, the more that the so-called committed nations have to canvass for the moral support of others, the greater are the chances of peace. No country which relies upon power or negotiation from strength should

* An Address to the General Assembly of the United Nations, October 17, 1960, *U.N. General Assembly Official Records*, 15th Session, Plenary 751-752 (A/PV. 906) (1960).

be able to take any other country for granted. That is, we should be able to decide, either in our wisdom or otherwise, as to what is good for ourselves in the world. We should be open to persuasion, because if we are not open to persuasion we should never be able to persuade anybody else. [751/752]

102. Therefore, our position is that we are uncommitted in regard to sides. We do not belong to one camp or another. That does not mean that where these issues are involved to which I have referred we would simply sit on the fence and not take sides. What is more, this uncommittedness is not an attempt to escape international responsibilities. My own country, in regard to the situation that arose later in Korea—or even during the Korean war—in Indo-China, in the Lebanon, in the Gaza Strip, and now in the Congo (Leopoldville), is heavily committed, committed far beyond our capacity. We committed ourselves because we think it is in the interests of peace at this time. We want it understood that we do not welcome this appellation of neutral, or neutralist, whatever it means. It means that, if we even accept the appellation, first of all we would accept the freezing of the cold war or the power blocs, which we do not want to see in the world. In this world we cannot continue to live in peace and security, or even survive, unless the great countries of Europe and America come together, not necessarily with an identity of thinking, but with tolerance and co-operation and lay down their arms. This is not possible if there are only two sides and they are ranged against each other, each canvassing against the other. If they are successful in their enlistment effort there may well be no areas in the world that are not precommitted to forceful action. This is a tragic state of affairs.

103. We are happy to think that, while at one time being non-aligned was regarded—as I have been told so many times —as sitting on the fence, or pronouncing a curse on both houses, or trying to canvass assistance from both sides, that day has fortunately disappeared. Today in the world, even in the United States of America, the Soviet Union or European countries, there is a greater appreciation of the integrity of purpose involved in this; and even of the political profit and the profit of the world that might arise from independent countries exercising their policies independently. This is not a counsel of anarchy, or a counsel against co-operation between peoples. We do not regard military alliances between Member States of the United Nations outside the Charter, and as against another group of nations as sanctioned by Article 51 of the Charter.

104. But at the same time, we have not carried on a campaign against it. As the world stands at present, these systems have come into existence and we hope that with the evolution of proposals for disarmament and collective security they will begin to disappear even though little by little. Therefore, our position in this regard is what is dictated by the Charter; the policy of the good neighbour, the policy that we try to practice in our own country by our democratic institutions, tolerance for differences of opinion. Then, while one does not want to speak for other countries who more or less follow the same policy, speaking for ourselves, our peoples are never able to accept the idea of exclusive good and exclusive evil. There are no individuals, no nations, no groups of people who can say that their policies, their actions, their thoughts, their commitments, or whatever they are, are exclusively one thing or the other. In this changing world of ours it is always necessary to have observation and examination of the opponents' proposals. There is always a chance that the opponent may be right, and if he is right and you reject him out of hand, you lose his contribution. Therefore, we will not contribute our strength, for what it is worth—it is worth very little in economic or military terms— for the promotion of world factions. We shall not be a party at any time to inter-

vening in any way, economically or otherwise, either in the developing continent of Africa and or in other parts of Asia with a view to profiting ourselves or in such a way as to stifle their progress, or anything of that character.

105. There are no troops, there is no soldier, no aeroplane, no horse and no gun belonging to the Republic of India anywhere outside our frontiers except at the behest of the United Nations or international agreements. The last of these were withdrawn on the last day of August 1947. Therefore, we stand, without any reservation whatsoever, as a country that does not want to be involved in the war blocs.

106. This takes me to another, perhaps more controversial question—the classification of uncommitted countries as a bloc. We are against the formation of isolated blocs in the United Nations, because it means that this Assembly has no capacity to decide in freedom; that decisions are reached elsewhere beforehand and that all that happens is degrees of master-minding. This would not lead to the prosperity of this world. Co-operation among like-minded nations, co-operation among people with like-minded experience past or present is both necessary and useful. But to say that we are a third force, or a neutralist bloc, the panacea for everything, is beside the point.

107. At the risk of being misunderstood, my country does not stand for the formation of blocs, because blocs mean isolationism. We stand for a universalist world. In fact, the position the United Nations is facing is what humanity has faced from almost the pre-Christian era, where on the one hand there was the doctrine or approach of universalism, one world and one family, whether on theological, political or other grounds—and on the other hand power for oneself. This has been the contradiction the whole time. In the sixth century B.C., the Chinese tried to bring about some degree of understanding among the rival areas of the Yangtse basin on the basis of peaceful settlements, and they ended up by imposing domination in the Yangtse region.

108. After that, in the Christian world at various times there were moves in this direction, and ultimately there was the Congress of Vienna of 1815. Tsar Alexander preached to the world the universal doctrine of Christendom and the great dreams that he had for the whole world, for the great human family. But he was torn between his dreams and his schemes for power, which ultimately resulted in the Holy Alliance. So here also is the great universal doctrine that has been explored by the fathers of our constitution—the Charter—including the representatives of the United States and of the Soviet Union whose speeches at the United Nations Conference in San Francisco I just read. On the one hand they try to reach universalism, while on the other hand keeping out a good little country like Outer Mongolia; and, on the other hand, not allowing the free play of independent nations through fear of one nation or the other. So unless this Organization remains not only universal in its membership, but universal in the conception pervading it, not divided by factionism, we are not likely to get much further.

. . . .

An Address to the Belgrade Conference of Nonaligned Countries, September 3, 1961*

SIRIMAVO R. BANDARANAIKE (1916-   ) is prime minister of Ceylon. She is the widow of S. W. R. D. Bandaranaike who was assassinated in September 1959 when he was prime minister. Leading the Sri Lanka Freedom Party to victory in the elections of July 1960, Madame Bandaranaike became head of the government on a pronounced nationalist and Buddhist platform. Her major governmental undertakings are nationalization of Western property and efforts to settle the Sino-Indian dispute.

Mr. Chairman and Friends,

I consider it a great honour to represent my country at this Conference which could prove to be of historic significance in the cause of world peace. I am happy to attend this great assembly not only as a representative of my country but also as a woman and mother who can understand the thoughts and feelings of those millions of women, the mothers of this world, who are deeply concerned with the preservation of the human race. I am also happy that we have chosen to hold the Conference in this beautiful city of Belgrade not only because of the warmth and hospitality of the Yugoslav people of which there is so much evidence but also because in holding it in a European city we have demonstrated to the world that the ideals and hopes which we all share are not confined to a continent or region but reflect an awareness on the part of human beings wherever they may be of the urgent need for international peace and security.

We in Ceylon count ourselves fortunate that the people of our land were spared the horrors of two world wars and that

we were able to throw off the shackles of colonial power without strife or bloodshed. But it was not until eight years after the attainment of independence, when my late husband was elected Prime Minister, that the foreign bases were taken over and a definite and positive policy of non-alignment with power blocs adopted in foreign affairs.

The experience of many countries represented around this conference table has not been so fortunate. Some countries, like Yugoslavia, have had to see their homelands made into battle-ground; others, like Cuba and Algeria have had to sacrifice their sons and daughters in order to be free; and some others, like Tunisia, are yet striving to exercise sovereign power over the bases situated within their territory.

This Conference at Belgrade has not been convened however, for the consideration of specific problems peculiar to individual nations; we are gathered here in the firm belief that the positive policy of non-alignment with power blocs followed by each of our several countries and that our common dedication to the cause of peace and peaceful co-existence

* Sirimavo R. Bandaranaike, An Address to the Belgrade Conference of Nonaligned Countries, September 3, 1961, *The Conference of Heads of State or Government of Nonaligned Countries* (Belgrade: Government of Yugoslavia, 1961), pp. 175-181.

gives us the right to raise our voices in common decisions and declarations in [175/176] a world divided into power blocs and moving rapidly towards the brink of a nuclear war.

Many of the Heads of States and Heads of Governments who addressed this Conference in plenary session have emphasized the point that our group of nations do not propose to become a third bloc or a third force. None of us can really disagree with that view, for that would be inconsistent with the very idea of nonalignment. But it is important to remember that in our anxiety to avoid becoming a third force we must not allow our spirit of unity and purpose which has been so evident at this Conference to disintegrate and fall apart. We should endeavour to maximize the influence of non-aligned thinking in world affairs. We cannot, in my view, rely on the haphazard form of consultation which we have employed in the past. We are meeting in challenging circumstances and in a critical hour in the world's history. We must adapt our procedures to meet that challenge. I would therefore suggest that some method should be devised by this Conference to enable our individual countries to ascertain the maximum area of agreement among ourselves, without the need of a formal conference of Heads of States and Heads of Governments. I am sure that this Conference does not wish to pass moral judgments on the policies of nations. We do not propose to be the guardians of international morality. Nor do we consider that our position of nonalignment makes us in any way morally superior to other nations in the international community.

We believe that the ideals which have drawn us together will continue to inspire our thinking on international problems. We must recognize, however, that national policy is seldom divorced from national interest and that it is in the nature of international politics that competitive interests should arise. It would be unreal for us to believe that such conflicts of interest can be resolved by any appeal to principles alone. It would be equally unreal, and indeed positively dangerous, to allow these conflicts to remain unresolved. It is in this spirit that I would like to express our thoughts on some of the problems which confront us.

None of the countries of the world, big or small, rich or poor, can afford to look with indifference at the increasing international tension and at the steady deterioration in mutual trust and understanding among the committed nations of the world, particularly the Great Powers. The present crisis in Berlin must be reviewed not as a separate question but as part of the larger problem of a divided Germany and against the background of the failure of the Great Powers to agree on i [a] firm peace settlement for that country.

The tensions which have grown in various parts of the world in recent years can be traced to the clash of interest between the two power blocs. Nowhere is this clash more pronounced than over Germany. Here we have the case of two governments, each of them committed to opposing military alliances, each of them dependent upon the policies pursued by their stronger allies. Is there no way of bridging the gulf between the two German States and of reconciling the interests of the two blocs which have created this [176/177] division? In my view, this problem will not be solved if the Governments concerned continue to insist on legal arguments of a technical kind. We have our own views on the legal status of the respective German Governments. We may hold differing opinions on whether the right of the Western Powers to have their forces in what has since become West Berlin gives with it also the right of access to their respective sectors. But we do not propose to air them here. A discussion of legal aspects will not, in our view, contribute towards a solution.

The fact remains that the German problem is one of the legacies of the last war, and the earlier this question is resolved of uniting the two sections, the better it will be for peace and understanding among nations.

We regret to note, however, that no satisfactory solution acceptable to all the parties concerned has yet been found. Fears and prejudices, some real and others imaginary, have stood in the way of a solution. A spirit of compromise and conciliation should therefore be adopted by the parties directly concerned in order to arrive at a settlement of this question. We believe that the situation in Germany today should not be regarded as a testing-ground for courage and will in the military sense, but as a practical challenge to the politics and strength of the forces of universal progress and of total peace.

It is our view that as a first step towards creating international confidence the Great Powers should firmly resolve and make it known to the world that they will not resort to military engagements and will depend solely on peaceful negotiations to arrive at a solution. The Great Powers must also agree to the withdrawal of all foreign armed forces from their respective sectors in Germany and to the demilitarization of Germany. The Great Powers must immediately get down to the task of reopening direct East—West negotiations designed to achieve a final settlements [sic] by peaceful means. For the success of such negotiations it would be essential for the two Germanies to participate in the discussions, since the future of Germany must be determined not in accordance with the cold war strategy to suit either of the Great Powers but in order to establish a unified state, insulated as far as possible from the cold war and unaligned with either of the existing power blocs. No lasting solution of the German problem can be found on the basis of unilateral abrogation of right and obligation. Likewise a rigid attachment to positions formulated by mere legal technicalities cannot pave the way towards an abiding settlement. The Great Powers must recognize that whatever rights and obligations they hold must be regarded as capable of modification in the face of existing realities.

We feel that a settlement on these lines would permit the reunification of Germany on conditions acceptable not only to the German people but also to those countries who, with good reason, have cause to fear a revival of German militarism. The world has been devastated by two major wars in the first half of this century and we cannot allow a third one to destroy mankind and all that we cherish in our civilization. A satisfactory solution must be found. That solution must reconcile the conflicting interests of the [177/178] various nations concerned if we are to move away from tension and war towards a lasting and abiding peace.

Ceylon has consistently advocated the eradication of colonialism in all its forms and manifestations. We share the view expressed at this Conference that colonialism is morally unjust and politically out of date. Though many of the countries of Asia and Africa have emerged as full fledged sovereign states in the past, none the less a few colonial powers today doggedly cling to their colonial positions on various pretexts, claiming peaceful motives but in practice resorting to rough and ruthless methods to retain them. The refusal of these powers to read the writing on the wall only causes human suffering and creates bitterness and hatred—a state of affairs which is not conducive to peaceful co-existence and which constitutes a threat to peace.

The United Nations General Assembly at its fifteenth session made a significant declaration on the granting of independence to colonial countries and peoples. That resolution called for immediate action to be taken to end the colonial issue in all dependent territories but did not specify a date line. One of the matters which this Conference may have to consider will be the desirability of translating that resolution into practical terms.

Disarmament is a crucial question of our times. An early settlement of this question will be of paramount importance in building confidence among nations and in decreasing the dangers of war. It would also be an important milestone in the improvement of relations between nations and would mark the end of two-power blocs with all this portends for the future peace and security of the world. Vast sums of money that are expended in manufacturing these weapons of destruction could usefully be spent on economic and social development in various countries of the world.

Unfortunately, no tangible results have followed. The mutual fear and suspicion of the powers concerned have prevented even a start being made in disarmament. We accept the need for an immediate treaty for general and complete disarmament, and this should be achieved in rapid stages. Every stage or phase should be established by having an effective mission of inspection and control over its operation and maintenance. In this connection I would commend to this Conference the statement on disarmament referred to in the final communiqué of the Commonwealth Prime Ministers' Conference held in March of this year. Cyprus, Ghana, and India, together with Ceylon, who are represented at this Conference, were parties to this statement. We felt at that time that an effective international agreement could be concluded on the lines indicated in that statement. The Commonwealth premiers statement on disarmament urged the reopening of disarmament negotiations at the earliest possible moment with the aim of completely eliminating all means of waging war. This document was later circulated to other members of the United Nations for their information. Unfortunately disarmament negotiations, regarding both nuclear tests and general disarmament, have come to a standstill, and, what is worse, nuclear tests have been resumed by the Soviet Union. [178/179]

As countries having a vested interest in peace we should make an immediate appeal to the Big Powers to resume negotiations with a view to the achievement of complete and general disarmament. In my view, it would help these negotiations if a certain number of the non-aligned countries are also included in the Disarmament Commission. This Conference of non-aligned states does not in any way act contrary to the aims and objectives for which the United Nations stands. On the contrary, this Conference supports and supplements the work of the United Nations. Since the founding of this Organization the membership of this body has considerably increased. Most of the new members have come from the Asian-African group, and they generally follow the policy of non-alignment. This change in the composition of this Organization has taken away the prestige and influence wielded by the West European group, and consequently there is a threat among certain members to undermine its authority. This attempt should be checked. The United Nations stands for the interests of all concerned, particularly the small countries, to maintain and strengthen this Organization.

We would prefer basic changes in the Charter in order to strengthen this Organization, but disagreement among the Big Powers makes this difficult. The failure to seat the representative of the People's Republic of China has contributed to this impasse. It is our earnest hope that wise counsels will prevail and that China will take her legitimate seat in the United Nations.

The office of the Secretary-General has in recent times come in for much criticism, and a new proposal has been made by the Soviet Union to change the office of the Secretary-General into a triumvirate of three persons having the same power and the right of veto. An alternative suggestion has been the appointment of three deputies on a similar basis. We do not conform to either viewpoint in spite of the mistakes made by the Secretary-General over the Congo situation last year. On the contrary, we feel that the Secretary-General should retain sole executive authority for carrying out the directives of the General Assembly, the Security Council and the other bodies of the United Nations. We also feel that the office and authority of the Secretary-General should be upheld and strengthened, and one of the positive ways to achieve this would be to reorganize the Security Council in such a way as to enable it to give directives to the Secretary-General.

The composition of the Security Council and the other institutions of the United Nations does not adequately reflect the present membership of the United Nations. When a satisfactory solution is reached as regards the representation of the People's Republic of China we feel a reallocation of seats could be made in those bodies so that greater representation might be given to the Asian-African group.

The existence of an economic imbalance and the problems of unequal economic development assume considerable significance in our exchange of views on the international situation. It is not coincidence that the majority of the under-developed nations believe in a policy of non-alignment. They are only too aware of the enormous tasks which confront them in the [179/180] economic field and the need to devote their slender resources to the fulfilment of these tasks. They also realize that the tension which exists between ideological blocs can be traced directly to the existence of economic imbalance. As long as there exists a gulf between the developed and the under-developed countries the possibilities of tension are immense. This tension is highlighted by the enormous resources which the more developed countries allocate to military expenditure. Conversely, if this tension could be reduced the resultant saving could be diverted to economic aid for the under-developed countries.

In most of the countries represented here there has been some acceleration in the process of development. In many cases, however, this acceleration does not keep pace with the increase in population, and even if it did it could not match the rate of growth which obtains in the more developed nations of the world. I need hardly say that what is required is that the process of equalization should be hastened. It would of course be absurd to suggest that the developed countries should slow down or even reverse their development. The alternative would therefore lie in the acceleration of the rate of growth of the under-developed countries. Increasing economic and political contacts between the peoples of the world make comparisons inevitable, and in the result a note of frustration has been introduced into the revolution of rising expectations. Of course, the solution to this problem lies primarily with the under-developed countries. We need to increase our productive capacity, widen our investment opportunities and plan our economic development. These tasks command our full attention but we need the assistance of the more developed countries. That assistance has been forthcoming but if it is to reduce the economic imbalance which exists today it must be on a considerably wider scale. Fortunately there is an increasing awareness of the urgency of this problem in the more enlightened countries, and this Conference would do well to consider what more we can do to widen the area of understanding.

I have very nearly finished what I have to say on the subjects of this Conference, but before I conclude I should like to express my firm conviction that there is no single country in the world at this moment that looks forward to the prospect of war without dismay. I do not for one moment believe that there is a single mother in the world who could bear to contemplate the possible danger of her children being exposed to atomic radiation and slow and lingering death, if not swift annihilation. The statesmen of the Great Powers, who have been placed in positions of trust and authority by millions of ordinary people who do not want war, have no right to assume that they have a mandate to precipitate a nuclear war and immense destructive power either to defend a way of life or to extend a political ideology. In the late nineteenth and early twentieth centuries sabre-rattling was sometimes an expensive political game for the bigger countries. Today, when a major conflict could be started off by accident or hysteria, the consequences of sabre-rattling could be disastrous. We talk of peaceful co-existence, but what kind of co-existence is possible between countries which maintain a battery of intercontinental ballistic missiles aimed prominently at one [**180/ 181**] another? The whole basis of peaceful co-existence depends on the premise that inconsistent ideologies in the modern world do not require an armoury for their survival.

We do not expect, nor have we any right to expect, that in the short space of five or six days we shall succeed in solving all the world problems, but we are here in Belgrade because it is our firm conviction that the non-aligned nations have a positive contribution to make in the cause of peace. If I may attempt to assess the contribution that the non-aligned countries can make at this time, I would say that our endeavour should be to influence world opinion to such an extent that governments, however powerful, cannot regard warfare as an alternative to negotiation. Too much is at stake today to allow us the luxury of considerations of prestige and honour. When human life is involved all else is secondary. Let us in our deliberations make this clear in no uncertain terms.

Brazil's New Foreign Policy*

JANIO DA SILVA QUADROS (1917-   ) became the president of Brazil on January 31, 1961. Pledged to solve internal economic problems through conservative reforms in domestic matters, Quadros deflected his nation leftward in foreign affairs by means of public sympathy for Castroism, disdain for American diplomacy, and economic agreements with the Communist bloc. He resigned on August 25, 1961, blaming reactionaries for his departure. After a brief exile he returned to Brazil, where political currents under his successor Joao Goulart prevented his political comeback. In 1964, a revolutionary regime suspended Quadros' political rights.

The interest shown in the position of Brazil in international affairs is in itself proof of the presence of a new force on the world stage. Obviously my country did not appear by magic, nor is it giving itself momentarily to a more or less felicitous exhibition of publicity seeking. When I refer to a "new force," I am not alluding to a military one, but to the fact that a nation, heretofore almost unknown, is prepared to bring to bear on the play of world pressures the economic and human potential it represents, and the knowledge reaped from experience that we have a right to believe is of positive value.

We are a nation of continental proportions, occupying almost half of South America, relatively close to Africa and, ethnically, having indigenous, European and African roots. Within the next decade, our population will amount to close to 100,000,000 inhabitants, and the rapid industrialization of some regions of the country heralds our development into an economic power.

At present we are still beset by the evils of underdevelopment which make of the greater part of our country the scene for quasi-Asiatic dramas. We have poverty-stricken areas which are over-populated, and we have vast regions—the largest in the world—still unconquered. And yet, great cities are becoming industrial and trade centers of major significance.

If Brazil is only now being heard of in international affairs, it is because on taking office I decided to reap the consequences of the position that we had achieved as a nation. We had been relegated unjustifiably to an obscure position, while—even in our own hemisphere—there were accumulating errors and problems in our way that jeopardized our very future. We gave up the subsidiary and innocuous diplomacy of a nation aligned with worthy though alien interests and, to protect our rights, placed ourselves in the forefront, convinced as we were of our ability to contribute with our own means to the understanding of peoples.

Before I undertake an objective analysis of Brazil's foreign policy, the reader will, I hope, bear with me in a somewhat subjective statement of views. It will serve to clarify the underlying [19/20] reasons why we have taken particular positions on world issues.

To be genuine, a nation's foreign policy, as such, must be the embodiment of the

* Janio da Silva Quadros, "Brazil's New Foreign Policy," Foreign Affairs, XL (October, 1961), 19-27. Used by permission of Foreign Affairs. Copyright by the Council on Foreign Relations, Inc., New York.

ideals and common interests that govern its existence. Idealistic aspirations are defined by the explicit or implicit establishment of the goals aimed at. They reflect the common interests and all those economic, social, historic and political circumstances that at a given moment influence the choice of immediate aims and the selection of ways and means of action.

The ideals of the community are the backdrop against which the national drama unfolds, and are the constant source of inspiration of true leadership. They generally permeate the means and resources for the enforcement of political decisions. A national policy—as a tool for action—seems at times to turn against the fundamental impetus that gave it birth, in order the better to serve it; but in terms of the very essence of that policy, the truth of certain realities cannot be refuted. In order to ensure that the formulation of a national strategy is viable, popular desires and ideals cannot be ignored; but the truth of the matter is that very often the tactics must be neutralized and divested of idealistic or sentimental content in order to meet urgent interests and strengthen the ideals of the community itself.

There are two moments in the life of nations when complete freedom is permitted in the expression of what might be called a national ideology: when they are undergoing dire poverty, as the sole romantic consolation left to the people; and when they are thriving in abundance, as a duty imposed upon the nation by the multitude of interests asserted but never entirely satisfied.

A nation which no longer is so poor or unprotected as to be able to indulge in the luxury of dreamy consolations, yet is struggling against mighty odds to achieve the full possession of its wealth and to develop the potentialities of its own nature, must ever remain in the arena —alert, aware and vigilant. Such a nation cannot lose sight of its objectives, yet must avoid jeopardizing them by submitting

to policies which—though in keeping with remote ideals—do not, at the moment, satisfy its true interests.

There can be no doubt that Brazil— thanks to a tremendous national effort— is making gigantic strides toward breaking the barrier of underdevelopment. The rate of national growth speaks for itself, and I am convinced that at the end of my term of office the country's rate of progress will be such as to make the population explosion no longer a somber prospect but rather an addi- [20/21] tional and deciding factor for advancement in the process of economic development.

We have no right to dream. Rather it is our duty to work—but at the same time to trust and hope—and work with our feet firmly on the ground.

In time, the foreign policy of Brazil will reflect the craving for developmental progress. Obviously, underlying the decisions which we are compelled to take in order to meet the problems of material growth inherent in the desire of the Brazilian people for economic, social, political and human freedom lies the interweaving of the country's material needs. Keeping our aims ever in mind, we must choose those of our country's sources of inspiration that can best be mobilized to assist the national effort.

II

Because of our historical, cultural and Christian background as well as our geographical situation, ours is a predominantly Western nation. Our national effort is directed toward the achievement of a democratic way of life, both politically and socially. It may not be idle to stress here that our dedication to democracy is greater than that of other nations of our same cultural sphere. We have thus become the most successful example of racial coexistence and integration known to history.

Common ideals of life and organization draw us close to the major nations of the Western bloc, and on many issues Brazil can, in a leading position, associate itself with this bloc. This affinity is underlined by our participation in the Inter-American regional system, which entails specific political commitments.

However, at the present juncture, we cannot accept a set national position exclusively on the basis of the above premises. It is undeniable that we have other points in common with Latin America in particular, and with the recently emancipated peoples of Asia and Africa, which cannot be ignored since they lie at the root of the readjustment of our policy, and on them converge many of the main lines of the development of Brazilian civilization. If it be true that we cannot relegate our devotion to democracy to a secondary place, it is no less true that we cannot repudiate ties and contacts offering great possibilities for national realization.

The closeness of Brazil's relations with neighboring countries of the continent and with the Afro-Asian nations, though based [21/22] on different reasons, tends to the selfsame end. Among these, in the majority of cases, are historical, geographic and cultural motives. Common to them all is the fact that our economic situation coincides with the duty of forming a single front in the battle against underdevelopment and all forms of oppression.

From all this, naturally, certain points stand out that may be deemed basic to the foreign policy of my government. One of these is the recognition of the legitimacy of the struggle for economic and political freedom. Development is an aim common to Brazil and to the nations with which we endeavor to have closer relations, and the rejection of colonialism is the inevitable and imperative corollary of that aim.

It is, furthermore, in the light of these political determinants that today we consider the future of the Inter-American regional system of first importance. The growth of Latin America as a whole and the safeguarding of the sovereignty of each nation of the hemisphere are the touchstones of a continental policy as the Brazilian government understands it.

The mistakes created by an erroneous equating of continental problems are only too well known. Insufficient or misdirected aid has increased regional disagreements. Nations at grips with grave problems in common—that is, all the countries of Latin America—must take stock of their needs and plan accordingly. Latin Americans are interested not in the prosperity of the small, leading groups, but in the national prosperity as a whole, which must be sought at all costs and regardless of the risks.

The United States must realize that today it confronts a challenge from the socialist world. The Western world must show and prove that it is not only Communist planning that promotes the prosperity of national economies. Democratic planning must also do so, with the assistance of those economically able, if the political system of a perplexed two-thirds of the Western world is to avoid the risk of bankruptcy.

We cannot too often stress the extent to which poverty separates us from North America and the leading European countries of the Western world. If by their success these represent, in the eyes of underdeveloped peoples, the ideal of achievement of the élite of European cultural origin, there nevertheless is taking root in the minds of the masses the conviction that this ideal, for a country without resources and hamstrung in its aspirations for progress is a mockery. What solidarity can there be between a [22/23] prosperous nation and a wretched people? What common ideals can, in the course of time, withstand the comparison between the rich, cultivated areas of the United States and the famine-ridden zones of the Brazilian Northeast?

Thinking of this sort irrevocably creates in us a sense of solidarity with those poverty-stricken peoples who, on three continents, are struggling against imperialist interests which, under the umbrella of democratic institutions, mislead

—if not destroy—attempts to organize popular economies. When nations competing with the democratic group make demonstrations of real or pretended and disinterested economic help, this problem seems more acute under the pressure of the conflict of interests.

At this point it might be appropriate to refer to the ideological prejudices of the capitalist democracies, ever ready to decry the idea of state intervention in countries where either the state controls and governs economic growth—which has become a question of sovereignty—or nothing at all is achieved. We are not in a position to allow the free play of economic forces in our territory, simply because those forces, controlled from outside, play their own game and not that of our country.

The Brazilian Government is not prejudiced against foreign capital—far from it. We stand in dire need of its help. The sole condition is that the gradual nationalization of profits be accepted, for otherwise it no longer is an element of progress but becomes a mere leech feeding on our national effort. Let it be known that the state in Brazil will not relinquish those controls that will benefit our economy by channeling and ensuring the efficiency of our progress.

III

Economic imbalance is doubtless the most critical of all the adverse factors that beset the Inter-American regional system, and from it almost all others stem. My government is convinced that it is fighting for the recovery of Pan Americanism and that this must start with the economic and social fields. Politically we are trying to give shape and content to the imperative principles of self-determination and non-intervention, and it is these principles that guide us in relation to the Americas as well as to the rest of the world.

The still dramatically present question of Cuba convinced us, once and for all, of the nature of the continental crisis. In defend- [23/24] ing with intransigence the sovereignty of Cuba against interpretations of an historical fact which cannot be controlled *a posteriori*, we believe we are helping to awaken the continent to a true awareness of its responsibilities. We stand by our position on Cuba, with all its implications. Surely the Brazilian attitude has been understood by other governments, and as it gains ground, the entire regional system shows signs of a regeneration in the assessment of the responsibilities of each member nation.

The government of the United States, through its recent aid programs, took an important step toward the revision of its classical and inoperative continental policy. We hope that President Kennedy, who is not lacking in the qualities of leadership, will carry the revision of his country's attitude to the very limit and will sweep away the considerable remaining obstacles on the road to a truly democratic, continental community.

As to Africa, we may say that today it represents a new dimension in Brazilian policy. We are linked to that continent by our ethnic and cultural roots and share in its desire to forge for itself an independent position in the world of today. The nations of Latin America that became politically independent in the course of the nineteenth century found the process of economic development delayed by historical circumstances, and Africa, which has only recently become politically free, joins us at this moment in the common struggle for freedom and well-being.

I believe that it is precisely in Africa that Brazil can render the best service to the concepts of Western life and political methods. Our country should become the link, the bridge, between Africa and the West, since we are so intimately bound to both peoples. In so far as we can give the nations of the Black continent an example of complete absence of racial prejudice, together with successful proof of progress without undermining the principles of freedom, we shall be decisively contributing to the effective integration of an entire continent in a system to which we are attached by our philosophy and historic tradition.

The attraction exerted by the Communist world, by Communist techniques and by the spirit of Communist organizations upon the countries but recently freed from the capitalist yoke is common knowledge. Generally speaking, all underdeveloped countries, including those of Latin America, are susceptible to that appeal. It must not be forgotten that whereas the independence of the Latin American nations was inspired by a liberation [24/25] movement rooted in the French Revolution, the autonomy obtained by the new Asian and African nations was preceded by a wave of hope aroused by the socialist revolution in Russia among the oppressed classes and peoples all over the world. The Afro-Asian liberation movement arose against the domination by nations that compose —if not lead—the Western bloc.

These historical factors are of decisive importance and must be borne in mind when gauging the role that a country such as Brazil can play in the task of reappraising the dynamic forces that are at work in the new world of today in Asia and Africa.

For many years Brazil made the mistake of supporting European colonialism in the United Nations. This attitude—which is only now fading—gave rise to a justified mistrust of Brazilian policy. Misinformed circles, overly impressed with European patterns of behavior, contributed to a mistake which must be attributed more to a disregard of the deeper commitments of our country than to political malice. Our fraternal relationship with Portugal played its part in the complacency shown by the Ministry of Foreign Affairs of Brazil in this matter.

Therefore, everything points to a necessary change of position with regard to colonialism, which in all its guises—even the most tenuous—will from now on meet with the determined opposition of Brazil. This is our policy, not merely in the interests of Africa, nor for the sake of a platonic solidarity, but because it is in keeping with Brazilian national interests. These to a certain extent are still influenced by the most disguised forms of colonialist pressure, but call for a rapprochement with Africa.

I might add that the raising of the economic standards of the African peoples is of vital importance to the economy of Brazil. Even from a purely selfish standpoint, we are interested in seeing the social betterment and improvement in the production techniques of Africa. The exploitation of Africans by European capital is detrimental to the Brazilian economy, permitting as it does the fostering of commercial competition on the basis of low-salaried Negro workers. Competition on a civilized and human level must be found to replace that of enslavement by underpayment of an entire race. Here and now, the industrial growth of my country guarantees to the Africans a most important source of supply, which could even serve as the basis for arrangements for the linking together of our respective production systems.

We are setting up regular diplomatic and trade relations with [25/26] several African countries and my government's emissaries have visited that continent to study concrete possibilities for coöperation and exchange. In time, the potentialities of this closer relationship, destined to be a milestone in the history of human affairs, will be fulfilled.

IV

Here I must underscore another important aspect of the new Brazilian foreign policy. My country has few international obligations: we are bound only by pacts and treaties of continental assistance which commit us to solidarity with any member of the hemisphere that may become the victim of extra-continental aggression. We have not subscribed to treaties of the nature of NATO, and are in no way forced formally to intervene in the cold war between East and West. We are therefore in a position to follow our national inclination to act energetically in the cause of peace and the relaxation of international tension.

Not being members of any bloc, not even of the Neutralist bloc, we preserve our absolute freedom to make our own decisions in specific cases and in the light of peaceful suggestions at one with our nature and history. A group of nations, notably of Asia, is also careful to remain on the sidelines in any clash of interests which are invariably those of the great powers and not necessarily those of our country, let alone of world peace.

The first step in making full use of the possibilities of our position in the world consists in maintaining normal relations with all nations. Brazil, either through misinterpretation or distortion of its better political judgment, spent many years without regular contacts with the countries of the Communist bloc, even to the point of having only roundabout and insufficient trade relations with them. As a part of my government's program, I decided to examine the possibility of renewing relations with Rumania, Hungary, Bulgaria and Albania; these have now been established. Negotiations for the reopening of relations with the Soviet Union are in progress and an official Brazilian mission is going to China to study exchange possibilities. Consistent with this revision of our foreign policy, my country, as is known, decided to vote in favor of including on the agenda of the U.N. General Assembly the question of the representation of China; this initial position will, in due course, have its logical consequences.

The possibilities of trade relations between Brazil and the [26/27] Orient are practically *terra incognita*. Even in the case of Japan, to which we are bound by so many ties, our barter relations are far from complete. China, Korea, Indonesia, India, Ceylon and all of Southeast Asia provide room for the development of our production and commercial endeavors, which neither distance nor political problems can discourage.

The world must be made aware of the fact that Brazil is intensively increasing its production, looking not only to the domestic market, but specifically seeking to attract other nations. Economically speaking, my government's motto is "Produce everything, for everything produced is marketable." We shall go out to conquer these markets: at home, in Latin America, in Africa, in Asia, in Oceania, in countries under democracy, and in those that have joined the Communist system. Material interests know no doctrine and Brazil is undergoing a period where its very survival as a nation occupying one of the most extensive and privileged areas of the globe depends on the solution of its economic problems. Our very faithfulness to the democratic way of life is at stake in this struggle for development. A nation such as ours, with 70,000,000 inhabitants and with the world's highest rate of population growth, will not permit even a slowing down of its movement toward the full utilization of its own wealth.

Without fear of error I can say that the experiment in democratic progress being carried out in Brazil is decisive both for Latin America and for all the underdeveloped areas of the world. Therefore, this experiment is of deep interest to prosperous nations which are also proud of being free. They will remain so to the extent that success crowns the efforts for economic emancipation of the underdeveloped nations living under the same system. Freedom once again becomes the outgrowth of equality.

It must be pointed out that the idea behind the foreign policy of Brazil, and its implementation, has now become the instrument for a national development policy. As part and parcel of our national life, foreign policy has ceased to be an unrealistic academic exercise carried out by oblivious and spellbound élites; it has become the main topic of daily concern.

With it we seek specific aims: at home, prosperity and well-being; elsewhere, to live together amicably and in world peace.

There is no need to spell out to Brazilians what we are in the world today. We are fully aware of the mission we must accomplish—and can accomplish.

Positive Neutralism and Nonalignment*

ALEX QUAISON-SACKEY (1924-   ) is the permanent representative of Ghana to the United Nations. He has had diplomatic assignments in London and at conferences on African affairs. A former teacher, he was educated in the Gold Coast and at Oxford University.

As the African personality asserts itself on the continent of Africa by searching for unity, so it asserts itself beyond its borders, among the nations of the world, by following a policy of positive neutrality and nonalignment. The two are, of course, related, as domestic and foreign policies so often are; but the latter policy is an unusual one in many ways, for it emerges from, and is consistent with, Africa's unique position as a continent not only struggling to free itself from European domination but unwilling to exchange a Western form of domination for an Eastern one. Positive neutralism, however, strikes many people as a contradiction in terms, especially since neutrality is usually associated with passivity. But the African policy is neither negative nor passive, as we shall see, although its development from earlier concepts may at first make it seem so. Dr. Kwame Nkrumah has said of positive neutralism, for example, that it does not "imply that the Government of Ghana will be a mere silent spectator of world events. On the contrary, the Government of Ghana will continue to take positive steps through the United Nations to promote and maintain peace and security among all nations. We shall always adopt whatever positive policies will do most to safeguard our independence and world peace." And President Modibo Keita of Mali has described the policy as "the refusal of a nation to lose its personality in a world [**100/101**] where assimilation is the objective of every great power." These two statements may seem to stress the negative, yet they take into account the two great realities, so to speak, of our time—the United Nations and the Cold War—and so revise the traditional concept of neutrality from an instrument of passivity into one of activity. [**101/102**]

. . . .

With . . . illusory forms of neutrality, the policy of positive neutrality and nonalignment has nothing in common, for it has continually concerned itself with political realities. In fact, it may be said to have been born in response to political realities, one of which, curiously enough, was the powerful current of thought that has consistently held, ever since the outbreak of the Korean War in 1950, that neutralism is not only outmoded but impossible. For when the United States and the Soviet Union took opposite sides in the war between the North and South Koreans, countries like India, which followed an avowed policy of neutrality, had to be careful, whatever the merits of the situation, not to incur the wrath of either of the two great protagonists. And yet they were being placed in the most difficult of situations simply because the protagonists themselves seemed to make it impossible for neutral nations to remain neutral.

* Alex Quaison-Sackey, from "Positive Neutralism and Nonalignment," *Africa Unbound* (New York: Frederick A. Praeger, 1963), pp. 100-106, 111-118. Reprinted by permission of Frederick A. Praeger, Inc. and Andre Deutsch, Ltd.

On the Communist side, for example, there were many declarations of policy in the Soviet Union that echoed the eras of Lenin and Stalin, revealing the view that he who is not for us is against us. . . . **[102/103]** It [Russia] has found fault with the policy of neutrality, and, as its overt hostility toward President Tito of Yugoslavia has indicated, it maintains that there can be no neutrality on the issue of capitalism versus Communism.

However, it must be said that Communist China's attitude toward positive neutralism is much more rigid than the Soviet Union's. While the Soviet Government is prepared to countenance a policy of positive neutrality and also coexistence as such, China has always been suspicious of countries following such policies. The recent border conflict between China and India may well have stemmed from the basic Chinese suspicion of India as a non-aligned country, as well as China's view of India as a "bourgeois," semicapitalist nation ideologically inclined toward the West rather than the East. There is no doubt that the India-China conflict did put to the test the whole policy of non-alignment. While there is bound to be an agonizing reappraisal of this policy by the Indian Government, I doubt whether the foreign policy of India will undergo any drastic change. I suspect, however, that India will refuse to support any Chinese causes and will remain basically hostile to the Peking Government for some time to come.

In the West, there have been equally strong opinions that neutralism is no longer tenable in the present ideological conflict. As a matter of fact, the late Secretary Dulles at one time raised this view nearly to the level of official Western policy; in 1956, he stated that the United States's mutual-security treaties with forty-two nations should "abolish, as between parties, the principle of neutrality which pretends that a nation can best gain safety for itself by being indifferent to the fate of others. This has increasingly become an obsolete conception, and, except under very special circumstances, it is an immoral and shortsighted conception." Although the Kennedy Administration has **[103/104]** since discarded this view, it seems, nonetheless, to linger on in the psyche of the Western nations. It appears so frequently, and in such a variety of contexts, that one could easily become convinced of an ulterior purpose—to "permit" the uncommitted nations to pursue a policy of neutrality in order to soothe the feelings of the Afro-Asians, who do not like to be reminded of the fact that they are, in the Western view, dependent upon the West. In this context, "neutralism" becomes an artificial but necessary screen that is erected by general consent to protect a pro-Western country from attack, either diplomatic or propagandistic, by the other side—a device as indefinable but as generally accepted as that which confers status on a Frenchman's mistress. It has even provided material for the American comedian Mort Sahl, who has asked his audiences, "A neutral country, did you say? Is it one of our neutrals or one of theirs?"

Such were the views of neutralism in the capitals of both the Eastern and Western power blocs at the time that Ghana achieved her independence on March 6, 1957, and the fact that these views have, publicly at least, been modified in the last five years is in itself a tribute to the growing force of positive neutralism. The new neutralism had, however, been foreshadowed in the final communiqué of the Bandung Conference, in April, 1955, just as that had, in turn, developed from the Indian predicament in the Korean War of 1950–53. **[104/105]**

. . . .

Ghana's contribution to the concept of neutrality has, in essence, been to provide it with a new attribute. The announcement at the first Conference of Independent African States, in April, 1958, when delegates expressed their common desire to pursue a foreign policy "with a view to safeguarding the hard-won independence, sovereignty, and territorial integrity of the participating states," deplored "the division of the greater part of the world into two antagonistic blocs," and affirmed certain fundamental principles, among which were loyalty to the United Nations and adherence to the principles enumerated at the Bandung Conference. The Accra Conference also affirmed its conviction that all participating governments "shall avoid being committed to any action which might entangle them to the detriment of their interest and freedom." This policy of nonalignment has since been followed by all the countries that attended the conference—all, that is, except Liberia, which has a traditional commitment to the United States, and Tunisia, which since her quarrel with France over the French base at Bizerte in July, 1961, has been moving in the direction of nonalignment. Of those African countries which became independent after the Accra Conference, only Guinea, Mali, Tanganyika, and, to some extent, Nigeria and Sierra Leone have followed a policy of nonalignment.

Later in 1958, Prime Minister Nkrumah made three statements that threw further light upon the concept of positive neutrality. On July 25, during an official visit to the United States, he told the U.S. House of Representatives: "Our policy is that of positive neutralism and nonalignment. This does not mean negative neutralism and should not be confused with the sort of neutralism which implies the suspension of judgment, but rather the conscientious exercise of it." In October, he expanded his views in an article published in the magazine *Western World*: [105/106] It has been made quite clear that so far as Ghana is concerned our policy toward all other nations will be based on one of independence and non-involvement in power blocs. Our desire to keep clear of such blocs is motivated by the fact that only in such a situation can we hope to exert our influence in the world. We are quite aware that in terms of military or economic strength no action of ours can make any difference strategi-

cally or otherwise in the world balance of power. On the other hand, our involvement in power blocs might draw us into areas of conflict which have so far not strayed below the Sahara. In other words, we do not wish to be involved in these conflicts because we know that we cannot affect their outcome. Primarily, we believe that the peace of the world is served, not harmed, by keeping at least one great continent free from the strife and rivalry of military blocs. But this attitude of non-involvement does not mean a suspension of judgment, nor does it imply indifference to the great issues of our day. It does not imply isolationism, neither is it anti-Western or anti-Eastern. [106/111]

. . . .

Since positive neutralism is a cornerstone of Ghana's foreign policy, it might be instructive, as a means of illustration and further definition, to examine past applications of the policy at the United Nations. Let us select three issues—Hungary, the reorganization of the United Nations Secretariat, and Cuba—to show how one African nation, Ghana, applied itself to resolving these problems. Two of them involved violence, bloodshed, and intervention, open or covert, by a foreign power; the third involved a drastic change in the post of the Secretary-General because of the Soviet proposal for a "troika."

The Hungarian situation first came before the General Assembly in November, 1956. Shortly before, the Hungarian people were reported to have revolted against their government; since the government appeared powerless to suppress the revolt, the Soviet Union, according to the reports, moved in troops and tanks to help the unpopular government put down the rebellion. It was this alleged Soviet intervention that led the United States and other Western countries to call for an emergency session of the General Assembly. After a heated debate, the Assembly decided to set up a special committee, which presented its report to the Eleventh Session of the General Assembly in September, 1957—six months after Ghana had been admitted to the United Nations. On the basis of the report, the General Assembly adopted a resolution which stated that since the Soviet Union had deprived the people of Hungary of their liberty and political independence and was responsible for other acts of repression, the United Nations condemned these acts.

The presentation of the committee's report confronted Ghana with the first major international question on which it was obliged to make a decision. On September 13, 1957, during the debate on the Hungarian situation, the representative of Ghana [111/112] stated: "As a nation which has only recently achieved its independence, we have a vested interest in orderly international intercourse and the rule of law, and we would always vehemently protest in any instance in which it was clearly demonstrated that one country had used its superior military power to crush a movement for freedom in another country." The representative then went on to say that the delegation of Ghana would support the resolution on Hungary, but pointed out that "we would be sorely disappointed if the adoption of the resolution were to be interpreted by any side as a political victory or defeat. We are here concerned only with principles and the suffering of humanity, wherever that may be."

The task of the reorganization of the Secretariat of the United Nations had been assigned to a Committee of Experts, which, according to Resolution 1446 of the Fourteenth Session of the General Assembly in 1959, was "to work with the Secretary-General in reviewing the activities and the reorganization of the Secretariat with a view to effecting or proposing further measures designed to ensure maximum economy and efficiency in the Secretariat." I served on this Committee together with Mr. Omar Loutfi, then the Permanent Representative of the United Arab Republic (now Under-Secretary under U Thant), Mr. Guillaume Georges-Picot of France, Mr. Francisco Urrutia of Colombia, Mr. A. A. Fomin of

the Soviet Union, Sir Harold Parker of the United Kingdom, Mr. C. S. Venkatachar of India, and Dr. Herman B. Wells (later replaced by Professor Leland M. Goodrich) of the United States.

The Committee of Experts was thus engaged in its work when Premier Nikita Khrushchev, Chairman of the Council of Ministers of the Soviet Union, raised the issue of the reorganization of the Secretariat in his statement before the General Assembly on September 23, 1960. The Russians had not been very happy with the handling of the Congo operations by Dag Hammarskjöld, and had come to the conclusion that the post of the [112/113] Secretary-General should be substituted by a triumvirate representing the three basic groups of states existing in the world—the socialist states, the nonaligned states, and the Allied Western states. According to Chairman Khrushchev, "there are no neutral men," and, therefore, the Secretary-General could not possibly be objective in his handling of issues that affect all member states. The Soviet Union also accused Hammarskjöld of being "a servant of the colonialists" and argued that the events of the world, especially those in the Congo at the time, had demonstrated the necessity of reorganizing the structure of the Secretariat and its management at the top level. In Khrushchev's view, the Secretariat did not reflect the change in the international balance of forces or take into account the emergence of a strong socialist world, the collapse of colonialism, and the emergence of a large number of nonaligned countries. The Soviet Union argued that by the adoption of the troika system, therefore, it would not be possible to favor this or that bloc of powers, and the decisions of the Security Council and the General Assembly would then be faithfully carried out by the Secretariat.

As was to be expected, the other great power, the United States, opposed this move with the valid argument that a change in the post of the Secretary-General would involve an amendment to the Charter, and that what was required in any case was one chief administrative officer at the helm of the Secretariat. The United States expressed its solid opposition to the troika proposal.

Ghana and other nonaligned countries did not take kindly to the open accusations leveled against the person of Secretary-General Hammarskjöld and other officials, although, on many occasions, we had had cause to complain about the way United Nations operations were being conducted in the Congo. The Soviet troika proposal took us all by surprise.

Therefore, when Chairman Khrushchev made his far-reaching proposal, the President of Ghana, who was then in New York, immediately decided that the nonaligned states should [113/114] take a position of their own. At a luncheon given in his honor by the United Nations Correspondents Association in September, 1960, Osagyefo Dr. Kwame Nkrumah proposed that there should be no change in the post of Secretary-General, but that there should be three Deputy Secretaries-General who would form a kind of cabinet presided over by the Secretary-General. Ghana's position was definitely in defense of the Charter of the United Nations, but our view was that account had to be taken of the prevailing circumstances in international life. If the Secretary-General was to carry out his functions properly, then he would have to consult regularly, and work in cooperation with, his top advisers, who may be designated as deputies but in fact are under-secretaries.

The idea of a cabinet system at the top echelons of the Secretariat was strongly supported by Premier Nehru of India, who, in his address before the Fifteenth Session of the General Assembly, made it clear that the troika proposal of the Soviet Union would not work. Thus, the nonaligned states became united in their search for a compromise that would not involve an amendment of the Charter and would avoid weakening the executive functions of the Secretary-General, who, after all, has overriding responsibility for the running of the Secretariat under Articles 97–101 of the Charter. [114/115]

. . . .

Therefore, the nonaligned states put their weight solidly behind the Charter and appealed to the Soviet Union not to press its troika system. We have argued that the responsibilities of the Secretary-General go beyond the concept of a nonpolitical civil servant and that, because he may take stands of a political and controversial nature, there was need for adequate and regular consultations between the Secretary-General and his top advisers, whose views must reflect the realities of international life.

Consequently, in the Committee of Experts dealing with the reorganization of the Secretariat, I pressed the proposal for Deputy Secretaries-General, and in this I was ably supported by Omar Loutfi and C. S. Venkatachar. Hammarskjöld agreed to the idea of a cabinet system, and a month before his untimely death he conferred with the three of us and proposed that there should be five or six under-secretaries—drawn from Africa, Asia, Europe, Latin America, the Soviet Union, and the United States—instead of three to form the Secretary-General's cabinet.

Of course, the issue of a troika persisted after Hammarskjöld's death, and for some time it seemed as if the United Nations was going to do without a Secretary-General. But the nonaligned states were determined to press the idea of one Secretary-General as defined by the Charter, assisted by a cabinet.

In retrospect, it is satisfying to realize that U Thant, who became the new Secretary-General of the world organization, had taken part in our deliberations as Ambassador of Burma.

Here, then, is an instance where positive neutralism as an active policy has contributed tremendously to the maintenance of peace and the settling of a Cold War issue.

The Cuban complaint of October, 1960, "regarding the vari- [115/116] ous plans of aggression and acts of intervention being executed by the government of the United States of America against the Republic of Cuba, constituting a manifest violation of territorial integrity, sovereignty, and independence and a clear threat to international peace and security" —this was a third issue on which Ghana and other nonaligned nations had to act circumspectly. Here was a small country, Cuba, which felt that a large one, the United States, was determined to destroy it, and under normal circumstances it should have had the full support of all other small countries. But Cuba's accusation against the United States was a grave one, and it was utterly repudiated by the United States, which argued not only that Cuba had become a Communist stronghold but that it was Cuban exiles who were acting to overthrow the government of Fidel Castro. The Cuban issue could not be considered simply as a Cold War issue of itself, but the fact that the Soviet Union stood forth as the champion of the Cuban case against the United States made tension run high indeed. Therefore, nonaligned countries like Ethiopia, Ghana, India, Indonesia, Sudan, United Arab Republic, and Yugoslavia were looked upon as possible mediators, and we all made every effort to be as objective as possible by counseling nonintervention.

Most of the representatives of the nonaligned countries who took the floor spoke, as I remember, in favor of an earlier resolution passed during the Fourth Session of the General Assembly, in 1949. This had called upon all states "to refrain from threats or acts, direct or indirect, aimed at impairing the freedom, independence, or integrity of any state, or at fomenting civil strife and subverting the will of the people in any state." Speaking on behalf of Ghana, I said:

Ghana has cordial relations with both the United States and Cuba. Apart from the mutual esteem and the friendly relations existing between Ghana and Cuba, on the one hand, and Ghana and the United States, on the other, there is a feeling of kinship all around due to the fact that in both Cuba and the United States [116/117]

there are large numbers of people of African descent whose welfare and progress cannot but engage our attention.

In April, 1961, as reports reached the United Nations that Cuba had been attacked by an invading force from outside Cuba, I spoke before the Political Committee of the General Assembly:

The delegation of Ghana is not in a position to be a judge in this matter, but we are painfully aware of the fact that there has indeed been an attack on Cuba from outside by planes which have taken off from places outside Cuba; and, in fact, Guatemala and the United States have been cited by the Foreign Minister of Cuba in his statement before this committee. We are painfully aware that Cubans have been killed in this escapade. My delegation expresses the sympathy of the people of Ghana to the families of those who have lost their lives in Cuba. . . . We therefore ask the Assembly to urge that all direct or indirect assistance for the armed intervention be discontinued and that, in accordance with the Charter of the United Nations, the parties concerned settle this dispute by peaceful means, a settlement which will lead to pacification and enable the Cuban peoples to work out their own destiny in complete freedom.

Although the Assembly did not adopt any resolution on the Cuban question, the debate was sufficient to emphasize the necessity for nonintervention in Cuba by any outside power.

The later, and far more serious, Cuban crisis of October, 1962—brought about by the United States "blockade" of Cuba in response to the installation of Soviet missile bases there—deserves some mention. This crisis nearly engulfed the world in a nuclear holocaust. Quick action was needed to save humanity from destruction. The nonaligned states at the United Nations played a decisive role. Mahmoud Riad (of the U.A.R.) and I became their unofficial spokesmen at the Security Council—in getting U Thant, Acting Secretary-General, to intervene between the two great powers. In the end, common sense prevailed. Khrushchev [117/118] and Kennedy reached an agreement that quickly averted the danger of war over Cuba. The bases were dismantled and the missiles taken back to the Soviet Union. The United States then lifted the "quarantine" or "blockade" of Cuba. And what remained was the still-unresolved bad relations between Cuba and the United States and the Latin American countries.

In all three of the cases cited, I have endeavored to show that positive neutralism is much more active a policy than that usually connoted by the word "neutrality." Any country that pursues such a policy of positive neutralism and nonalignment must be prepared to work hard, for it must undertake the most assiduous and objective analyses in order to decide how that country may, by word and deed, best aid the cause of peace. And as long as the Soviet Union and the United States assume antipodal positions on world problems and attempt to entice into their orbits any number of other countries, so long will there be a need for a group of countries to remain outside the two camps —a group of countries that will approach international issues as objectively as possible and speak out for justice, morality, and human rights. Here, then, is Africa's opportunity to serve, and that is the reason I hope that all African nations will adopt the policy of positive neutralism and nonalignment.

. . . .

The South Vietnam Liberation Front's Policy Statement on Independence and Neutrality*

THE SOUTH VIETNAM LIBERATION FRONT is the Communist-dominated insurgency movement that seeks to overthrow anti-Communist governments of South Vietnam and to displace American and SEATO power in Southeast Asia.

A 14-point policy of independence and neutrality has been adopted by the South Vietnam Liberation National Front.

In a statement . . . the Front's central committee declares that "the Front will strive resolutely and persistently for the establishment in South Vietnam of an administration pursuing a policy of independence, and strict and positive neutrality." The statement makes clear the following points:

1. As a state having sovereignty, independence and territorial integrity, South Vietnam will not join any military bloc or treaty, or any bloc or treaty of a military character, and will not accept the protection of any military bloc or treaty. It will not enter into [a] military alliance or alliance of a military character, with any country, and will not sign with any country treaties contrary or harmful to South Vietnam's neutrality.

2. All foreign troops and military personnel must withdraw from South Vietnam. South Vietnam will not accept the presence on its territory of foreign armed forces, military personnel and military bases.

3. South Vietnam will carry out a fully independent and sovereign internal and foreign policy. All blocs and states must neither intervene in the internal affairs of South Vietnat [sic], nor bring pressure to bear upon it, in whatever forms and whatever fields, political or military, economic or cultural, diplomatic or internal.

4. South Vietnam will carry out the 5 principles of peaceful co-existence in its relations with all countries, regardless of their ideological system and political regime. It will establish friendship and diplomatic relations with all countries on condition that they respect its sovereignty and treat it on an equal footing. South Vietnam will no[t] allow any country to use its territory to threaten other countries' security.

As for the neighbouring Kingdoms of Cambodia and Laos in particular, South Vietnam will maintain friendly relations with them and thoroughly respect their sovereignty, independence and territorial integrity.

5. South Vietnam will build an army with the sole aim to safeguard the fatherland's sovereignty, independence, territorial integrity and security. With adequate effectives and equipment, the army of neutral South Vietnam will be a defensive and peaceful army.

6. South Vietnam will thoroughly realise democratic liberties for the people. Freedom of thought, worship, opinion and organisation will be guaranteed to all citizens, political parties, mass organisations, religions and nationalities.

* From "The South Vietnam Liberation Front's Policy Statement on Independence and Neutrality," Afro-Asian Bulletin, IV (May-June-July-August, 1962), 55-57.

7. South Vietnam will receive aid from all countries, directly and without any political conditions attached . . . provided such aid aims to help develop the economy, culture and welfare of the South Vietnamese people.

8. South Vietnam will carry out a policy of [building a] democratic and independent economy, free itself from foreign manipulation, and prohibit all forms of monopoly by foreign capitalists.

9. Foreign nationals of any citizenship will be allowed to reside and earn their living in South Vietnam, and will be protected by South Vietnam laws, provided they do not harm the South Vietnamese people's interests. [55/56]

Foreign capitalists of any citizenship will be permitted to do business in South Vietnam, and their interests will be guaranteed, provided they respect South Vietnam's laws.

10. South Vietnam will carry out cultural exchanges and broaden cultural cooperation with all countries.

11. The Vietnamese nation is one. But, in view of the fact that Vietnam has been divided into two zones with different political regimes, due concern must be shown to the question of Vietnam's reunification and adequate consideration given to the characteristics of this situation and of the two zones. This question will be decided by the people of the two zones, on the principle of equality, non-annexation of one zone by the other, negotiations between the authorities of the two zones, and step-by-step reunifications.

Priority must be given to the consideration of the question of restoration of normal relations between the two zones in view of the readjustment and development of the economy and because of the sacred sentiment and urge of the people in both zones.

The future political regime of unified Vietnam will be decided by the people of both zones.

12. South Vietnam is ready to form with the Kingdoms of Cambodia and Laos a peace and neutral zone in South East Asia, in which each member enjoys full sovereignty.

13. South Vietnam will actively unite with all states and organisations working for peace and friendship among nations. It will contribute to the realisation of general disarmament throughout the world, liquidation of nuclear weapons, cessation of A-bomb tests, and dissolution of hostile military blocs.

14. South Vietnam's independence and neutrality must be respected and guaranteed by the 1954 Geneva Agreement on Vietnam, and by all countries and parties concerned.

The statement notes that the Front's policy of independence and neutrality has enjoyed ever stronger support from the South Vietnamese people, and ever wider approval from organisations and personalities of various political tendencies, at home or in exile, including prominent figures and senior officers of the South Vietnam army.

Its [*sic*] pays tribute to the understanding shown to the Front's policy by public opinion the world over, particularly in Asia and Africa. "The peaceful settlement of the Laotian problem and the declaration of neutrality of the Laotian coalition government has strongly inspired us", it states.

It thanks Cambodia's Head of State, Prince Sihanouk, for his constructive proposals concerning the South Vietnam situation.

The statement denounces the U.S. for deliberately imposing upon the South Vietnamese people the so-called "protection" of SEATO. The South Vietnamese people do not recognize SEATO's "protection", it stresses. "The South Vietnamese people", it goes on "hate, and are fed up with the fascist, dictatorial, family rule installed by U.S. imperialists in South Vietnam. We only want democracy. The crude war of aggression launched and expanded by U.S. imperialism must be ended and peace restored at once in South Vietnam".

"The South Vietnamese people demand

the establishment in South Vietnam of a national and democratic coalition gonvernment [*sic*] representing the interests of all strata, factions, tendencies and nationalities there. An independent and neutral South Vietnam can only be a friend to the U.S., but the South Vietnamese people are determined not to be enslaved by the warlike financiers from **[56/57]** the other shore of the Pacific and are resolved to throw off at all costs the yoke imposed by the U.S. imperialism upon them".

The statement points out that honest public opinion in the U.S. has shown ever greater understanding of South Vietnam realities, and that more and more Americans have sternly condemned the dark designs and adventurous moves of the Kennedy administration.

"The South Vietnam war is taking a heavy toll of lives from both Vietnamese and Americans and is threatening to take more. We believe that the American people are strong enough to compel their rulers to give up the criminal path and recognise the sovereignty, independence and neutrality of the South Vietnamese people, in the interests of both nations", the statement says.

"Of late", it goes on, "the American imperialists and their henchmen are worrying much about the development of the neutrality tendency among the South Vietnamese people. They angrily slander neutral nations and the neutrality policy of the South Vietnam Liberation Front. They threaten and even ruthlessly repress organisations and individuals favouring neutrality in South Vietnam. However, their acts only betray their confusion, and prove the correctness of the Front's policy", the statement remarks.

It stresses: "The South Vietnam Liberation National Front central Committee holds that those in the South Vietnam administration who have always styled themselves as nationalists are having the best opportunity to prove their good will and patriotism before the people at home and world public opinion. Should they deny the country peace, independence, democracy, neutrality and prosperity, they would once more lay bare their true colours, and this would only drive them into complete isolation".

The statement expressed the "hope to contact all patriotic forces in South Vietnam to exchange views on the policy of independence and neutrality, and attain practical action serving this noble and urgent goal, first of all, to strive to remove the obstacles to South Vietnam's independence and neutrality, the U.S. aggressors and their hangers-on".

The statement calls on all governments and peoples of the world to support the Front's policy.

An Address to the General Assembly of the
United Nations, October 22, 1963*

JOSEPH BROZ TITO (1892-   ) is the president of Yugoslavia. A veteran Communist, during World War II he led a resistance movement against Italian and German invaders and conducted a civil war. With victory, he established a dictatorship, but soon Stalin's interference caused a rupture with the Soviet Union. Tito's regime began an independent foreign policy which fluctuates within limits set by economic and ideological factors, although on arms, German, and colonial issues, it is seldom distant from Russian thinking after Stalin. He climaxed his diplomatic efforts with the new states when he was host to the 1961 meeting of nonaligned nations in Belgrade. In 1963 he visited North and South America and addressed the United Nations.

. . . .

One of the most significant characteristics of our epoch undoubtedly resides in the fact that the capitalist and the socialist social system[s] exist side by side. It should, however, be borne in mind that what is involved here are essentially social and political contradictions in the broader sense of the term and not conflicts between states, although, under certain conditions and under the influence of various circumstances, and more especially of subjective factors, these contradictions acquire many of the elements of an opposition between states or between groupings of states. However, in order correctly to comprehend the policy of coexistence, it is essential to distinguish between ideological relations and contradictions, on the one hand, and relations between states and peoples, on the other. Contradictions and differences of opinion exist within the individual states themselves, and it is a matter pertaining to their internal development. Such differences should be settled without any outside interference. They will, of course, be settled in various ways according to the specific conditions prevailing in the different countries. Otherwise, the struggle would be transferred to the international arena and would assume the form of inter-state differences, thus leading to an aggravation of international relations. It is a well-known fact that political and ideological differences and contradictions have existed through the centuries. They reflected the fact that human society is moving forward. The momentous scientific and technical achievements of mankind have a more decisive bearing than ever before upon such a movement, and this includes the advance, in the most various forms, towards more progressive social relations and systems.

There are also many disputes and unsettled questions in the relations between states, such as questions of frontiers, of national minorities, and so forth. These numerous bilateral problems of lesser or greater importance, place a considerable strain upon international relations. An

* Joseph Broz Tito, An Address to the General Assembly of the United Nations, October 22, 1963, *Yugoslav Facts and Views*, No. 158, October 31, 1963, pp. 1-7.

improvement of the international situation and the settlement of major international problems would, however, also bring about more favourable conditions for the peaceful solution of such questions.

Of particular importance is a consistent compliance with the policy of non-interference in the internal affairs of other countries. What I am thinking of her[e], of course, is not only interference involving the use of armed force and direct pressure, as these are swiftly exposed at the present time and encounter general and resolute condemnation in the world. Pressure and interference still continue under various pretexts and in various guises, whereby the economic and other difficulties of some of the independent countries are exploited and all sorts of "ideological", political and other forms of justification invoked. The smaller, the developing and the newly independent countries are especially exposed to such forms of interference, because they have not yet been able to build their economic strength and achieve political stability. What I have in mind here are not only the remnants of colonialism which should be urgently eliminated, but also the manifestations of neo-colonialism. I therefore attach great value to the suggestion recently put forward by the President of the United States of Mexico, Mr. Adolfo Lopez Mateos, that the United Nations should take the initiative towards the conclusion of an agreement of all states on non-interference and non-intervention. [3/4]

As I have already mentioned, an awareness is, after many extremely difficult years, beginning to prevail of the necessity not only to renounce policies and methods which lead to war, but to discard the cold war itself, because it is only thus that a more determined step towards the strengthening of peace can be taken.

The Moscow Agreement [of 1963 on nuclear testing] and the other steps that have recently been taken are vivid evidence of the existing trends towards the **overcoming** of the division which has hitherto split the world into military and political groupings. I may say that we have, for our part, always considered that such a division of the world, whatever its historical explanation might be, is neither unavoidable nor permanent. It was precisely therein that lay the vast historical significance of the policy of non-alignment and of the activity of the non-aligned countries, which through their peace-loving policy, acted, among other things, to prevent the complete division of the world into hostile groupings. Under the new conditions, their activity acquires a broader basis and an increased significance.

Under the present improved conditions, when the forces of peace have been vitally strengthened, we see that policies are gauged today above all in function of their relationship to contemporary processes and changes, i.e. to peaceful coexistence. People and countries in the world today take their stand more and more in relation to this fundamental question and less and less according to their formal adherence to one side or the other in the cold war, which is slowly but gradually abating and to which an end should be put as soon as possible.

We welcome these positive changes and the growth of the forces which desire an end of the cold war. We also pay tribute to the prominent statesmen who have contributed to this. We, for our part, are prepared fully to contribute to facilitating this process and to ensuring its continuation.

In this new phase in the evolution of international relations, the conditions under which the policy of non-alignment had come into being are also changing. We had even in the past emphasized that this policy did not imply a passive attitude towards international events, still less an attempt to establish any kind of a third bloc. Nor have the non-aligned countries arrogated unto themselves the role of sole protector of peace. In view of the changed international situation, it may be said that the term non-alignment has in a way been superseded by the new and positive evolution of international relations.

The question of non-alignment is posed today in a far broader sense, in view of the growing number of states and peoples that are participating in the active struggle for peace. The polarization of the forces of peace, on the one hand, and of the forces of cold war on the other, is taking place at an accelerated pace, practically in all the countries of the world, with the forces of peace in ascendency. Non-alignment is thus changing, both in quantitative and in qualitative terms, and is transforming itself into a general movement for peace and for the finding of peaceful and constructive means for the settlement of various problems among nations. Active "non-alignment" is thus becoming an increasingly broad and active participation in the struggle for the triumph of [4/5] the principles of the United Nations Charter, as was so powerfully expressed by the Heads of states and governments of 25 countries at the Belgrade Conference in 1961. These principles are endorsed by the overwhelming majority of nations. That is understandable, because we all bear a responsibility for the fate of the international community. The participation of all peace-loving forces in this process should be constructive and realistic and be inspired by a desire to find a solution to existing problems.

We stand on historical cross-roads branching out towards new more constructive and more humane international relations which should make it possible for mankind to live without fear for its fate to develop and to harness towards peaceful ends all the achievements of the human mind so far. The atomic age calls for a radical change in our outlook on international relations and on the solution of the problems of the present day world.

Voices are still heard that such expectations are naive—the voices of those who feel the cold war to be in their interest and the voices of those who are still unable to grasp that lack of faith and faint-heartedness also serve the purpose of those who believe in the primacy of force. To this I cannot agree for the following simple but profoundly genuine reasons. Mankind has moved forward because the masses of the people and the individuals looked forward, because they did not reconcile themselves to their hardships and misfortunes. We too, in Yugoslavia, must have appeared naive to many when in 1941 we came to grips with the awesome hitlerite machine which was then at the height of its power. The further course of events showed however that it was those who did not believe in the possibility of successful resistance who were the "naive" ones. I could cite a number of other examples from our recent common experience. I shall merely mention this year's Test Agreement, which many only a few years or months ago probably felt to be unattainable. It is therefore not correct to identify—as is only too frequently done—political realism with the capacity of observing only that which is static, inert, negative and, in fact, transient. Realism, on the contrary, requires a comprehensive view and understanding of phenomena and processes, and this means of those factors also which impede the movement forward, but even more so of those which stimulate and compel that movement.

. . . .

PART TWO

TESTIMONY—NEUTRALISM AND DISENGAGEMENT
IN THE DEVELOPED NATIONS

A Defense of Neutralism*

HENRI BARTOLI (1918-   ) is professor of political economy at the School of Law of the University of Grenoble, member of the editorial board of *Esprit*, and author of several political and economic studies. Writing a decade ago, he clarified some of the intellectual and political currents aiding European, and especially French, neutralism.

. . . .

Neutralism represents neither the political expression of intellectuals misled by theories nor of parliamentarians who strive for originality. It reflects instead the vague aspiration of the masses who do not want war, who fear inflation and its consequences, and who feel an immense disgust with the so-called solutions they are offered [61/62] —yesterday Pétain, today German rearmament . . . Above all, neutralism reflects, in France as in Germany, a cry of the outraged conscience, and it is not by chance that the protestations of Pastor Niemöller and Karl Barth have been echoed by men who were prominent in the French resistance movement. To understand French neutralism one must not only recognize what it rejects, but also sense its commitments.

I

French neutralism represents, in the first instance, a reaction against fear. We all know how difficult it is to escape from collective fears. A man can resist the fear he feels deep in himself, but not the fear he sees in others. Fear nourishes itself; fear drives men mad. Are we quite certain that fear does not today motivate most of our leaders? The exploitation of fear represents an easy means of control, all the more effective in preparing people for war because it becomes transformed into hatred of the "enemy." It facilitates, and then consecrates, a good conscience—by force of lies. "When a people believe themselves the repository of the values of civilization, this collective self-esteem leads them to imagine that the adversary represents the powers of darkness. The crusading spirit is born in this manner."[6]

French neutralists observe with anxiety the progressive crystallization of opinion in the United States. They believe that it is creating the psychological conditions for a kind of prefascism among a profoundly democratic people seemingly unaware of the danger. They are afraid that the "American way of life" may gradually assume the proportions of an almost religious bond among the members of a chosen people. The efforts of the press, the radio, and of the Franco-American clubs to spread this conception of life irritate them all the more because they sense in it a philosophical emptiness, "the absence of Man and the silence of God."[7] If they [62/63] are believers, French neutralists refuse to confound Western civilization with Christendom, or Christendom with Christiantiy. "The regime of the Christian world, more and more worm-eaten, is breaking away from its moorings;

[6] P. Ricoeur, "Pour la coexistence pacifique," *Esprit*, March, 1951, p. 410.
[7] A. Beguin, "Réflexions sur l'Amérique, l'Europe, la neutralité," *Esprit*, June, 1951.

* Henri Bartoli, from "A Defense of Neutralism," *Confluence*, I (June, 1952), 61-69. Reprinted by permission of Henri Bartoli.

it is adrift, leaving behind it the pioneers of a new Christendom," writes Mounier. Do people really believe that those who want with all their hearts to begin building the new world are suddenly going to decide to defend a way of life which they have felt compelled to abandon? Protestants and Catholics agree, if they are neutralists, in putting aside the very idea of a crusade which would "hide fear under an appearance of nobility."[8] Can we presume to cast the first stone at another and to impose on him the Christian spirit before we have established it within ourselves?

The Russians, too, are afraid: the terrifying trials for espionage and the odious denunciations of "traitors" are an obvious proof. The psychosis of encirclement, the dread of plots—these are the lot of the communists. The neutralists are aware of this, and they also deplore, especially if believers, the excesses of the police regimes. They reject the distortion of certain of the highest commands of the Gospels which are applied in the people's democracies, but emptied of their content and turned into mockeries. A believer cannot enter into such a system to the slightest degree without being devoured to the very soul.

Since they refuse to yield to fear and its intoxication, the French neutralists will not allow themselves to be bound by the dialectic of either camp. They are aware of the existence of capitalist imperialism, and of an international communism which aims to spread throughout humanity the inevitable revolution which must put an end to the capitalist contradictions. They know that "the logic of economic systems can work against men's aspirations, and that today there are two great systems which confront each other."[9] They do not, however, admit the inevitability of conflict. Realism does not demand alignment with one side or the other, but rather [63/64] that we ignore all opportunities for war and do everything in our power to abolish it altogether.

The attitude of the French neutralists toward the Atlantic Pact and toward the rearming of Germany is a case in point. When the pact was signed, Beuve-Méry denounced it as an illusory protection and a compromise.[10] The Pact commits the nations of western Europe to a definite camp, but fails to provide them with the weapons and other means which this choice involves. The impregnable atomic curtain will prove just as ineffectual as the Maginot Line in June 1940. "Whatever the Pact may accomplish, it seems fairly certain that America would have an invasion of western Europe to contend with, and improbable that she would be able to neutralize its home bases."[11] In a more hostile vein, J. M. Domenach and P. Fraisse ask what the American attitude would be "if the West Indies were occupied by the Russians and if Mexico belonged to some Baltic Pact."[12] Lapierre insists that the provocative nature of the Pact makes it necessary for France to denounce it, and with it the Dunquerque Treaty, the Brussels Pact—and also the Franco-Soviet Treaty.[13]

All French neutralists agree that we must not surrender our fate into the hands of foreigners. The Korean War has taught the people of Europe the price of liberaiton; this does not mean that they prefer slavery to death, but that they wish to be masters of their own destiny. They have not forgotten that it was at Yalta that the agreements were signed which opened Austria and the Balkans to the Russians. It seems to them to have been, at the least, adventuresome to assert in 1950 that the South Koreans had nothing to fear, when every means of preventing aggression had

[8] J. Lacroix, "Faire la paix," *Esprit*, March, 1951, p. 328.
[9] H. Bartoli, "Deux systèmes économiques," *Esprit*, March, 1951.
[10] Beuve-Méry, "Le Pacte Atlantique et la Paix," *Le Monde*, March 17, 1949: "Un nouveau pilier de la paix?" *Le Monde*, April 6, 1949; "Guerre ou Paix?" *Le Monde*, May 5, 1950.
[11] Beuve-Méry, "Le Pacte Atlantique et la Paix," *Le Monde*, March 17, 1949.
[12] J. M. Domenach and P. Fraisse, "De la paix à la coexistence," *Esprit*, March, 1951, p. 335.
[13] J. W. Lapierre, "La neutralité française," *Esprit*, March, 1951, p. 380.

disappeared two years [64/65] earlier.[14] They are little anxious to bind their fate to the moods of a General MacArthur.

The rearming of Germany "is contained in the Atlantic Pact like the seed in an egg."[15] All French neutralists agree in opposing it, even if they differ on other means of assuring the defense of Europe. The rearming of Germany, whether or not it is carried out under the aegis of a European army, will inevitably lead to the resurgence of the German military caste and of the German national army. The very powers who for the past several years have been engaged in castigating Germany's cult of war now insist on imposing rearmament. This is a violation of promises made to the community of nations which had united to strike down German fascism and German militarism. It leaves the preservation of the peace of Europe in the hands of the very men who instigated the aggressions of 1939 and who are today already talking about the reconquest of Eastern Germany and the re-establishment of the old boundaries of the Reich. The opposition of the French neutralists to the rearming of Germany coincides with the opposition of the vast majority of the French people. The Americans should understand this, and they should learn from those who have been the actual victims of repeated German aggression how great a risk of war they run in rearming Germany.

II

The attitude of the French neutralists could justly be taxed with idealism were it limited to negative criticism. Our time is not one for dreaming; beyond their negations French neutralists have a positive program, excellently summed up by P. Ricoeur: "We must," he writes, "exercise our influence on public opinion with the aim of preventing panic; we must practice a kind of counter-magic which consists essentially of directing attention away from the so-called [65/66] external threats of aggression to the disequilibriums of our own Western society."[16]

The U.S.S.R. is not the Third Reich. One does not have to be a specialist in Marxist theory to know that the communists do not expect their ultimate victory from war but from the disintegration of capitalism. To be sure, the communists believe that the normal result of the maladjustments of capitalism is imperialism and war,[17] but they also hold that the masses have the power to prevent war. The ultimate triumph of communism, because it represents an historical necessity, is possible in a peaceful world—this is the communist doctrine.

Anticommunist hysteria opens the way to war; we must overcome it, and to this end give our support to all the forces which are working for peace, wherever they may be. On the other hand, the communists must be brought to make a clear statement about the limits of their pacifism and about the meaning of the "revolutionary war."

. . . .

[14] Beuve-Méry, "Combats en retraite," *Le Monde*, Dec. 13, 1950.
[15] Beuve-Méry, "Un nouveau pilier de la paix?" *Le Monde*, April 6, 1949.
[16] *Op. cit.*, p. 412.
[17] The American reader may profitably consult P. M. Sweezy's *Theory of Capitalist Development* (New York: Oxford University Press, 1942) or M. Dobb's *Political Economy and Capitalism* (London: Routledge, 1950).

The Future of Soviet Communism*

GEORGE F. KENNAN (1904-   ), American diplomat and historian, has held several high positions in the Department of State, among them ambassadorships to the Soviet Union and Yugoslavia. He is the author of *Realities of American Foreign Policy* (1954), *Russia and the West under Lenin and Stalin* (1961), and other books on foreign affairs.

It is often suggested that great changes are due in American foreign policy as a result of, and by way of, adjustment to changes that have recently occurred in the attitudes and policies of the Soviet Government. The President [Eisenhower] appeared to be endorsing this same thought when he recently said that policies that were good six months ago were not necessarily now of any validity. This suggestion seems to me to reflect in large part a misunderstanding of the true situation. There have indeed been important changes in the attitude and policies of the Soviet Government. But their relationship to the problem of our own foreign policy is, in my opinion, somewhat different than is generally supposed.

In the first place, there is an impression that Stalin was a man of war, aiming to launch a military onslaught against the non-Communist world, whereas his successors are men of peace. Therefore, it is urged, we no longer need to orient our policies exclusively to the danger of war. This is a great oversimplification. Stalin was not what you would call a nice man, and his intentions toward ourselves were strictly dishonorable. But the image of a Stalinist Russia poised and yearning to attack the West, and deterred only by our possession of atomic weapons, was largely a creation of our own imagination, against which some of us who were familiar with

Russian matters tried in vain, over the course of years, to make our voices heard. In this respect, the change that has come about has been more a change in the American attitude than in any external reality.

Secondly, while the changes that have occurred in the Soviet Union do indeed suggest and emphasize the need for certain alterations in American policies, these alterations are ones the need for which ought to have been visible to us years ago and the implementation of which is decidedly overdue. It should not have required the effectiveness of recent Soviet appeals to the neutral bloc to bring us to realize that the extreme bipolarity of world power which marked the immediate postwar period was bound to break down at a relatively early date, and that this breakdown would give increased importance on the world scene to the attitudes and reactions of the neutral powers. It should not have required the evidence that [3/4] the Russians were actually testing atomic explosives to make us recognize that weapons of such vast destructiveness were bound to become, sooner or later, suicidal and prohibitive for mankind at large. It should not have required things like the Geneva meeting to bring home to us that it was foolish for America to take a stance in world affairs that appeared to be oriented exclusively to the winning of

* George F. Kennan, from "The Future of Soviet Communism," *The New Leader*, XXXIX (June 18, 1956), 3-6. Reprinted with the permission of George F. Kennan and *The New Leader*.

a future war and that would plainly leave us empty-handed and devoid of suggestion in case, as so many hundreds of millions of people desperately continued to hope, a new world war did *not* materialize and tensions were reduced rather than increased.

As one who has pleaded for these recognitions on many earlier occasions—rather futilely and often with a great sense of loneliness—I find it hard to share, today, the view that things have quite recently occurred in the Soviet Union that change drastically the assumptions underlying American policy.

I do not mean to belittle what has occurred. No one is more pleased and encouraged than I am about these recent changes in Russia. They have unquestionably helped to reduce world tension. They represent, I think, the beginning of that mellowing process which overtakes sooner or later all militant movements and which has been a source of hope for many of us who refused, in the darker moments, to take a despairing view of the Soviet problem. These changes point the way to a lifting, in considerable degree, of the Iron Curtain—to the restoration of a more normal and more hopeful relationship of the Russian people to their world environment, and to us in particular. I think all this has important and even, in some respects, exciting possibilities.

But we should not exaggerate them. We would be ill advised to ignore the very real differences of historical experience and tradition and outlook that still divide us from the Russian people and would continue to divide us even under the most liberal conceivable Russian regime. We Americans have a tendency to hazy and exalted dreams of intimacy with other peoples; and the farther away those peoples are from us both in physical distance and in historical tradition, the more we like to picture ourselves as associated with them in some sort of rosy nirvana of intimacy and comradeship. This has applied particularly, over the past hundred years, to our feelings about the Rus-

sians and the Chinese. Woodrow Wilson pictured the Russian people as a great mass of appealing, downtrodden liberals, cherishing in their hearts the same ideals that animated the people of this country, waiting only for liberation from the strictures of political oppression to add what he conceived to be their "thrilling voice" to the aspirations of American democracy. The number of Americans who have entertained similar illusions and daydreams with respect to the Chinese is legion.

I sometimes wonder whether these dreams of intimacy with what we regard as the humble and oppressed peoples of the earth do not represent a form of rebellion against the older European peoples who were, in a sense, the parents of this country. Perhaps we Americans, having once been the child of older nations, have a subconscious yearning, now, to play the father to someone else, in order to prove to ourselves the reality of our maturity and the finality of our liberation from the apron-strings of old Europe. However this may be, our dreams of possible association with the Russian and Chinese peoples have been unrealistic and a little silly: unjust to those peoples, because we attributed to them by implication a helplessness and weakness and dependence—an inferiority, really—that did not exist; unworthy of ourselves, since most of us are intelligent enough to be aware, on reflection, of the unreality of such visions. Perhaps we may regard the profoundly anti-American spirit of the political revolutions that have swept both these great countries during the past half a century as in part a just reproof to ourselves for this childishness and wishfulness in our approach to them.

Great damage can be done in international life, as in personal life, by the attempt to push intimacy beyond the point warranted by the real prerequisites of taste and outlook and experience. There are ways of looking at things and reacting to things among the Russian people which will always be strange to Americans and will always tend to arouse our resentment if we become too closely involved in their affairs. The same is no less true conversely. [4/5]

. . . .

So much for the main figures in the Communist camp. Now for the satellites. There can be no argument here about the hideous injustices committed some years ago in the forcing of Communist regimes upon these people and in the cynical exploitation of them by Stalin for his particular purposes. But if American foreign policy were to be addressed exclusively to righting the wrongs of the past rather than to developing the possibilities of the present, it would have a long way to go. Much of world history is little more than a recital of the injustices and brutalities committed by minorities of willful, power-thirsty men on the more docile majority of mankind, and most of these wrongs will never be righted. What we must recognize today, in the case of the satellites, is that evil, like good, produces it[s] own vested interests. Where regimes of this nature have been in power for more than a decade, there can be no question of putting humpty-dumpty together again and restoring the *status quo ante*.

No one in this country has deeper sympathy than myself with those moderate and democratically minded people—many of them my good friends—who have been driven into exile by the sickening intolerance of these Communist regimes. But there is a finality, for better or for worse, about what has now occurred in Eastern Europe; and it is no service to these people to encourage them to believe that they could return and pick up again where they left off ten or twenty years ago. Whether we like it or not, the gradual evolution of these Communist regimes to a position of greater independence and greater responsiveness to domestic opinion is the best we can [5/6] hope for as the next phase of development in that area. It is through this process that the respective peoples will best be able to return to something resembling a normal and independent participation in world affairs. But this transition will be effected most

easily and most rapidly if it does not come as a military or an ideological issue—if the satellite countries, in other words, are not asked to challenge in any way Russia's military interests or to embrace abruptly, in deference to any external pressure, ideologies conflicting with that which is dominant in that region today. The Soviet leaders have recently shown a greater liberality in their attitude toward these regimes, and this makes it all the more important that we should not allow ourselves to appear as the barrier to tendencies that are actually in everyone's interests.

This has an important bearing on our policies toward the countries that border on the Communist orbit. I have always felt that the release of Eastern Europe from the abnormal sort of bondage in which it has been held in these recent years will be best facilitated if the line that divides American and Russian military power in Central Europe is not too strongly accentuated and if there can be an increase, rather than a reduction, in the neutral zone that stands between. I think it, in other words, a good thing rather than a bad thing that Sweden has never joined the Atlantic Pact, that Switzerland has preserved in every respect her traditional neutrality, that Austria has been effectively neutralized, and that Yugoslavia is not wholly committed either to West or to East. I would wish that this neutral zone might be widened, rather than narrowed. While I realize that the concept of neutrality can be, and has been, exploited for Communist purposes, I don't think that should deter us from recognizing the real advantages it may hold. I, in any case, am a protagonist of neutralism in general, and feel that what we should wish from many other countries is not that they make promises to defend us in case of war but that they hold an enlightened view of their own self-interest and then firmly resist improper pressure from any quarter, in war or in peace.

For this reason, I have always doubted the wisdom of the decision to rearm West

Germany and to bring her into the Atlantic Pact. It seems to me that American policy should be aimed at the reunification of Germany and the earliest possible re-establishment of that country as a neutral factor that can blunt the sharp edge of military bipolarity in Europe and help, eventually, to mitigate the intensity of conflict between East and West. I am aware of the memories and inhibitions that cause the French and many other Europeans to contemplate such a prospect with unmitigated horror, and to fear that a Germany so re-established would eventually rework itself into the attitudes and aspirations of Hitlerism. But I think these fears ignore the real changes that have taken place in the mentality and aspirations of the German people in the past fifteen years. If our European allies insist that we must try to solve the European problem of today on the basis of the conditions that prevailed twenty years ago, then I am bound to say I see no solution of that problem at all and no very good reason why the United States should continue to commit resources to the vain hope of its solution.

It is frequently observed to me by friends here and in Europe that the Russians don't want German unification and that therefore there is no point in pressing it more seriously as an objective of United States policy. About the soundness of this assertion I just don't know; I suspect it to be something of an oversimplification. But I see no reason, in any case, why Russia's attitude of the moment should be the binding determinant of Western policy. I recognize that it may be too late to undo a portion of what we have done in our German policy, and I am not arguing for any abrupt or dramatic changes of policy. But I believe that, before we can hope to make much further headway in the European situation, the three Western powers will have to show a more genuine interest in German unification than they have shown to date and

a readiness to take greater chances, and to contemplate more realistic concessions, to achieve it.

The same principle applies, in my mind, to Japan. Again, I thought it regrettable, at the time, that it should have been necessary for us to conclude with the Japanese this particular sort of peace treaty, which settled nothing with respect to the adjacent areas and provided for an indefinite stationing of American forces on Japanese territory. I suspect that this may have had more to do than we suppose with the outbreak of the Korean War—by which observation I do not mean to condone in any way the cynicism and irresponsibility that led to the unleashing of that conflict. What troubles me particularly about the present arrangement is the maintenance of our bases in Japan. I have no illusion about the motives behind the Soviet agitation against our bases abroad; but again I see no reason why this should prevent us from recognizing that the prolonged stationing of American forces on the territory of any foreign country is always going to represent to some extent an unnatural situation and a burden on our relations with the people of that country. I can think of nothing more important for the peace and stability of the entire Pacific area than the relations between the Japanese people and ourselves. It seems to me a pity that these relations should be encumbered by any unnecessary burden. I fear that the prolonged presence of our forces in Japan, with all the minor inconveniences and irritations for the Japanese that this inevitably involves, will, even with the best of intentions on both sides, constitute just such a burden. I think American policy ought to be pointed toward a solution in which the Japanese archipelago, like Central Europe, could eventually come to constitute a bridge and an area of reconciliation, rather than a bone of contention, between the two great world systems.

[Elaboration of the Rapacki Plan]*

The following memorandum expanded an earlier Polish proposal, often known as the First Rapacki Plan after Foreign Minister Adam Rapacki. The expanded Rapacki proposal was resubmitted to the West at the General Disarmament Conference in Geneva on March 28, 1962. A new version of the Rapacki Plan appeared on March 5, 1964, but the one following is basic.

. . . .

On October 2, 1957, the Government of the Polish People's Republic presented to the General Assembly of the United Nations a proposal concerning the establishment of a denuclearized zone in Central Europe. The governments of Czechoslovakia and of the German Democratic Republic declared their readiness to accede to that zone.

The Government of the Polish People's Republic proceeded with the conviction that the establishment of the proposed denuclearized zone could lead to an improvement in the international atmosphere and facilitate broader discussions on disarmament as well as the solution of other controversial internal issues, while the continuation of nuclear armaments and making them universal could only lead to a further solidifying of the division of Europe into opposing blocks and to a further complication of this situation, especially in Central Europe.

In December 1957 the Government of the Polish People's Republic renewed its proposal through diplomatic channels.

Considering the wide repercussions which the Polish initiative has evoked and taking into account the propositions emerging from the discussion which has developed on this proposal, the Government of the Polish People's Republic hereby presents a more detailed elaboration of its proposal, which may facilitate

the opening of negotiations and reaching of an agreement on this subject. [822/823]

I. The proposed zones should include the territory of: Poland, Czechoslovakia, German Democratic Republic and German Federal Republic. In this territory nuclear weapons would neither be manufactured nor stockpiled, the equipment and installations designed for their servicing would not be located there; the use of nuclear weapons against the territory of this zone would be prohibited.

II. The contents of the obligations arising from the establishment of the denuclearized zone would be based upon the following premises:

1. The states included in this zone would undertake the obligation not to manufacture, maintain nor import for their own use and not to permit the location on their territories of nuclear weapons of any type, as well as not to install nor to admit to their territories of installations and equipment designed for servicing nuclear weapons, including missiles' launching equipment.

2. The four powers (France, United States, Great Britain, and U.S.S.R.) would undertake the following obligations:

(A) Not to maintain nuclear weapons in the armaments of their forces stationed on the territories of states included in this zone; neither to maintain nor to install on the territories of these states any installations or equipment designed for serv-

* From "Polish Note of February 14," *Department of State Bulletin,* XXXVIII (May 19, 1958), 822-823.

icing nuclear weapons, including missiles' launching equipment.

(B) Not to transfer in any manner and under any reason whatsoever, nuclear weapons nor installations and equipment designed for servicing nuclear weapons—to governments or other organs in this area.

3. The powers which have at their disposal nuclear weapons should undertake the obligation not to use these weapons against the territory of the zone or against any targets situated in this zone.

Thus the powers would undertake the obligation to respect the status of the zone as an area in which there should be no nuclear weapons and against which nuclear weapons should not be used.

4. Other states, whose forces are stationed on the territory of any state included in the zone, would also undertake the obligation not to maintain nuclear weapons in the armaments of these forces and not to transfer such weapons to governments or to other organs in this area. Neither will they install equipment or installations designed for the servicing of nuclear weapons, including missiles' launching equipment, on the territories of states in the zone nor will they transfer them to governments or other organs in this area.

The manner and procedure for the implementation of these obligations could be the subject of detailed mutual stipulations.

III. In order to ensure the effectiveness and implementation of the obligations contained in Part II, paragraphs 1–2 and 4, the states concerned would undertake to create a system of broad and effective control in the area of the proposed zone and submit themselves to its functioning.

1. This system could comprise ground as well as aerial control. Adequate control posts, with rights and possibilities of action which would ensure the effectiveness of inspection, could also be established.

The details and forms of the implementation of control can be agreed upon on the basis of the experience acquired up to the present time in this field, as well as on the basis of proposals submitted by various states in the course of the disarmament negotiations, in the form and to the extent in which they can be adapted to the area of the zone.

The system of control established for the denuclearized zone could provide useful experience for the realization of broader disarmament agreement.

2. For the purpose of supervising the implementation of the proposed obligations an adequate control machinery should be established. There could participate in it, for example, representatives appointed/not excluding additional personal appointments/by organs of the North Atlantic Treaty Organization and of the Warsaw Treaty. Nationals or representatives of states, which do not belong to any military grouping in Europe, could also participate in it.

The procedure of the establishment, operation and reporting of the control organs can be the subject of further mutual stipulations.

IV. The most simple form of embodying the obligations of states included in the zone would be the conclusion of an appropriate international convention. To avoid, however, implications, which some states might find in such a solution, it can be arranged that:

1. These obligations be embodied in the form of four unilateral declarations, bearing the character of an international obligation deposited with a mutually agreed upon depository state.

2. The obligations of great powers be embodied in the form of a mutual document or unilateral declaration/as mentioned above in paragraph 1/;

3. The obligations of other states, whose armed forces are stationed in the area of the zone, be embodied in the form of unilateral declarations/as mentioned above in paragraph 1/.

On the basis of the above proposals the government of the Polish People's Republic suggests to initiate negotiations for the purpose of a further detailed elaboration of the plan for the establishment of the denuclearized zone, of the documents and guarantees related to it as well as of the means of implementation of the undertaken obligations.

The government of the Polish People's Republic has reasons to state that acceptance of the proposal concerning the establishment of a denuclearized zone in Central Europe will facilitate the reaching of an agreement relating to the adequate reduction of conventional armaments and of foreign armed forces stationed on the territory of the states included in the zone.

A Neutral Belt in Europe?*

DENIS HEALEY (1917-   ) is defense spokesman for the British Labour Party and member of Parliament for the Leeds East district. An Oxford graduate, he served in the British Army in World War II and entered politics in 1945. He is identified with the moderates of his party, formerly led by Hugh Gaitskell.

. . . .
2. A PLAN FOR DISENGAGEMENT

What I am going to do now is to put forward a model for a neutral belt in the middle of Europe. I fully admit that it is not the only model which we can construct. But I think that if you are seriously concerned to advocate a policy of disengagement you have got to work it out in some detail. It is no good saying, like the German Social Democrats, that you want a European Security Pact and then not being able to answer the first question about who is in it, how it operates, what military forces are involved and how they would be used in case of emergency. You have got to be able to answer these concrete questions. But, as I say, I fully admit that the model I am going to put forward is not the only possible one, and it may well be defective in certain respects.

GEOGRAPHICAL LIMITS OF A NEUTRAL BELT

I do not believe it would be wise to aim at neutralising Germany alone, as has been suggested by many in the past, including Sir Winston Churchill in his speech at Aachen.

In the first place this would mean much greater concessions by the West than by the Soviet Union. The Federal Republic is nearly three times larger and more populous than the Soviet zone of Germany—and many times more wealthy. The manpower and territory of the Federal Republic are at the moment vital to NATO's strategy, whereas East German territory and resources are only marginal to Soviet strategy.

In my opinion the political case against neutralising Germany alone is even stronger than the purely military one. If you had a neutral Germany which was actually next door to the Soviet Union—which had Soviet power, the Soviet policy, the Soviet empire, immediately on its Eastern flank—then I think it would be too easy for some future German government to make a deal with the Soviet Union without Western agreement and mainly, of course, at the expense of Poland. Indeed, so long as the Polish-German frontier is not settled by the free agreement of an independent Polish and an independent German government, the Soviet Union has a trump card, through her occupation of Poland, to play for the allegiance of Germany. This second reason, I think, is absolutely decisive; if you try to neutralise Germany alone, you put Germany in the one situation in which she could exploit her bargaining power to upset whatever *status quo* is agreed.

* Denis Healey, from *A Neutral Belt in Europe?* (London: Fabian Society, 1958), pp. 7-13. Reprinted by permission of the Fabian Society and Denis Healey.

A FOOTHOLD IN EUROPE

It is vital, I think, if you have a neutral zone which includes the whole of Germany, that it should also include countries east of Germany, which could form both a counter weight to Germany inside the neutral area and would constitute a physical as well as a political barrier to direct contact between Germany and the Soviet Union.

So that I don't think you could restrict the zone to Germany alone. A surprising number of people have suggested that you should neutralise the [7/8] whole of continental Europe. Not only Mr. Krushchev [sic], but Sir John Slessor and Mr. George Kennan, have both at various times in the last few years suggested that the West could afford to accept what in effect the Russians have proposed, that is to say, the complete withdrawal of British and American forces from Western Europe in return for the complete withdrawal of the Red Army from Eastern Europe. Sir John Slessor has described this particular proposal as 'an air Locarno.' Now the weaknesses about that are two. Once again the West would be giving up far more than the Russians. Because once the British and American forces left the continent, and their bases left the continent, the British would go back across the North Sea, the Americans across the Atlantic, whereas the Russians would simply withdraw 500 miles across land to their own country. The disparity between the ease with which the Russians could return and that with which the West could return would be too great. And consequently, the only Western sanction against a Soviet violation of Europe's neutrality would be massive retaliation, because the West would not be in a physical position to do anything to counter a Soviet advance other than drop H-bombs on the Soviet Union itself.

Now, as I have already said, I do not think that a policy of massive retaliation —involving race suicide as well as the destruction of the country which initiates it—is a practical policy, quite apart from the fact that it is grossly immoral. And if a policy of massive retaliation is not a practical policy for defending an ally, it is certainly not a practical policy for defending a neutral. It seems to me that the great weakness of Sir John Slessor's proposal for an air Locarno is that it is inconceivable that Britain or the United States would expose their own territory to thermo-nuclear annihilation simply because there had been an infringement of the neutrality of an area in which they had no longer any direct physical involvement at all. If you are going to have an effective military sanction to protect the neutral belt, the West will have to keep a foothold on the continent of Europe from which it can exert military power short of total war.

I think the most obvious line for constructing a neutral belt would have to include the Federal Republic on the western side and Eastern Germany, Poland, Czechoslovakia and Hungary on the Soviet side; and then, in addition, as many other states as you could get in by bargaining. It might be, for example, that you could bring in Denmark against Rumania, and so on. But you would have to guarantee some physical foothold on the continent for the West as a base for military sanctions against a possible military violation of the neutral zone by the Soviet Union.

LIMITATION AND CONTROL OF ARMAMENTS

The second question is what arms should the countries in the neutral belt have and how should their arms be kept within the limits agreed. I think it is obvious that you could not afford to allow countries in the neutral zone any atomic weapons. A country with the power for thermo-nuclear attack and probably even with the power for small scale atomic attack has total freedom in its foreign policy. If it wants to blackmail other countries [8/9] —even large countries—it probably can. If you are going to keep the countries in the middle neutral, it means that you cannot give them that freedom *vis-a-vis* the guaranteeing powers outside. The Soviet Union would insist on that, and I think we should be wise to insist on it too. On the other hand, though these countries shouldn't have atomic weapons, I think they would have to have quite substantial conventional forces. They would have to have enough conventional forces to defend their frontiers against a local infraction, an infraction which is not serious enough to call in whatever external sanction may be envisaged to deal with a violation of neutrality. And, very much the same as NATO today, they must have conventional forces which are large enough to prevent a rapid *fait accompli* by the Russians, which would face the West with the alternative between starting up the war again or letting the thing go. In other words they would have to be able to start the fighting and to keep it going some time if there was a Soviet invasion. So I think you would have to have substantial conventional forces in the neutral area.

The question of how you control and inspect the limitations which are agreed is a soluble one. If it isn't soluble, then of course all the discussions that have taken place on disarmament in history are nonsense. But I believe that you could in fact have effective inspection by the Russians and the West of the armaments in the neutral zone by ground control teams along the lines that were discussed in the Disarmament Sub-Committee last summer. In addition to that I think you would allow the Russians to move their radar system to the western frontier of the neutral zone, and the West to move its radar system to the eastern frontier of the neutral zone. In addition, if it is still relevant after the development of earth satellites, you would have a system of aerial inspection beyond the frontiers of the neutral zone, including most of Britain and some part of European Russia. This would give you substantial protection against a surprise attack by either side.

All these provisions were under serious discussion between Russia and the West this year.

MILITARY SANCTIONS

The most difficult problem, it seems to me, and the one on which I confess I haven't been able to come to a conclusion which satisfies me fully, is this: assuming you have a neutral zone with limited armaments and mutual inspection, and then, in spite of that, a country on one side or the other tries to violate the neutral zone, either peacefully or by war, what physical sanctions could you impose to compel withdrawal? Alternatively, what military deterrent could you offer against an attempt at such a violation? My own opinion is that you could not really rely on the threat of massive thermo-nuclear retaliation to protect the neutral zone. Indeed it is doubtful if we shall be able much longer to rely on it even to protect some of our allies. This raises the whole question of the possibility of limited warfare and in particular the possibility of limited nuclear warfare.

What I think you must aim at is replacing the deterrent of thermo-nuclear annihilation in all-out war by what I would call the disincentive of punishment in limited atomic war. In other words, instead of threatening the other [9/10] side that you will blow the world up if he moves, you simply say: if you move, we will hit you so hard that it will cost you more to keep on fighting than you can possibly gain by carrying your aggression through to the end. Of course, this type of limited disincentive may not be a deterrent to all-out war; it may be that the capacity for massive retaliation is the only final deterrent to all-out war; but we assume that this capacity does remain in existence on both sides. Indeed its existence gives the best guarantee that if an armed conflict does break out, both sides will try to keep it limited.

If you want to deter limited aggression

into the neutral area, then I think you must have the capacity for limited retaliation and this will involve, I am sure, the limited use of atomic weapons from air bases in Western Europe and possibly also from missile bases in Western Europe on our side, and conversely, of course, for the Russians. This is a frightfully difficult problem; it is probably the most difficult problem in the history of modern defence policy, but it is a problem that must be solved, and I think that the Western governments, whatever their diplomatic policies for Europe, are going to spend most of the next five or ten years trying to solve it. The problem of limited war is just as urgent and important for NATO in the present situation as it would be for what remains of NATO under this new European settlement.

AN ALTERNATIVE TO MASSIVE RETALIATION

Somehow or other we must find an alternative to massive retaliation which is still an effective deterrent to local aggression, and which if the deterrent fails makes it possible to smother a local war without suddenly expanding it into all-out war. It is, as I say, the essential military problem for NATO today, when Europe is divided, just as much as it would be if we had a European neutral belt.

Although the problem of finding a deterrent which is both severe and convincing, because it does not mean suicide, is the same in principle for protecting Western Europe today, in practice it is very much simpler if you have a neutral belt. The biggest problem that NATO faces today in a divided Europe is that there is just not enough room on this side of the Iron Curtain to organise any sort of defence in depth at all. The Iron Curtain is too far west. But if you had a neutral belt, the fighting, if fighting began, would begin on the Soviet frontier, and you would have a buffer of substantial conventional forces to cross

before you got to the atomic forces of the West. If there is a solution to this problem, as I believe there is, it is easier to find it if you have this conventional arms buffer between the Soviet Union and the West, starting at the Soviet frontier, than it is if you have a general mingling of nuclear and conventional weapons, starting in the middle of Europe, as at the moment. Moreover, the risks of world war starting from spontaneous combustion in Central Europe are infinitely less if the whole of Central Europe is limited to conventional arms. And I think it is also worth pointing out that, as time passes, both the Soviet Union and the West will have less and less of a military incentive to violate the neutral area. In so far as they are worried about one another's aggressive intentions, they are [10/11] worrying more about long-range missile attack, and of course, who occupies what part of Europe is becoming increasingly irrelevant there. If they are really worried about one another's intentions, then they won't worry so much about the middle of Europe. The real fight will be in the laboratories of their homelands, rather than in the territories between them.

THE SOVIET UNION'S INTEREST IN DISENGAGEMENT

I believe that the sort of considerations I have put forward make a very strong case for the West to take the initiative in proposing a disengagement in central Europe along these lines. The big question is whether the Soviet Union would be prepared to negotiate seriously for such a settlement. The Soviet leaders have said they would, about once every two months, for the last two years. We have never taken up their proposals, and so we have not been able to find out whether or not they are sincere. But it is at least a starting point that they have said that they want to talk about this. In fact, on one occasion Krushchev [*sic*], who, I admit, does not always guard his words as carefully as he might, actually suggested a neutral zone along the sort of lines I have suggested. That is to say, if Western troops would only leave the Federal Republic, the Red Army would be prepared to leave the whole of Eastern Europe. Perhaps this was one of Krushchev's [*sic*] *obiter dicta*; one does not know how seriously one should take it.

But I do believe that the Soviet interest in staying in Eastern Europe is dwindling all the time. In the first place, the events of autumn 1956 showed that the satellites are not a source of military strength to the Soviet Union but a source of military danger. During the Hungarian revolution, there was considerable fraternisation between the Hungarian rebels and the Red Army. As you know, the Russians were unable to organise effective intervention until they had replaced almost the whole of their occupation forces by new troops, mainly from central Asia. The satellite manpower is not a military asset to the Soviet Union. There is evidence that since last year the Russians have been systematically starving the satellite armies because they don't regard them as reliable.

ECONOMIC FACTORS

In the second place, the Russians know that they cannot hope to prevent another explosion in [E]astern Europe unless they prevent the economic suffering of the people from becoming too great. Consequently, since the events of 1956, the Russians have probably been giving more economically to Eastern Europe than they have been getting. This is a complete reversal of the situation ever since 1944. The Soviet economic and military interest in staying in Eastern Europe is nothing like as great as it was a few years ago. For that reason they might be prepared to consider leaving Eastern Europe, providing it was within a system which gave them the sort of military safeguards which I have been describing. On the other hand, fear of change, conservatism in the Foreign

Office and the Army are probably just as powerful a force in the Soviet Union as in Britain and the United States. Perhaps the situation may be a little easier now that Zhukov has gone, because what little one does know about Zhukov's personal views suggest that he would not be prepared to withdraw the Red Army [11/12] from any of its existing positions, nor would he be prepared to consider any strategy other than all-out war. But the evidence is too poor to be conclusive.

My own opinion is that the dwindling of the Soviet Union's interest in Eastern Europe may not by itself be sufficient to induce the Russians to negotiate seriously about a neutral belt. What may finally turn the scale in favour of negotiations is the fear that unless the Soviet Union can organise a completely new sort of European settlement with Western agreement, each of the Western countries on the Soviet frontier will be equipped with atomic weapons. And I would venture to predict that within the next twelve months there will be serious public discussion about giving atomic weapons to Western Germany. And as that discussion approaches the point of decision, I think the Russians will make a really serious attempt to reach an alternative settlement of the whole European situation. It may well take the fear of a nuclear-armed Germany to force the Russians to consider so drastic a revision of their European policy as a whole. And unless the Western governments show far more imagination, I would expect to see the first real spasm of negotiations on this issue develop in one or two years' time.

A PILOT SCHEME FOR DISARMAMENT

I think it is worth pointing out at this stage that what we are really discussing is what is often called disarmament but is really the limitation of armaments. It is the same sort of problem that the Disarmament Sub-Committee has been discussing in the last few years. That is to say, a situation in which you try to reduce the level of armaments while maintaining the same balance of military power between the opposing groups. I believe some general factors will come into play to promote progress on both sides towards negotiation on disarmament. First of all, some agreement on arms limitation is immediately desirable for economic reasons. The cost of new weapons is increasing in geometric progression, on both sides. In the second place, providing that countries on both sides of the Iron Curtain adapt their strategy to meet the demands and possibilities of the new weapons, I think you can produce a situation in which war can be abolished altogether in so far as the deterrence of calculated aggression is concerned. There isn't much point in having a lot of arms if no situation is ever likely to arise in which you can use them either physically or diplomatically—by threatening to use them physically.

I think the Soviet Union and America at least, as the two countries which are most concerned with the arms race, have realised this already, and that is why they gingerly started getting to grips this year in the Disarmament Sub-Committee for the first time. But I think what has happened in the Disarmament Sub-Committee this year has underlined two lessons. Firstly, I don't believe the great powers will accept a disarmament agreement which involves control of their own internal system until the effectiveness of control has been proved on the little powers first. It seems to me absurd to imagine that the Soviet Union and the United States will agree to receive one [12/13] another's spies in their own atomic arms installations before they have first satisfied themselves in practice that this type of control can be made to work.

They can only satisfy themselves of this through a pilot scheme in other countries.

DANGER ON THE PERIPHERY

Secondly, I think that the dislocations and the changes in attitude involved in any effective arms inspection and control are so great that countries are not going to agree to it except in areas and on issues where there is a very great danger unless you have arms control. Nobody believes there is very much danger of either America or the Soviet Union starting an all-out thermo-nuclear war. In this sense people are less afraid of an H-bomb attack than ever before, because it is so obviously suicidal to the attacker as well as the attacked. Moreover, once you have got missiles you can put in submarines and hide in the ground there is no possibility of any surprise attack destroying the enemy's capacity to retaliate. What the big powers are worried about—and they are the powers, of course, which count most in disarmament negotiations, and they are the powers most engaged in the arms race—what they fear most is a war starting without their volition in a dangerous unstable peripheral area between them. Therefore the process of arms limitation and control will have to start in these peripheral areas. The two obvious areas are, of course, Central Europe, which we have been discussing, and the Middle East.

I think it is increasingly recognised by the big powers that the problem of preventing war now is essentially the problem of preventing small wars and, if small wars do break out, of preventing small wars from turning into big wars. That problem can only be solved by mutual agreement and I think that a European neutral zone along the lines I have discussed would be an admirable start, as a precedent for other such agreements.

An Address to the General Assembly of the United Nations, September 19, 1959*

NIKITA S. KHRUSHCHEV (1894-   ) became chairman of the Council of Ministers of the Soviet Union in 1958 when he displaced N. A. Bulganin in the post-Stalin struggle for power. Since 1953 he has been first secretary of the Communist Party of the Soviet state, succeeding Stalin in that key position. The following selection is taken from his proposal for general disarmament made in the United Nations General Assembly in September 1959.

. . . .

70. What does the Soviet Government propose?

71. The essence of our proposals is that, over a period of four years, all States should carry out complete disarmament and should divest themselves of the means of waging war.

72. The result of this is that land armies, naval fleets and air forces will cease to exist, that general staffs and war ministries will be abolished, and that military training establishments will close down. Tens of millions of people will return to peaceful, constructive work.

73. Military bases in foreign territories will be done away with.

74. All atomic and hydrogen bombs at the disposal of States will be destroyed, and all further production of such bombs will cease. The energy of fissionable materials will be devoted exclusively to peaceful economic and scientific purposes.

75. Military rockets, whatever their range, will be abolished, and rocket technology will remain solely in the service of transport and the conquest of cosmic space for the benefit of all mankind.

76. States should be allowed to retain only strictly limited police (militia) contingents —of a strength agreed upon for each country—equipped with light firearms and intended solely for the maintenance of internal order and the protection of the citizens' personal safety.

77. In order that no one may violate his undertakings, we propose the creation of an international control organ in which all States would participate. There should be established, for the control of all disarmament measures, a system which would be set up and operated in conformity with the stages in which disarmament was carried out.

78. If disarmament is general and complete, then, once it is accomplished, control will also be general and complete. States will have nothing to hide from each other; none of them will have a weapon to raise against another; and the controllers will then be able to display their zeal to the maximum.

79. This solution of disarmament questions will provide complete security for all States. It will create favourable conditions for the peaceful coexistence of States. All international problems will then be solved, not by force of arms, but by peaceful means.

80. We are political realists, and we ap-

* An Address to the General Assembly of the United Nations, September 19, 1959, *U.N. General Assembly Official Records*, 14th Session, Plenary 36-37 (A/PV. 799) (1959).

preciate that a certain time will be required in which to work out so broad a disarmament programme. While this programme is being evolved, and while the various issues are being settled by agreement, we must not sit with folded hands and wait. [**36/37**]

. . . .

90. In the conviction that these great aims can and must be achieved by the joint efforts of all States, united under the banner of the peaceful principles of the United Nations Charter, the Government of the Union of Soviet Socialist Republics is presenting, for the consideration of the United Nations, a declaration on general and complete disarmament, together with specific proposals on the subject.[1]

91. It goes without saying that, if at present the Western Powers do not, for one reason or another, express their readiness to embark upon general and complete disarmament, the Soviet Government is prepared to come to terms with other States on appropriate partial measures relating to disarmament and the strengthening of security. In the view of the Soviet Government, the most important steps are the following:

(1) The establishment of a control and inspection zone, and the reduction of foreign troops in the territories of the Western European countries concerned;

(2) The establishment of an "atom-free" zone in Central Europe;

(3) The withdrawal of all foreign troops from the territories of European States and the abolition of military bases on the territories of foreign States;

(4) The conclusion of a non-aggression pact between the member States of NATO and the member States of the Warsaw Treaty;

(5) The conclusion of an agreement on the prevention of surprise attack by one State upon another.

92. The Soviet Government considers it appropriate to recall its disarmament proposals of 10 May 1955,[2] which outlined a specific scheme for partial measures in the field of disarmament. It is convinced that these proposals constitute a sound basis for agreement on this vitally important issue.

93. This is not the first time that the idea of general and complete disarmament has been put forward by the Soviet Union. Our Government presented an extensive programme for complete disarmament in the period between the two world wars.[3] Opponents of disarmament were then wont to say that the Soviet Union had made the proposals because it was economically and militarily weak. This false argument may have misled some people at that time, but today it is obvious to everyone that to talk of the weakness of the Soviet Union is absurd.

94. The new proposal of the Soviet Government is prompted solely by the desire to ensure lasting peace between nations.

. . . .

[1] Subsequently distributed as document A/4219.
[2] *Official Records of the Disarmament Commission, Supplement for April to December 1955*, document DC/71, annex 15.
[3] See League of Nations publications, *IX. Disarmament*, 1932.IX.63 (documents Conf.D. 82 and 87), pp. 124-137.

Democratic-Socialist Party: Its Status and Policy*

N I S H I O   S U E H I R O (1891-   ) is chairman of the Central Executive Committee, Democratic-Socialist Party of Japan. This party, founded in 1960 after a split in the Japan Socialist Party, stands to the right of the older party and is the smaller of the two. Nishio is a veteran politician, having served in many party, union, and governmental posts since 1915.

. . . .
The Party advocates independent diplomacy. Its foreign policy follows an independent course neither in the direction of an exclusively pro-American foreign policy, such as adopted by the Conservative Liberal- [29/30] Democratic Party, nor in the direction of an indiscriminately pro-Communist attitude as assumed by the Social Democratic Party, or by the Communist Party. Rather, the foreign policy of this Party is formulated on the basis of the following principles.

First, it is laid out with a view to maintaining close relations and promoting cooperation with other free nations. This, however, does not necessarily mean that the Party is indiscriminately taking sides with free nations; it proposes, instead, that Japan should, above all, remain firm in maintaining its standpoint, voicing its convictions, unafraid and independent. Basically, it opposes the foreign policy currently adopted by the Government and the Conservatives who tend to fall in step invariably with the policy of the United States, pleading the necessity for promoting cooperation with the Free World. The Democratic-Socialist Party proposes to offer to the United States a frank explanation of Japan's justifiable claims; particularly, in respect to the U.S.-Japan Security Treaty, the Party supports a gradual annulment of this treaty and calls for the opening of negotiations for that purpose.

Secondly, in respect to the Communist states, the Party upholds the policy of promoting both cultural and economic relations with these countries, although they maintain an entirely different standpoint, ideologically and politically. On the basis of this policy, the Party would spare no effort in bringing about an early normalization of relations with Communist China and the Soviet Union.

Thirdly, the Party opposes, in practice, to [sic] an unarmed, defenseless neutralism, which is no more, no less, than an unwise measure to ingratiate this country with Communist China and the Soviet Union. Neu- [30/31] trality becomes a possibility only when its maintenance is ensured either with the existence of sufficiently strong armed forces; or with such an exceptional geographic advantage as being a country in a remote corner of the world, where the influence of the two confronting powers fails to reach; or with its guarantee of neutrality accorded to it by the two great powers of the world themselves. None of these exceptional cases is applicable to Japan. Therefore, the Party considers unarmed, defenseless neutrality to be an irresponsible argument put forward in complete disregard of Japan's political, economic and geographic conditions.

It is the basic objective of this Party to

* Nishio Suehiro, from "Democratic-Socialist Party: Its Status and Policy," *Contemporary Japan*, XXVII (May, 1961), 25-34. Reprinted with the permission of Nishio Suehiro and *Contemporary Japan*.

promote independent diplomacy on the basis of the recognition that Japan's peaceful independence can be ensured only through adhering firmly to the above-

stated principles of independent foreign policy.

Text of Peking Letter*

CHOU EN-LAI (1898-   ) is head of the Communist Chinese government and a member of the Politburo of the ruling party. He represented Peking at the Geneva Conference of 1954 and the Bandung Conference of 1955. After the Americans, British, and Russians reached agreement on a nuclear test-ban treaty in July 1963, Communist China denounced the accord as a fraud and asked for destruction of all nuclear weapons. Pursuing its own diplomatic and propaganda objectives, the Peking regime, over Chou's signature, sent the following letter to heads of governments, including the American president.

The Chinese Government issued July 31, 1963, a statement proposing a conference of the government heads of all countries of the world to discuss the question of complete, thorough, total and resolute prohibition and destruction of nuclear weapons. The text of the proposal reads as follows:

The Government of the People's Republic of China hereby proposes the following:

[1]

All countries in the world, both nuclear and non-nuclear, solemnly declare they will prohibit and destory [sic] nuclear weapons completely, thoroughly, totally and resolutely.

Concretely speaking, they will not use nuclear weapons nor export nor import nor manufacture nor test nor stockpile them; and they will destroy all the existing nuclear weapons and their means of delivery in the world, and disband all the existing establishments for the research, testing and manufacture of nuclear weapons in the world.

[2]

In order to fulfill the above undertakings step by step, the following measures shall be adopted first:

A. Dismantle all military bases, on foreign soil, and withdraw from abroad all nuclear weapons and their means of delivery.

B. Establish a nuclear weapon-free zone of the Asian and Pacific region, including the United States, the Soviet Union, China and Japan; a nuclear weapon-free zone of Central Europe; a nuclear weapon-free zone of Africa; and a nuclear weapon-free zone of Latin America. The countries possessing nuclear weapons shall undertake due obligatioons [sic] with regard to each of the nuclear weapon-free zones.

C. Refrain from exporting and importing in any form nuclear weapons and technical data for their manufacture.

[3]

A conference of the government heads of all the countries of the world shall be convened to discuss the question of complete prohibition and thorough destruction of nuclear weapons and the question of taking the above-mentioned four measures in order to realize step by step the complee prohibiion [sic] and thorough destruction of nuclear weapons.

In view of the urgent desire of the people of the world for the removal of the threat of nuclear war and for the safe-

* "Text of Peking Letter," New York Times (August 5, 1963), p. 4.

guarding of the peace and security of the world, the Chinese government earnestly hopes that its proposal will receive the favorable consideration and positive response of the Government of your country.

Please accept the assurances of my highest consideration.

CHOU EN-LAI,
President of the State Council of the People's Republic of China. [4]

PART THREE

EVALUATION—NEUTRALISM IN

THE DEVELOPING NATIONS

The Forces of Democracy and Socialism Are Growing and Winning*

IZVESTIA, the original source of this selection, is the government newspaper of the Soviet Union published in Moscow. The entire article from which an excerpt is reprinted here appeared in *Izvestia* on February 22, 1949.

. . . Thirty years ago—on Feb. 22, 1919—Izvestia printed Comrade Stalin's article, "The Two Camps." In this article Comrade Stalin described the deployment of political forces on the international arena as a result of the victory of the great October socialist revolution.

On the basis of a deep Marxist analysis of the inter-relationship of the forces of the camp of imperialist reaction and the camp of socialism, Comrade Stalin with great perspicuity defined the historical prospects of the development of the two camps and the inevitability of the victory of the forces of democracy and socialism over the imperialist camp.

Through the decades Comrade Stalin's work has retained all its acuteness and timeliness, to this very day. It arms the Party and the Soviet people with theory, helps us to understand the complex circumstances of the present struggle on the international arena, strengthens in the minds of millions of working people of the capitalist countries faith in the inevitability of the downfall of imperialism and the destruction of the regime of slavery and oppression of the peoples.

"The world has decisively and irrevocably split into two camps: the camp of imperialism and the camp of socialism," wrote Comrade Stalin, describing the new distribution of forces following the victory of the Soviet revolution.

. . . The struggle of these two camps, pointed out Comrade Stalin, constitutes the axis of contemporary life and provides the whole substance of the internal and foreign policy of the figures of the old and new worlds.

Analyzing the sources of strength of both camps, Comrade Stalin came to the firm conclusion of the coming victory of the forces of democracy and socialism. . . .

At that time the enemies were prophesying the speedy downfall of the Soviet state. And not only prophesying. The imperialists of the Entente, headed by one of the worst enemies of Soviet Russia, W. Churchill, organized the "campaign of the fourteen states" against our Motherland, with the aim of strangling the October revolution and returning the overthrown landowners and capitalists to power.

In these circumstances Comrade Stalin, with great perspicuity, outlined the further course of historical development. ". . . At the present moment of 'storm and stress,'" he wrote, "Russia is the *only* country where social-economic life is proceeding 'normally,' without strikes or demonstrations hostile to the Government, and the Soviet Government is the

* From "The Forces of Democracy and Socialism Are Growing and Winning," *The Current Digest of the Soviet Press*, I (March 22, 1949), 15-17. Reprinted by permission of *The Current Digest of the Soviet Press*, published weekly at Columbia University by the Joint Committee on Slavic Studies, appointed by the American Council of Learned Societies and the Social Science Research Council. Copyright 1949, the Joint Committee on Slavic Studies.

strongest of all the governments now existing in Europe, while the strength and weight of Soviet Russia, both domestically and without, are growing from day to day in direct relation to the decline of the strength of the imperialist governments. . . .

"Dying imperialism is seizing the last means, the 'League of Nations,' in an effort to save the situation by rallying the plunderers of all countries in a single alliance. But its efforts are in vain, for circumstances and time are working against it and for socialism."

This forecast by Comrade Stalin has been brilliantly confirmed by the entire course of world history. Guided by the great party of Lenin-Stalin, [15/16] the Soviet people smashed the foreign and domestic foes and won a long breathing spell. During the years of peacetime construction great historic transformations were carried out in the U.S.S.R. on the basis of the Stalinist policy of socialist industrialization of the country and collectivization of agriculture.

Time, as Comrade Stalin pointed out, works for socialism. Our country marched and continues to march along a path of ascending development.

. . . .

Thirty years ago Comrade Stalin wrote prophetically: "The waves of the socialist revolution are mounting irresistably, [*sic*] laying siege to the strongholds of imperialism. Their roar is echoed in the countries of the oppressed East." The second world war extremely aggravated the crisis of the colonial system of imperialism. Today the national liberation struggle has gripped millions of working people of the East. The victorious struggle of the Chinese people against the rapacious Kuomintang clique and American domination has already led to the liberation of enormous territory in China and to the establishment of genuine liberty and democracy in the liberated regions. The peoples of Indonesia, Vietnam, Burma and Malaya are fighting bravely for liberation from the domination of the Dutch, French and British colonizers. The drive of hundreds of millions of working people of Asia toward the revolutionary struggle against the colonial yoke still further strengthens the forces of the democratic camp and weakens the domination of imperialism. . . .

Today a fierce struggle of the two camps—the anti-democratic, imperialist camp and the anti-imperialist, democratic —is in progress in the international arena. But, as Comrade Stalin foresaw, deep changes have occurred in the relation of forces of the fighting camps. These changes reflect a tremendous growth of the forces of the democratic camp and brilliantly confirm the correctness of the Leninist-Stalinist doctrine of the inevitable downfall of the capitalist system and the victory of socialism.

The imperialist camp of the reactionary bourgeoisie is today opposed by the tremendously increased forces of democracy and socialism. Our great Motherland is the bulwark and leading force of the democratic camp. . . . Hundreds of millions of working people, both in the colonies and in the capitalist countries themselves, are taking an active part in the struggle of the democratic camp. . . .

At the head of the movement of the popular masses against capitalist slavery abroad stand the battle-tempered Communist and united workers' parties numbering more than 18,000,000 persons. . . .

The policy of aggression and of unleashing a new war, which the present leaders of the U.S.A. and England are pursuing, is based on a struggle against the U.S.S.R. and the countries of people's democracy, against the national liberation movement of the colonial peoples, and against the forces of democracy throughout the world.

. . . .

On the Dictatorship of the People's Democracy*

MAO TSE-TUNG (1893-   ) is chairman of the Central Committee of the Communist Party of China. He wrote the following article in 1949 to commemorate the twenty-eighth anniversary of the revolutionary party he led to power in mainland China. From 1954-1958 he was chairman of the People's Republic of China. Mao has made substantial contributions to Marxism-Leninism in theory and practice and is the author of *On New Democracy* and other writings including poetry. This selection originally appeared in *Pravda* (July 6, 1949).

. . . .
The only path for eliminating classes, for establishing world communism, goes through the people's republic under the leadership of the working class. All other ways have been tried and all of them ended in failure. Those who assimilated any other teachings were either smashed, or they recognized their errors, or they are changing their convictions. Events developed so rapidly that many were taken by surprise and these people's striving to learn anew is understandable. We welcome this yearning to learn anew. The vanguard of the Chinese proletariat studied Marxism-Leninism after the October revolution and created the Chinese Communist Party. Following this the vanguard of the Chinese proletariat began a political struggle and went through twenty-eight years of ups and downs before achieving victory. Basing ourselves on the experience of twenty-eight years, as well as on the "experience of forty years" referred to in Sun Yat-sen's testament, we may formulate the following general conclusion:

"One must firmly believe that, in order to attain victory, we must arouse the masses of the people and unite in a common struggle with those people of the world who regard us an equal nation."

Sun Yat-sen adhered to a world view different [4/5] from ours and based himself on another class point of view in determining and resolving problems. But in the problem of struggle against imperialism in the 20th century he came to a conclusion which basically accords with ours.

Since the death of Sun Yat-sen, 24 years ago, Chinese revolutionary theory and practice have, directed by the Chinese Communist Party, taken a tremendous step forward, radically altering the face of China. At the present time the Chinese people have mastered two basic problems:

(1) the awakening of the popular masses of the country: this means the unification of the working class, the peasantry, the petty bourgeoisie and the national bourgeoisie under the leadership of the working class, and the establishment of a dictatorship of people's democracy, led by the working class and based on an alliance of workers and peasants;

(2) the unification, in the common struggle, with countries of the world re-

* Mao Tse-tung, from "On the Dictatorship of the People's Democracy," *The Current Digest of the Soviet Press*, I (August 9, 1949), 4-5. Reprinted by permission of *The Current Digest of the Soviet Press*, published weekly at Columbia University by the Joint Committee on Slavic Studies, appointed by the American Council of Learned Societies and the Social Science Research Council. Copyright 1949, the Joint Committee on Slavic Studies.

garding us as an equal nation, and with the peoples of all countries: this means alliance with the U.S.S.R., with the countries of the new democracy in Europe, and alliance with the proletariat and masses of the people in all other countries for the creation of an international united front.

We are told: "You are leaning to one side." Exactly. Sun Yat-sen's 40 years of experience and the Communist Party's 28 years of experience have firmly convinced us that we must adhere to one side in order to achieve and consolidate victory. The 40 years and 28 years of experiences show that the Chinese people must, with no exception, take either the side of imperialism or that of socialism. It is impossible to remain in between the two. There is no third way. We are fighting against the reactionary clique of Chiang Kai-shek, who leans toward imperialism; in exactly the same way we are opposed to illusions about a third way. It is possible to adhere either to imperialism or to socialism, without exception, not only in China, but throughout the world. Neutrality is a camouflage and a third way a mirage.

We are told: "Your behavior is too provocative." The question involved is treatment of Chinese and foreign reactionaries, that is, imperialists and their watchdogs, no one else. As far as foreign and Chinese reactionaries are concerned, the question of provocative behavior does not arise; since they are reactionaries, it makes no difference. Only by distinguishing between reactionaries and revolutionaries, by exposing the purposes and conspiracies of the reactionaries, while maintaining vigilance in the revolutionary ranks, and only

by raising our own morale, can the reactionaries be isolated, subdued and suppressed. One cannot show the slightest fear when facing a wild beast. We must learn from Wu Sung (one of the 108 heroes of the known historical work, "All Men Are Brothers"), who killed a tiger on the Ching Yang Bridge. Wu Sung believed that the tiger on Ching Yang Bridge would devour people regardless of provocation. It was necessary to choose either to kill the tiger or to be eaten by him.

We are told that "we must engage in trade." Very true! There must be trade. We are only against our own and foreign reactionaries who prevent us from conducting trade, but we are not against anyone else. It should be known that it is none other than the imperialists and their lackeys, Chiang Kai-shek's reactionary clique, who are hindering us from conducting trade with foreign powers and from establishing diplomatic relations. When we have united all the forces in the country and abroad to destroy the Chinese and foreign reactionaries, then trade will begin and it will be possible to establish diplomatic relations with foreign powers on the basis of equality, mutual benefit and mutual respect for territorial sovereignty.

We are told: "Victory is also possible without international help." This is not true. In the age of imperialism real people's democracy cannot win in any country without various types of aid from international revolutionary forces. In the same way it is impossible to consolidate the victory even if it is won.

. . . .

The Political Report of the Central Committee of the Communist Party of China to the Eighth National Congress of the Party*

LIU SHAO-CH'I (1900-   ) became chairman of the People's Republic of China in 1959, succeeding Mao Tse-tung, whose policies he has long endorsed. In 1963 Liu made his first trip outside of the Communist world, to Southeast Asia. A veteran political organizer and theorist with high party rank, he is the author of On Internationalism and Nationalism and other basic works. He was chairman of the Standing Committee of the National People's Congress, when on September 15, 1956 he presented the report from which this selection is taken.

. . . .

Another development of great historic significance after the Second World War is the extensive victories gained in the movement for national independence. Besides the Democratic Republic of Vietnam, the Democratic People's Republic of Korea and the People's Republic of China which have already taken the road to socialism, there are a number of countries in Asia and Africa which have shaken off the colonial bondage and achieved national independence. These nationally independent countries, our great neighbour India included, have a total population of more than 600 million, or one-fourth of the human race. The overwhelming majority of these countries are all pursuing a peaceful, neutral foreign policy. They are playing a growing role in world affairs. The success of the Asian and African Conference at Bandung, and the new developments in the national independence movements in many Asian and African countries, especially the recent world-shaking event—the nationalization of the Suez Canal Company by Egypt—prove that the movement for national independence has become a formidable world force. In the past, most of the countries in Asia and Africa were colonies or semi-colonies of imperialism and were converted by the imperialists into their rear in preparing and waging wars. But now these countries have become forces opposing colonialism and war, and upholding peaceful co-existence. In the meantime, the struggle against colonialism is also spreading in the Latin American countries. The imperialists are doing their utmost to hold back the rising tide of the national independence movement. But this tide cannot be held back. It will, in the end, sweep over the whole of Asia, Africa and Latin [77/78] America, and thus end the rule of colonialism once and for all.

There can be no doubt that the existence of the socialist countries and their sympathy and support for the national independence movement have greatly facilitated the development and victory of this movement. At the same time, the upsurge of the national independence movement has likewise weakened the imperialist forces of aggression. This is fa-

* Liu Shao-ch'i, from "The Political Report of the Central Committee of the Communist Party of China to the Eighth National Congress of the Party," Eighth National Congress of the Communist Party of China (Peking: Foreign Languages Press, 1956), 77-80, 83.

vourable to the cause of world peace, and therefore favourable to the peaceful construction of the socialist countries. That is why the friendship and co-operation between the socialist countries and the nationally independent countries conform not only to their common interests but to the interests of world peace as well.

These great historical changes run counter to the desires of imperialism, especially U.S. imperialism. . . . [**78/79**]

. . . Naturally the imperialists nurse extreme hatred for the socialist countries. But they too know that the socialist countries, strong and united as one, cannot be shaken. Therefore, the main activities of U.S. imperialism at the present time are actually, under the pretext of "fighting communism," to suppress its own people, and, as far as possible, to control and interfere in the vast areas lying between the socialist countries and the United States.

These activities of the U.S. imperialists have met with increasing opposition from all quarters, and have further intensified the inherent contradictions within the capitalist system itself. The countries and peoples which once suffered, or are suffering, from colonialism are now becoming increasingly aware that U.S. imperialists are today the biggest colonialists, and the most predatory. In Asia and in Africa, an ever-growing number of nationally independent countries have adopted the policy of peace and neutrality, refusing to join the aggressive military blocs of the United States. This has put a powerful check on the colonial [**79/80**] aggrandizement of U.S. imperialism. Among the Western nations, too, an ever larger number have gradually come to realize the real damage done to them by the expansionist policy of the United States, and neutralist tendencies on the part of these nations to refuse to let themselves be tied to the American war-chariot and to favour, instead, peaceful co-existence with socialist countries, are also growing with each passing day. Britain and France, the two major allies of the United States, once hoped to maintain their vested interests by relying upon the power of the United States. But in fact, trailing after the U.S. policy of arms drive and war preparations has only exposed them to penetration by American influence, while the heavy burden of military expenditure has an increasingly harmful effect on the development of their national economies. This has in turn intensified the dissatisfaction with and opposition to American monopoly and American domination on the part of the major allies of the United States, and has particularly intensified the contradictions between Britain and the United States. At the same time, among the broad masses of the people in various Western countries, the movements for peace and democracy, in opposition to the U.S. policy of arms drive and war preparations, are expanding on an ever wider scale. The American people themselves have gradually come to realize what back-breaking burdens this policy has imposed on them, and the peril of war it has brought. Even inside the ruling circles of the United States, there are some sober-minded people who are becoming more and more aware that the policy of war may not, after all, be to America's advantage. [**80/83**]

. . . .

In past experience, in present circumstances, and in cherished hopes, China has much in common with the other countries of Asia and Africa which have just freed themselves from the rule of colonialism. In international relations in general, and in our mutual relations in particular, we all share the desire for mutual respect for territorial integrity and sovereignty, non-aggression, non-interference in each other's internal affairs, equality and mutual benefit, and peaceful co-existence. These common desires are embodied in the five principles initiated by China and India. Acting on these principles, we have already established ties of friendship and co-operation with many Asian and African countries, thereby promoting peace in this area.

. . . .

Statement of Conference of Representatives of Communist and Workers' Parties*

THE CONFERENCE OF REPRESENTATIVES OF COMMUNIST AND WORKERS' PARTIES met in Moscow in November 1960 to observe the forty-second anniversary of the Bolshevik Revolution and to discuss the common principles and internal differences in the Communist camp. Members of the Russian and Chinese parties differed, for example, about whether local Communists should seize power in underdeveloped countries (Peking favoring seizure) and about the relative urgency of the national liberation movement against colonialism (Moscow supporting a lower priority). The eighty-one participating Communist parties made adjustments on these and other questions and united in support of the final declaration, which follows in excerpted form. The final declaration was originally published in *Pravda* (December 6, 1960).

. . . .
. . . National-liberation revolutions have triumphed in vast areas of the world. In the 15 years since the war, approximately 40 new sovereign states have sprung up in Asia and Africa. The victory of the Cuban revolution has given a powerful impetus to the struggle of the peoples of Latin America for complete national liberation. A new historical period has begun in the life of mankind: The peoples of Asia, Africa and Latin America who have won their freedom have begun to take an active part in international politics.

The complete collapse of colonialism is inevitable. The downfall of the system of colonial slavery under the impact of the national-liberation movement is a phenomenon ranking second in historical importance after the formation of the world system of socialism.

The Great October Socialist Revolution aroused the East and drew the colonial peoples into the common stream of the world revolutionary movement. The victory of the U.S.S.R. in the second world war, the establishment of people's democracy in a number of countries of Europe and Asia, the triumph of the socialist revolution in China and the formation of a world socialist system greatly accelerated the development of this process. The forces of world socialism have contributed decisively to the struggle of the peoples of the colonies and dependent countries for liberation from the yoke of imperialism. The socialist system has become a reliable shield of the independent national development of the peoples who have won freedom. The international workers' movement is giving great support to the national-liberation movement.

The face of Asia has changed radically. The colonial systems in Africa are collapsing. A front of active struggle against imperialism has been opened in Latin

* From "Statement of Conference of Representatives of Communist and Workers' Parties," *The Current Digest of the Soviet Press*, XII (January 1, 1961), 3-4. Reprinted by permission of *The Current Digest of the Soviet Press*, published weekly at Columbia University by the Joint Committee on Slavic Studies, appointed by the American Council of Learned Societies and the Social Science Research Council. Copyright 1961, the Joint Committee on Slavic Studies.

America. Hundreds of millions of people in Asia, Africa and other parts of the world have won independence in fierce battles with imperialism. Communists have always recognized the progressive, revolutionary importance of national-liberation wars and are the most active fighters for national independence. The existence of the world socialist system and the weakening of the positions of imperialism have opened up to the oppressed peoples new possibilities for winning independence.

The peoples of the colonial countries are winning their independence both through armed struggle and by nonmilitary means, taking into account the specific conditions in the country concerned. They are working for a lasting victory on the basis of a powerful national-liberation movement. The colonial powers do not bestow freedom on the colonial peoples, and they do not depart of their own free will from the countries they are exploiting.

The United States of America is the chief bulwark of present-day colonialism. The imperialists, headed by the U.S.A., are making desperate efforts to preserve colonial exploitation of the peoples of former colonies by new methods and in new forms. The monopolies are trying to retain their hold on the levers of economic control and political influence in the countries of Asia, Africa and Latin America. These efforts are aimed at preserving the old positions in the economies of the countries that have gained freedom and seizing new positions under the guise of economic "aid," drawing these countries into military blocs, implanting military dictatorships in them and establishing military bases. The imperialists are trying to emasculate and undermine the national sovereignty of the countries that have liberated themselves, to distort the meaning of self-determination of nations, to impose new forms of colonial domination under the guise of so-called "mutual dependence," to put their puppets in power in these countries and to bribe a certain segment of the bourgeoisie, and they are using the poisoned weapon of national dissension to weaken the forces of young states that are not yet strong. Aggressive military blocs and bilateral aggressive military alliances are being used toward these ends. The most reactionary circles of the local exploiting classes serve as accomplices of the imperialists.

The urgent tasks of national rebirth in the countries that have cast off the colonial yoke can be successfully accomplished only given a resolute struggle against imperialism and the vestiges of feudalism through the unification of all patriotic forces of the nation in a single national democratic front. The strengthening of political independence, the carrying out of agrarian reforms in the interests of the peasantry, the elimination of the vestiges and survivals of feudalism, the eradication of the economic roots of imperialist domination, the restriction of foreign monopolies and their expulsion from the national economy, the creation and development of national industry, the raising of the people's living standard, the democratization of public life, the implementation of an independent peaceful foreign policy and the development of economic and cultural cooperation with the socialist countries and other friendly countries—these national democratic tasks form the basis on which the progressive forces of the nation can and do unite in the countries that have won freedom.

The working class, which has played an outstanding role in the struggle for national freedom, demands the consistent and complete accomplishment of the tasks of national, anti-imperialist, democratic revolution and resists the attempts of the reactionary forces to impede the cause of social progress.

The solution of the peasant problem, which directly affects the interests of the vast majority of the population, is of prime importance for these countries. Without far-reaching agrarian reforms, it is impossible to solve the food problem and to sweep away all the vestiges of the Middle Ages that impede the development of production forces in agriculture and industry. Of great importance in these countries is the establishment and expansion on a democratic basis of a state sector in the national economy, especially in industry, a sector that is independent of foreign monopolies and that steadily grows into a determining factor in the country's economy.

The alliance of the working class and the peasantry is a major force in winning and defending national independence, carrying out far-reaching democratic transformations and ensuring social progress. This alliance is called upon to be the basis of a broad national front. The extent to which the national bourgeoisie participates in the liberation struggle also depends to no small degree on the strength and stability of this alliance. A large role can be played by all national-patriotic forces, all elements of the nation that are ready to fight for national independence and against imperialism.

In present conditions the national bourgeoisie of the colonial and dependent countries that is not connected with imperialist circles is objectively interested in accomplishing the main tasks of anti-imperialist, antifeudal revolution and therefore retains the capacity of participating in the revolutionary struggles against imperialism and feudalism. In this sense it is progressive. But it is unstable; although progressive, it is inclined to be conciliatory toward imperialism and feudalism. Because of the dual nature of the national bourgeoisie, the extent of its participation in revolution differs from country to country, depending on specific conditions, on changes in the correlation of class forces, on the sharpness of the contradictions between imperialism, feudalism and the masses and on the depth of the contradictions between imperialism, feudalism and the national bourgeoisie.

After winning political independence, the peoples seek answers to the social problems raised by life and to questions of strengthening national independence. Different classes and parties offer different solutions. Which course of development to choose is the internal affair of the peoples themselves. As social contradictions sharpen, the national bourgeoisie becomes more and more inclined to conciliate internal reaction and imperialism. But the masses of the people become convinced that the best way to eliminate age-old backwardness and to improve the conditions of their life is that of noncapitalist development. Only on this path can the peoples free themselves from exploitation, poverty and [3/4] hunger. The working class and the broad masses of the peasantry are called upon to play a major role in the solution of this fundamental social problem.

In the present historical situation favorable international and internal conditions are being created in many countries for the formation of an independent national-democratic state, that is, a state that consistently defends its political and economic independence, struggles against imperialism and its military blocs, against military bases on its territory; a state that struggles against new forms of colonialism and the penetration of imperialist capital; a state that rejects dictatorial and despotic methods of government; a state in which the people are assured broad democratic rights and freedoms (freedom of speech, press, assembly, demonstrations, and establishment of political parties and public organizations) and the opportunity to work for agrarian reform and the satisfaction of other demands in the sphere of democratic and social transformations and for participation in the determination of state policy. The formation and consolidation of national-democratic states ensures these states the possibility of rapidly developing along the path of social progress and playing an active role in the struggle of the peoples for peace, against the aggressive policy of the imperialist camp and for complete abolition of the colonial yoke.

The Communist Parties are actively struggling for the consistent and complete accomplishment of the anti-imperialist, antifeudal, democratic revolution, for the establishment of national-democratic states and for decisive improvement of the living standard of the masses. They support the actions of national governments leading to the consolidation of gains achieved and the undermining of the positions of imperialism. At the same time, they vigorously oppose antidemocratic, antipopular acts and measures of the ruling circles that endanger national independence. Communists are exposing the attempts of the reactionary wing of the bourgeoisie to pass off their selfish, narrow class interests as the interests of the entire nation and the demagogic use by bourgeois politicians of socialist slogans toward the same end; they are working for true democratization of public life and uniting all progressive forces for the struggle against despotic regimes and for halting tendencies toward the establishment of such regimes.

The aims of the Communists accord with the highest aims of the nation. The effort of reactionary circles to break up the national front under the guise of "anticommunism" and to isolate the Communists—the most advanced segment of the liberation movement—weakens the forces of the national movement, contradicts the national interests of the peoples and threatens the loss of national gains.

The socialist countries are the sincere and true friends of the peoples who are fighting for liberation or who have already won freedom from the imperialist yoke and oppression. While rejecting in principle any interference in the internal affairs of young national states, they consider it their international duty to help the peoples in their struggle to strengthen national independence. They are giving all-round assistance and support to these countries in their development along the path of progress, in establishing a national industry, developing and strengthening the national economy and training their own personnel, and are cooperating with them in the struggle for peace throughout the world and against imperialist aggression.

The politically conscious workers of the parent states, realizing that "no nation can be free that oppresses other nations," consistently fought for the self-determination of the nations oppressed by imperialism. Now that these nations are taking the path of national independence, the international duty of workers and of all the democratic forces of the industrially developed countries of capitalism is to give them all-round support in the struggle against the imperialists and for national independence and its consolidation, and to help them successfully solve the problems of economic and cultural rebirth. In so doing, they are defending the interests of the masses in their own countries.

The complete and final abolition of the colonial regime in all its forms and manifestations is dictated by the entire course of world history in recent decades. All the peoples who are still languishing in the chains of colonialism must be given every support in winning their national independence! All forms of colonial oppression must be abolished. The abolition of colonialism will also have great importance for relaxing international tension and strengthening universal peace. The conference expresses solidarity with all the peoples of Asia, Africa, Latin America and Oceania who are carrying on a heroic anti-imperialist struggle. The conference greets the peoples of the young African states who have won political independence—an important step toward complete liberation. The conference expresses warm sympathy for and support of the heroic Algerian people in their struggle for freedom and national independence and demands an immediate cessation of the aggressive war against Algeria. It angrily condemns the inhuman system of racial persecutions and tyranny in the Union of South Africa ("apartheid") and calls upon the international democratic community to give active support to the peoples of South Africa in their struggle for freedom and equality. The conference demands noninterference in the sovereign rights of the peoples of Cuba, the Congo and all countries that have won freedom.

All the socialist countries and the international workers' and Communist movement consider it their duty to give all-round moral and material support to the peoples struggling to free themselves from imperialist and colonial oppression.

. . . .

More on Nehru's Philosophy in the Light of the Sino-Indian Boundary Question*

JEN-MIN JIH-PAO, the original source of the following article, is the daily organ of the Central Committee of the Communist Party of China. This periodical frequently presents major evaluations of foreign and domestic issues, sometimes prepared by high governmental and party officials.

. . . .

It is true that historically China had been powerful and had invaded other countries, but that occurred under the rule of the feudal landlord class. China today is a people's China, a socialist China; its social system is fundamentally different and its domestic and foreign policies are fundamentally different. A powerful and prosperous socialist China can only benefit peace and the fight against aggression, can only be of benefit to its neighbours and to friendship among nations. It will be a disadvantage only to the imperialists, who are aggressive by nature, and their lackeys. People throughout the world who love peace and uphold justice hold this view, and they believe that the more powerful and prosperous socialist China is, the better. Since Nehru so hates to see a powerful and prosperous socialist China, where does he stand? Has he not put himself in the very position of a lackey of the imperialists?

China has all along pursued a foreign policy of peace and stood for peaceful co-existence on the basis of the Five Principles with all countries having different social systems. China has signed treaties of friendship and mutual non-aggression or treaties of peace and friendship with the Yemen, Burma, Nepal, Afghanistan,

Guinea, Cambodia, Indonesia and Ghana. Similarly, China has always wanted to live in friendship with India. But Nehru, on the contrary, holds that India cannot live in [106/107] friendship with China. This runs diametrically counter to the wishes and interests of the Indian people.

China has had boundary questions left over from history with a number of its neighbours. For example, with Burma and Nepal too, China has very long boundaries which were not formally delimited in the past. But on the basis of the Five Principles of Peaceful Co-existence, in the spirit of mutual understanding and mutual accommodation, and through full consultations, boundary treaties have been signed between the Governments of China and Burma and between the Governments of China and Nepal, thus bringing about a reasonable and friendly settlement of the complicated questions left over from history. Why then should it be impossible to settle the Sino-Indian boundary question? If Nehru really wanted to settle the boundary question, it should not have been difficult to do so. And even if it were to remain unsolved for the time being, this should not prevent the two countries from maintaining the status quo of the boundary and living in peace with each other. And what need could there be to

* From "More on Nehru's Philosophy in the Light of the Sino-Indian Boundary Question," *The Sino-Indian Boundary Question,* 2nd ed. (Peking: Foreign Languages Press, 1962), pp. 106-107, 116-117, 120-121, 123-124, 126-127, 133-134.

slander and attack China endlessly and even to cross swords with China? [**107/116**]

. . . .

Nehru wrote in his book *Glimpses of World History* in 1934 that "so long as capitalism can use the machinery of democratic institutions to hold power and keep down labour, democracy is allowed to flourish. When this is not possible, then capitalism discards democracy and adopts the open fascist method of violence and terror." (Lindsay Drummond Ltd., London, 4th ed., 1949, p. 826.) At that time Nehru did not know that these words, after a number of years, would serve as an apt description of his own policy.

In view of the actual economic and political conditions in India, is not the building of a "socialist pattern of society" in India, as advertised by Nehru, an out-and-out hoax? Commenting on Nehru's "socialism," Harriman, spokesman for the U.S. monopoly groups, said on May 4, 1959:

I think it is a good thing that they [Nehru and his like] use this word ["socialism"]. It is a highly popular word among the Asian peoples, where capitalism has become closely identified—almost synonymous—with colonialism. The indians [Nehru and his like] have taken it away from the Communists.

Harriman's remarks serve to show what Nehru's "socialist pattern of society" is really worth.

With any country, a given foreign policy is necessarily the continuation of a given domestic policy. Like its domestic policy, the foreign policy of the Nehru government reflects its reactionary class nature.

At one time some actions of the Nehru government were helpful to world peace. It refused to join imperialist military blocs, turned down the imperialists' request [**116/117**] to establish military bases in India and declared its adherence to the policy of "non-alignment." It stood for peaceful co-existence with socialist countries and joined with China in initiating the Five Principles of Peaceful Co-exist-

ence. The Nehru government played a positive role in sponsoring the first Asian-African Conference.

However, even in that period, Nehru seldom voiced opposition to the major acts of aggression by imperialism, especially U.S. imperialism, but constantly came out against the just struggles of the people of various countries, and against the socialist countries. On many important, key international questions, Nehru always stood on the side of imperialism, adopting in the main a policy of "criticizing in a small way and helping in a big way" towards imperialism. For instance, during the war of U.S. aggression in Korea, the Indian Government put forward a proposal in the United Nations in November 1952, supporting the forcible retention of prisoners of war by the United States. In the counter-revolutionary event in Hungary in 1956, Nehru maliciously slandered the Soviet Union and attacked the Hungarian Workers' and Peasants' Revolutionary Government. [**117/120**]

. . . .

In September 1961 at the conference of the heads of state of the non-aligned countries, Nehru, going contrary to the opinions of the heads of many countries, held that the question of opposing imperialism and colonialism should occupy "a secondary place"; he disagreed with the adoption of "brave declarations" condemning imperialism and colonialism, and thus helped in a big way the Western countries, especially U.S. imperialism.

On May 29, 1961, the *U.S. News and World Report* in an article entitled "A Close Look at the Man U.S. Is Betting On in Asia" said that "Jawaharlal Nehru, Prime Minister of India, is turning out to be a top favourite of the Kennedy administration among statesmen of the world." But public opinion in Asia and Africa indicates that the role played by Nehru in international affairs has given him "a bad name." Even the *Ananda Bazar Patrika* admitted in its September 14, 1962 editorial that the Indian Government is "in an isolated position in international relations" and that "India has almost no friend in Asia." On September 22, 1962, the Indian weekly *Blitz* also said regretfully that among the Asian [120/121] and African countries, "we Indians [read Nehru and his like] are becoming conservative, if not reactionary."

Thus it can be seen that the policy of "non-alignment" publicized by Nehru has obviously become more and more a mere facade behind which he is actually carrying out a policy of opposing the national revolutionary movements of various countries, opposing socialism, and serving imperialism.

It is at a time when their entire home and foreign policy has become increasingly reactionary that the Indian ruling circles headed by Nehru have instigated the Sino-Indian boundary dispute, provoked China and finally launched large-scale armed attacks on China. They have done so because they persist in their expansionist policy and, by sabotaging Sino-Indian friendship and stirring up reactionary nationalist sentiment, attempt to divert the attention of the Indian people, intensify their exploitation and oppression of the people, and strike at the progressive forces. They have done so, too, because they seek to make use of the anti-China campaign to curry favour with U.S. imperialism and get more U.S. dollars. In a word, in the effort to satisfy their own needs and meet the demands of U.S. imperialism, the Indian ruling circles headed by Nehru have become pawns in the international anti-China campaign. This is the root cause and background of the Sino-Indian boundary dispute. [121/123]

. . . .

The basis of China's policy towards the nationalist countries is this: Firstly, the primary common task of China and all nationalist countries is to oppose their common enemy, imperialism and colonialism, especially U.S. imperialism. They must support one another in the struggle against imperialism and colonialism. China has consistently given active

support to the struggles waged by the various nationalist states against imperialism and colonialism. Secondly, it is necessary and entirely pos- [123/124] sible to establish and develop, between China and these countries, relations of friendship and co-operation on the basis of the Five Principles of Peaceful Coexistence. It is necessary and fully possible to bring about, through friendly consultations, a reasonable settlement of all outstanding disputes among them in accordance with the Five Principles and the Bandung spirit.

Similarly, China stands firm in its desire to live for ever in friendship with India. The relations of friendship between the Chinese and Indian peoples have a long history. There is no conflict of vital interests whatsoever between the peoples of our two countries. In 1954 the Chinese and Indian Governments jointly initiated the Five Principles of Peaceful Co-existence, and Sino-Indian relations built on this basis were once good. The Chinese people, like the Indian people, cherish the memory of the years when the two countries were on friendly terms.

But even in the period when Sino-Indian relations were good, the Indian ruling circles headed by Nehru repeatedly interfered in China's Tibet and harboured expansionist designs against it, thereby revealing their policy of reactionary nationalism. Then in 1959, when the rebellion of the reactionary clique of the upper social strata of the Tibet region instigated by Nehru was defeated and Nehru's expansionist dream about Tibet was shattered, and when he took a more reactionary line in all his home and foreign policies, Nehru immediately turned against his friend, switching from professions of friendship for China to frantic hostility to China. [124/126]

. . . .

The principles of China's foreign policy and of its policy towards India have been consistent. Despite incessant provocation by the Nehru government, China has still maintained an attitude of maximum restraint. It was only when the Nehru government had recently launched [126/127] large-scale attacks that China was compelled to hit back in self-defence to safeguard its sovereignty and territorial integrity and to repulse the attacks of the Indian reactionaries. It is fully necessary and perfectly just for China to do so, and it is the least a sovereign state should do. It is precisely for this reason that China has won the sympathy and support of the people of the world who cherish peace and uphold justice.

After the Nehru government started the Sino-Indian boundary dispute, the Yugoslav modern revisionists, renegades to Marxism-Leninism and lackeys of the imperialists, in utter disregard of the truth about the Sino-Indian boundary question, openly shielded and supported the outrageous anti-China policy of the Nehru government. On the Sino-Indian boundary question, Tito and his ilk have always hurled shameless slanders against China and become an echo of the imperialists and the Indian reactionaries. Moreover, Tito said that the Soviet Union should play a "pacifying" role in relation to China on the Sino-Indian boundary question. Does the Tito clique think that when a socialist country is invaded by the bourgeois reactionaries of a foreign country, another socialist country should stand by the bourgeois reactionaries and play a "pacifying" role in relation to the invaded socialist country? By this fallacy the Tito clique has further exposed itself as a group of renegades betraying socialism, hating socialist China and sowing dissension among the socialist countries. [127/133]

. . . .

We are firmly convinced that all complicated questions between China and India left over from history can be settled, provided friendly negotiations are conducted in accordance with the Five Principles of Peaceful Co-existence. Like the Sino-Burmese and Sino-Nepalese boundary questions, the Sino-Indian boundary question can be settled in a friendly way through peaceful negotiations. The Chinese people have never wavered in this conviction. We are willing to do everything possible and, together with the Indian people and all countries and people concerned with Asian peace and Afro-Asian solidarity, continue to work for the cessation of the border clashes, for the reopening of peaceful negotiations and for the settlement of the Sino-Indian boundary question. The Nehru [133/134] government should make corresponding efforts on its part if it still has some respect for India's national interests and for the aspirations of the Indian people, and if it does not want to bruise its head against a stone wall in further expanding the border clashes to the advantage of the imperialists.

To safeguard and strengthen the friendship between the Chinese and Indian peoples not only accords with the common interests of the 1,100 million people of the two countries but also conforms to the common wish of the peace-loving people in Asia and throughout the world. No force can undermine or shake this great friendship. Nor can the clashes provoked by the Indian reactionary circles on the Sino-Indian border in any way undermine or shake the true friendship between the people of China and India. It can be said that those people, whether inside or outside India, who whipped up anti-China campaigns in an attempt to sabotage Sino-Indian friendship, can never gain anything from it; they will only meet with utter defeat.

May the Himalaya and Karakoram Mountains bear witness to the great friendship between the peoples of China and India. Sino-Indian friendship which dates back to the immemorial past, though beclouded for the time being, will tower for ever like the Himalaya and the Karakoram.

The Nonaligned Countries and World Politics*

M I K H A I L   K R E M N Y E V (1923-   ) is a member of the staff of the *World Marxist Review*, an English language journal of international Communism, published in Prague. A citizen of Russia, Mr. Kremnyev is known especially for his articles on African affairs.

. . . .
Our times are times of revolutionary changes in the life of humanity. Socialism, advancing triumphantly, is destroying the exploitation of man by man and the unequal relations among nations. The national-liberation revolutions are sweeping away the last remnants of the old colonial empires; new sovereign states are arising in place of the former colonies and semi-colonies.

The emergence on the world arena of these independent states, a significant feature of our times, is changing the world balance of forces, narrowing imperialism's sphere of domination and undermining its positions.

1. True, the winning of political independence by the Afro-Asian peoples has not as yet brought them complete liberation from imperialist exploitation. The bulk of the new countries remains in the orbit of the world capitalist economy, although they now occupy a different place in it. They are still faced with the task of smashing the colonial economic structure, of achieving economic independence, and of ensuring democracy in the socio-political life of their countries.

On the international arena, however, the majority of the new sovereign states of Asia and Africa pursue an independent foreign policy and act as an independent force in world politics. In other words, they follow what is commonly known as

a *neutralist line.* The substance of this line is:

(a) support for peaceful coexistence, disarmament and prohibition of nuclear weapons;
(b) steadfast support for all movements for national independence;
(c) refusal to take part in military blocs;
(d) refusal to allow their territories to be used by foreign powers as military bases.

The neutralist line or, as it is sometimes called, the policy of non-alignment, is based on the principle of peaceful coexistence. The non-aligned countries, standing for friendly co-operation among all states on an equal footing, are making a contribution to the solution of the major international problems. Their stand on international issues objectively restricts the sphere of action of aggressive imperialist circles, narrows their chances of unleashing military conflicts.

This constructive role of the non-aligned states in working for peace and for peaceful coexistence was strikingly evident at the time of the Caribbean crisis, engendered by the aggressive designs of the United States against Cuba. When the world was on the brink of a thermonuclear world war the new Afro-Asian countries keenly realised that peace was indivisible, that they, together with the Great Powers, bore responsibility for it, and that now they would have to be more active in the fight against the war danger.

* Mikhail Kremnyev, from "The Nonaligned Countries and World Politics," *World Marxist Review*, VI (April, 1963), 28-34.

On the initiative of forty-five countries supporting a neutralist policy, U Thant, the U.N. General Secretary, appealed to the heads of government of the U.S.S.R. and the U.S.A. to settle the Cuban conflict in a peaceful way, to conduct talks in the spirit of mutual concessions and compromise. The positive role played by the neutral U.N. members was acclaimed by world public opinion.

The policy of non-alignment, which bears a distinctly anti-imperialist character, is in substance one of the forms of the anti-imperialist struggle. It is spearheaded against colonial oppression, and against the imperialist policy of military blocs and of encroaching on the freedom and independence of the peoples. The new sovereign states are co-ordinating their policy in order to render more effective assistance to the peoples still fighting for their liberation from the colonial yoke. They were, in particular, the initiators of the Bandung Conference which cemented the powerful anti-imperialist movement of Afro-Asian solidarity. The principles of Bandung are the bedrock basis of the non-alignment concept, and to a large extent determine the foreign policy of the young national states of Asia and Africa.

The non-aligned countries are opposed to the imperialist military blocs, which they [28/29] consider inimical to their interests. And for very good reason. On the one hand, the imperialists are still trying to inveigle them into these blocs and thereby prevent them from pursuing an independent policy, on the other, they are using the military blocs as an instrument to undermine the independence of the new countries and to crush the national-liberation struggle. One has only to recall the role played by NATO during the Suez crisis in 1956, or the aggressive action of SEATO against Indonesia, to see this. Many Asian and African leaders have voiced their sharp criticism of SEATO and CENTO, and of the other military blocs.

The non-aligned states are opposed to military bases on foreign territory. The Belgrade Conference of non-aligned states underscored this in its decisions. That conference, it will be remembered, supported Cuba's just demand for the closing of the American naval base at Guantanamo, retained by the United States against the will of the Cuban people. It is pertinent in this connection to recall that Tunisia's attempt in the summer of 1961 to abolish the French naval base at Bizerta [*sic*] led to an armed clash between Tunisian patriots and the French colonialists.

Many of the non-aligned states pursue an active, dynamic policy. There is nothing passive about the neutralism of India or Indonesia, for example. Theirs is not a neutralism that is indifferent to the pressing problems of the day, that keeps aloof from contemporary issues.

"Non-alignment is not a policy of seeking a neutral position in case of war," said President Sukarno at the Belgrade Conference. "Non-alignment is active devotion to the lofty cause of independence, abiding peace and social justice. . . ."

Many of the neutral countries effectively aided the Algerian people in their struggle against the French colonialists. India resorted to arms to drive the Portuguese colonialists from its territory only after having exhausted all peaceful ways and means; Indonesia was prepared to wage an armed struggle for the liberation of West Irian.

In the light of these examples one can hardly agree with those who identify the neutralist policy of the new states with the "perpetual neutrality" pursued by some European countries. Non-alignment, the sequence to the long national-liberation struggle waged by the peoples of the colonial and dependent countries, is an intrinsic part of this struggle, whereas the policy of "perpetual neutrality" is in most cases dictated by the geography of the country in question, or by its historical traditions. Such countries as a rule try to keep out of international affairs (Switzerland, for example, is not even a member of the United Nations), prefer not to wage an active struggle for peaceful coexistence, let alone against imperialism. In the final analysis what distinguishes the new neutralism from the older "perpetual neutrality" is the active, and not passive stand taken by the former in support of peace. It is not without reason, therefore, that the leaders of the neutralist states, when wishing to emphasize the difference, refer to their foreign policy as a policy of *active, or dynamic, neutrality.*

It does not follow from this, of course, that the neutrality of states like Austria or Sweden does not play a positive role in international life. Their neutrality serves the cause of peace, for it denotes a refusal to be involved in military blocs, or to allow their territory to be used for foreign military bases. It is a step forward compared with the policy of participation in imperialist military blocs. The growing sentiment in favour of neutrality observed of late in a number of capitalist states of Europe and America (Canada, Denmark, Norway, etc.) is proof of the vitality and growing popularity of the principles of peaceful coexistence and non-alignment, is a sign of the growing influence exerted by the people on foreign policy issues. [**29/32**]

. . . .

5. One of the favourite arguments of the opponents of non-alignment is that the neutralist states are not neutral at all, that in most cases they support the socialist camp, particularly when it is a matter of the fight against colonialism and for disarmament and peace. There has been talk of late in the imperialist camp about the neutralist policy being in general "an instrument of international communism."

The disciples of John Foster Dulles refuse to recognise the fact that the joint actions of the socialist and neutralist states to settle outstanding international issues are not the result of a compact between them, but the logical development following from the community of interests of the socialist world system and the worldwide national-liberation movement. In international politics the socialist countries pursue the aim of friendship and co-operation with the countries of Asia, Africa and Latin America fighting to achieve and consolidate their national independence.

The socialist camp guards the interests of the world liberation movement and bars the road to the imperialist aggressors every time they attempt to export counterrevolution. The events in the Caribbean demonstrated that the *Soviet Union and the other socialist countries consider it their internationalist duty to support national-liberation movements.*

The political, economic and military might of the socialist camp is the guarantee of the independence of the young states. The policy of non-alignment became possible only when the socialist system began to be a decisive factor in world developments. The Socialist countries support the neutralist policy of the young states because they consider that this policy corresponds to the interests of these countries, that it is an important factor in ensuring world peace.

The Soviet Union and all the socialist countries render extensive economic, technical and financial aid to the non-aligned countries, thereby helping them to achieve economic independence. This aid also strengthens the position of the young national states on the international arena, and is a paramount factor making for their security.

6. The policy of non-alignment took shape in the course of the struggle waged by the Afro-Asian countries against the imperialist military blocs. In the initial stage this policy simply meant non-alignment with the military blocs established by the imperialists. Egypt's refusal to enter the so-called Middle East Command in 1951, the resolute rebuff administered by Indonesia to all attempts to inveigle it into SEATO, the reluctance of the majority of the Arab states to be ensnared in the Baghdad Pact (now CENTO)— these were [**32/33**] the first shoots of the non-alignment policy which sprang from the soil of the struggle against imperialist intrigue.

Unfortunately, some statesmen in the

non-aligned countries close their eyes to this fact. In their criticism of the policy of military blocs they do not in all cases proceed from a realistic estimation of the situation but from general objective premises, making a fetish of the "non-bloc policy". Saying they are opposed to blocs in general, they equate the aggressive military alignments of the imperialist states and their allies with the defensive association of the socialist countries, the Warsaw Treaty.

But it is common knowledge that the establishment of the aggressive blocs was initiated by the imperialist powers. In the face of the threat to their security on the part of U.S. imperialism which began, immediately after the Second World War, to revive militarism and revenge sentiments, especially in Western Germany and Japan, the socialist countries had no choice but to strengthen their military might and form a defensive alliance. The Warsaw Treaty organisation appeared after the aggressive NATO and SEATO blocs were established, and after the foundation was laid for the Baghdad Pact. These were military alignments against the socialist states, designed to suppress also the national-liberation movement in the countries of Asia and Africa.

There is a fundamental difference between these aggressive pacts and the military organisation of the socialist states. "It will be pertinent to recall," said N. S. Khrushchov at the Sixth Congress of the Socialist Unity Party of Germany, "that right after the Warsaw Treaty organisation was founded the socialist countries declared that they stood as before for the dissolution of all military blocs and were prepared to abolish the Warsaw Treaty forthwith if the imperialist powers agreed to abolish their military alignments. We have repeated this many times since, and we adhere to the same viewpoint today."

Fetishism of the "non-bloc policy" has another aspect. Some advocates of this policy divide the present balance of strength into two military blocs—the imperialist and the socialist, placing the non-aligned states in a class of its own. They hold that the main trend in international relations will be an increase in the number of non-aligned states, primarily at the expense of the military bloc countries which, in their opinion, will gradually pass over to a "non-bloc policy". These theoreticians see non-alignment as a kind of remedy for all ills, as a lever for lessening international tensions and removing the danger of a new world war.

Non-alignment is the alternative to a pro-imperialist foreign policy, and is a gain *only* compared with the latter. A new type of international relations is being moulded by the socialist system, relations based on the principles of peace, equality, self-determination, respect for the independence of all countries, and on a fundamentally new type of diplomacy.

Failure to understand this can but lead away from the general path of contemporary international relations. It would be tantamount to disregarding the fact that the world is divided into two opposed social systems—the socialist and the capitalist; it would be tantamount to ignoring that in our age the socialist world system is a cardinal factor ensuring peace, and that the socialist countries will steadily increase in number, while the capitalist world will continue to shrink.

To be sure, the number of non-aligned countries has grown of late, and will continue to grow. This increase is primarily due to the appearance of new sovereign states. Independent Tanganyika, Uganda and Sierra Leone have declared that they will pursue an independent policy.

Although some countries in Asia and Africa still listen to the voice of their former masters, and have aligned themselves with the Western military blocs, it would be incorrect to assume that they have done so for all time, or that they have become reconciled to a subordinate role. Realisation of the fact that the peoples of these countries were able to win political independence has awakened powerful liberating forces which in the end will win for their countries a genuinely independent foreign policy.

Neutralist trends are manifesting themselves in the foreign policy of some of the Latin American states too. In this connection it should be noted that the policy of non-alignment, which crystallised as a result of the long struggle waged by the peoples of Asia and Africa for national liberation, is *not at all* the monopoly of these countries. Non-participation in aggressive military alignments and active struggle for peace are the underlying principles of the foreign policy of all countries anxious to get rid of imperialist dependence and to play an independent role on the international arena.

There is a growing sentiment for a neutralist policy in Brazil and Mexico, and, to some [33/34] extent, in Bolivia and Ecuador. On a number of questions connected with the struggle for peace, and, in particular, on the question of banning nuclear tests, some of the Latin American countries support the neutralist states.

* * *

The non-aligned states are playing an active role in world politics. Objectively, most of them act as a revolutionary and anti-imperialist force on the international arena. Together with the socialist states they form the vast peace zone, which is steadily expanding and vigorously countering the policy of war preparation. When assessing the policy of the non-aligned states the decisive criterion for Communists in all countries should be the part taken by these states in the powerful front of fighters for peace, which in our day can avert world war.

Socialism and Neutrality*

SATO NOBORU (1916-   ) is a theorist of the Japanese Socialist Party. He is associated with the wing which advocates "structural reform" (based on ideas from Togliatti of the Italian Communist Party) and a policy of "positive neutrality." Formerly a member of Japan's Communist Party, Sato was ousted in 1961 because of his membership in a faction which opposed Stalinism.

. . . .
The fundamental military alignments today are those of an imperialist bloc and a socialist bloc, centered respectively on the United States and the Soviet Union. The meaning of neutrality at the present time, therefore, is *principally* that of neutrality in *war* and in *military* confrontation between imperialist countries and socialist countries. It is theoretically possible even now to envisage war between imperialist countries, but the probability is slight, and the danger of such a war is not an urgent problem.

Thus apart from the fact that it is a military confrontation between imperialist and socialist countries that typifies the present age, in order to clarify the significance and role of present-day neutrality we must begin by studying the nature of the military confrontation between these two sets of nations.

In order to understand correctly the character of the situation which is known as the "American-Soviet conflict" or the "East-West conflict," it is necessary to distinguish three separate but related levels at which antagonism may be said to exist. The first is antagonism at the level of systems—between that of capitalism (imperialism) and that of socialism. The second is antagonism at what we may call the level of policy—between the peaceful policies of socialism and the warlike policies of imperialism. The third is antagonism at the military level—the relationship of opposition between two military blocs centered on America and the Soviet Union. The "United States-Soviet conflict" exists as a three-dimensional structure comprising these three sets of conflicting relationships. [34/35] Failure to appreciate this point leads inevitably to needless confusion in the understanding of problems of neutrality. First of all, how should we characterize the first of these conflicts, that between systems? A prevailing view is to see it as a class struggle. Therefore peaceful competition (coexistence), which is one of the forms taken by the conflict or struggle, between both systems, is seen as one form of the class struggle. "Peaceful coexistence between nations with differing social systems is one form of the class struggle between socialism and capitalism." (Declaration of the Representatives of Communist Parties of 81 Nations). This opinion is not necessarily mistaken, but it is not possible simply to regard a struggle between classes within one society as the same as a struggle between two systems, manifested as a national conflict. Even if we may take both in a broad sense as class struggles, we must not overlook their relative internal differences. They

* Sato Noboru, from "Socialism and Neutrality," *Shiso* (October, 1961) 34-43. Reprinted with permission of Sato Noboru. This selection was translated from the Japanese especially for this anthology by J. A. A. Stockwin.

are different in their historical origins, since the struggle between the capitalist class and the working class within one society—a class struggle in the strict sense—is as old as capitalism itself, while the conflict between capitalist and socialist systems, and the struggle between capitalist and socialist nations, has actually existed since the Russian revolution gave birth to a socialist system. Strictly, a struggle between systems is an extension and continuation of the class struggle in a narrow sense, and the class struggle within one country must be seen as externalized in a struggle between nations. For this very reason peaceful coexistence, which is unthinkable in the class struggle within one country, is extremely desirable in a struggle between systems.

Some may admit that conflict or struggle between systems is not confined to the one aspect of military confrontation. It can take the form of military conflict such as the Cold War or an actual war, but it can also take the form of peaceful competition or coexistence. Because of the confrontation of the two systems, however, it is not possible to eliminate the necessity of military conflict between them. This kind of thinking entails the Dullesian conclusion that peaceful coexistence between the two systems is impossible.

In two important senses neutrality is out of the question in the conflict and struggle between socialism and capitalism at the level of their systems. Firstly, it is impossible between socialist and capitalist ideologies. It is naturally impossible for there to be a third system or viewpoint belonging to neither of the other systems and occupying an intermediate position between them. This form of neutrality differs from the type of neutrality which is now proposed on the stage of world politics, namely, military neutrality. Military neutrality is a concept relevant only to military conflict between nations, and it can cause nothing but confusion to include the concept of military neutrality within the conflict at the level of systems. Even if the conflict between the two sys-

tems continues, there will not necessarily always be a question of military neutrality. [35/36]

. . . .

The second type of conflict is that at the level of policy—the conflict between war policy and peace policy. The origin of war and aggression is rooted in the oppressive nature of the capitalist system and is based on the rule of imperialism. On the other hand, socialism lacks in its system elements necessarily giving rise to war, and it must rather be admitted that it is a system for which peace is both necessary and profitable. In other words, if we look at the essence of the systems, we see that a war policy is basically a thing of imperialism, while the socialist side fundamentally takes a policy of peace, and within these limits it is not mistaken to call imperialism a war force and socialism a peace force.

It is clear that neutrality is impossible between a war policy and a peace policy. If such neutrality were not a policy of war it would also not be a policy of peace, but would have the meaning of a third policy between the two, and such a policy is clearly out of the question. Military neutrality is a policy of non-intervention, consisting of neither joining nor allying oneself with either of the military blocs; it is thus itself one sort of peace policy, not a third policy between those of war and peace. The very concept of military neutrality on the plane of the conflict between a war policy and a peace policy is misleading. The connotation of military neutrality is only at the level of military conflict.

Finally we will look at the third level, that of military conflict between imperialist countries and socialist countries. Today it is an undoubted fact that the imperialist countries centered on America, and the socialist countries centered on the Soviet Union have consolidated rival military blocs and are conducting stiff competition in the expansion of armaments. This military confrontation is on a different plane from the conflict of systems (between socialism and capitalism) and the conflict of policies (between a war policy and a peace policy), and it is on this plane that military neutrality becomes relevant. Conflict and struggle between a socialist regime and a capitalist regime is unavoidable within the limits of coexistence between the two systems; but whether the struggle will take the form of cold war or hot war, or whether it will take the form of peaceful competition, is the question which determines the main spheres of struggle between the two systems. In these circumstances, it is the imperialist side which denies the possibility of peaceful coexistence between the two systems and gives a military form to the conflict. It is the socialist side which affirms the possibility of peaceful coexistence, and tries to turn the struggle of the two systems into peaceful competition. What takes to extremes the struggle between the war policy of imperialism and the peace policy of socialism are the alternatives of total nuclear war and total disarmament, and this is the crux of the present struggle over war and peace.

Although the possibility has now very much increased that it will be possible to prevent war without either the peace policy of socialism or the war policy of imperialism completely overwhelming the other, and the prospects for stable peaceful coexistence are gradually brightening, it is nevertheless true that at present the world is beset by a bitter Cold War. [**36/37**]

What gives a military character to the conflict between socialism and imperialism is the policy of war and aggression on the part of the imperialists, based on the essence of the imperialist system, and it is imperialism, especially American imperialism, which bears the responsibility for starting the Cold War. Accordingly the socialist side has a basically defensive position in this military conflict, and if it has increased its armed forces and built a military bloc, this must be seen as a necessary evil.

. . . .

Although at present it is the conflict of military blocs centered on the United States and the Soviet Union, and the danger of war between them, that makes neutrality necessary, the most important factor which makes it possible for many countries to maintain neutrality is the peace policies of the socialist countries. . . . The fact that socialism has become a world system . . . provokes the imperialist countries and makes them resort to the policy of Cold War. Consequently the conflict of the two systems takes the form of a military confrontation between two blocs. From this springs the necessity for neutrality, but it is the peace-enforcing strength of the socialist system which makes it possible for many countries to maintain neutrality, [**37/38**] and prevents infringements of it by imperialist countries. The armaments of the socialist countries are thus included in their peace-enforcing strength. Although the military strength of the socialist countries serves to maintain and protect peace, it only plays the limited role of preventing aggression in the arena of conflict with the forces built up by the imperialist countries. It is thus merely a negative factor in securing peace. We may not simply conclude that the stronger the military strength of the socialist countries, the stronger will be the prospects for peace. As is now seen in the Soviet example, the socialist countries themselves, for the sake of peace, have repeatedly reduced their forces. If, however, they were to undertake total unilateral disarmament, it is clearly impossible to say that this would strengthen peace. The problem is that if socialist countries were content to disarm and thus create the conditions for dissolving military blocs, it would be necessary to persuade (more correctly speaking, to force) the imperialists to accept disarmament and the abolition of military blocs. Total disarmament is proposed for this very purpose. In other words, socialist countries have to strive for two things in order to maintain and strengthen peace; firstly, they have to maintain predominance in the arena of military confrontation, created originally by imperialism; they need to keep a defence establishment of sufficient strength so that they will not be overrun by the imperialists. Secondly, they have to try to abolish the arena itself, stop the military conflict between the two blocs and turn the struggle between the two systems into the less dangerous channel of peaceful competition. This is a positive peace policy suitable for the socialist systems. . . .

. . . .

One of the outstanding characteristics of contemporary neutrality is non-alignment with military blocs, combined with the peace policy of trying to eliminate these blocs. "Positive neutrality" means precisely the combination of neutrality with a peace policy. Of course, neutrality itself has a "peaceful" significance in that it objectively prevents the further expansion of military blocs and dampens their conflict. Although the objectively peaceful role of non-participation in military blocs, and the function of positively strengthening peace which is implied by the policy of dissolving military blocs, are in fact combined, a relative distinction must be made between them. [38/39] We must understand, for instance, the different role played in international politics by the neutrality of Switzerland and Austria, from that of India or Ghana.

The neutral policies of many countries, particularly those which are newly developing, are an amalgam of both policies of non-participation in military blocs and efforts to dissolve those blocs. . . . Peace policies designed to dissolve military blocs are seen not only in neutral countries, but also are a basic characteristic of the foreign policies of socialist countries. It is now possible for neutral countries to try to dissolve military blocs mainly because socialist countries themselves are aiming at this. . . .

In this way the neutral countries do not cooperate with the military strength of the socialist countries, but do cooperate with their positive peace policies. For the socialist countries themselves the disadvantages of the former are outweighed by the advantages of the latter. This is because world war is no longer inevitable in the present world situation. If war were at present inevitable, as it previously was, the socialist countries would have to do all they could to increase the number of their allies for a time of war. Now, however, that there is a prospect of preventing war, it is more profitable for the socialist countries that the number of countries with a neutral policy increase, and in this way the expansion of military blocs is prevented and it becomes more possible to abolish them. This shows that the interests of neutral countries and the interests of socialist countries are fundamentally the same, but it does not mean that neutral countries adopt a neutral policy for the sake of the socialist countries. Thus the socialist countries welcome as profitable to themselves the fact that the number of neutral countries is increasing, that the expansion of military blocs is halted, and that progress is being made toward their abolition. There is no contradiction in newly developing, independent countries and capitalist countries allying themselves with socialist countries for the maintenance and achievement of neutrality. . . . Such alliances, however, should not be made so much because the countries concerned are socialist, but rather because their policy of peace and support of neutrality lays the basis for an alliance; it is necessary not to overlook the relative distinction between the level of systems and the level of policies. At the same time there is certainly a limit to such alliances, since so long as a country has neutrality as an aim, it clearly cannot enter into a military alliance with socialist countries.

In connection with this point we must examine how to evaluate the neutrality of Yugoslavia. While socialist countries welcome and prize the neutrality of capitalist countries, what they criticize in the neutrality of Yugoslavia is its partiality, and that it is demonstrably designed to expand Yugoslav influence. [**39/40**] The real reason why Yugoslav neutralism is criticized is not that she is a socialist country, but that in present international politics, and especially in the Cold War conflict, despite the fact that she is geographically and historically connected with the Soviet Union and Eastern European countries, she neglects her special duties of solidarity, and particularly those of collective defence. Therefore if Cuba, in her advance to socialism, in the future should maintain a neutral position, this will not necessarily be criticized. Socialist countries have joined in a military bloc for their own security, and if many newly independent and capitalist countries see their security to lie in military neutrality, this is basically because of a difference in international viewpoints. The difference lies in whether it is best to face the Cold War directly, or whether involvement in military blocs presents grave dangers. Various geographical, historical and economic conditions have, however, had an important secondary effect. This is why in the capitalist countries of Western Europe (excluding Germany), neutrality has never been put forward as a concrete question in the way that it has been in Japan. As for America and the Soviet Union, which are the extreme examples of the Cold War conflict, neutrality is absolutely out of the question, but instead of neutrality, peaceful coexistence should be put forward. [**40/41**]

. . . .

Concerning the relations between the achievement of neutrality and national independence, there are differences between countries which have had their total national sovereignty taken away under colonial control by imperialist countries, countries of a colonial type which have been robbed of their existence as national states, and countries of an imperialist type which, like postwar Japan, have signed unequal military treaties with imperialist countries (American imperialism) and have suffered restrictions of

their sovereignty. In the first case the achievement of national independence is the prior condition for a neutral policy, and these countries have to take the course of "neutrality through independence," or "without independence no neutrality." For the latter type (e.g. Japan) it is necessary to adopt the method of independence through neutrality. The idea that there can be no neutrality without independence, thus postponing advocacy of neutrality until after independence is achieved, involves abandoning the neutralist movement as a road to independence. [**41/42**]

. . . .

. . . The neutralist movement itself, whose aim is to get out of the military bloc, is the road to the restoration of sovereignty, and a separate independence movement is not possible. Before the achievement of complete restoration of sovereignty by secession from its military bloc, the government can take measures leading to neutrality. (In Japan this could be done by concluding a peace treaty with the Soviet Union and restoring relations between Japan and China.) The problem of turning the government's policy in that direction is one of the most important questions of neutrality.

The achievement of the type of neutrality that is proposed in Japan—the movement for secession from an imperialist military bloc—is a national problem. In a broad sense it can be said to belong to the democratic movement, but it does not directly aim at socialist revolution. At present, however, this movement with its democratic nature, has become a constituent element in socialist revolution. In what sense is this true? First of all, the neutralist movement is not something which aims directly at socialist revolution, and it may be said that the two should not be combined. Nevertheless in a capitalist country such as Japan the neutralist movement is necessarily involved in a struggle with imperialism which has invaded her sovereignty, and with its ally, the monopoly bourgeoisie, which is advancing towards a revival of militarism, especially the extreme reactionary elements of this bourgeoisie. It thus has the same opponent as the socialist movement. In other words, if the most reactionary forces in the nation are isolated and their control weakened by movements other than the neutralist movement, this will objectively facilitate the achievement of neutrality. This, however, does not mean that all opposition to imperialism and the monopoly bourgeoisie should be included within the neutralist movement. The neutralist movement is purely a movement for the achievement of neutrality and is not capable of resolving the struggle against imperialism and against monopoly generally.

Secondly, the demand for neutrality, and the emergent basis of the neutralist struggle, operate within the capitalist (imperialist) system. The demand for neutrality is similar to the demand for peace, but the danger of war which gives rise to it is rooted in the exploitive nature of capitalism and in the rules of imperialism. In this sense the demand for neutrality and for peace is objectively opposed to the capitalist system. National security, which is the aim of neutrality, will be achieved for the first time when the essentially aggressive and warlike attributes of imperialism have been suppressed and its scope restricted, and when total disarmament and stable peaceful coexistence are realized. The neutralist movement is one aspect of the struggle against the results of a capitalist system. The socialist movement is a struggle to sweep away the cause as such (the system itself), and in this sense both are internally connected.

Thirdly, in the neutralist movement, as in the case of other democratic movements, the main bearer of the load is the working class and the labouring masses. [**42/43**] These classes are the main strength of the socialist movement, and the fact that it is they who provide the leadership and backing gives both movements a common basis.

. . . .

Lastly, the victory of the neutralist movement in many countries has resulted in the balance of power between imperialism and socialism being tilted in favour of socialism. We should not overlook the fact that by strengthening peaceful coexistence it has facilitated socialist revolution, and especially that [it] has increased the possibility of peaceful transition to socialism.

On the possibility of peaceful transition to socialism, Sakamoto Yoshikazu, in the previous issue of *Shiso*, writes as follows: "The conditions for peaceful transition are that the ruling class, which holds the State organs of compulsion, should not resort to Fascist violence. In other words, democratic principles must permeate the effective part of the ruling class. The ruling class must not betray the people by requesting aid from abroad to intervene against the revolution. In other words, nationalistic principles must permeate the effective part of the working class."

This argument maintains that the possibility of achieving peaceful revolution may be reduced to the question of "one's enemy's attitude"—whether the ruling class will turn to Fascism, and whether it will appeal for help from abroad in order to intervene against revolution. This, however, is not necessarily correct, since the requirements and motivating force of the ruling class in resorting to Fascism or asking for foreign counter-revolutionary help are not here distinguished from the capacity of the ruling class or the capacity of imperialism to give such counter-revolutionary help. This is because insufficient attention has been paid to the fundamental capacity of the international and domestic forces of revolution to resist both of these dangers. Today the masses in many countries are fighting for neutrality, and the fact that success has been achieved in maintaining neutrality shows how important this has come to be. This same capacity, and power relationships, point to the possibility of a peaceful transition to socialism.

President Eisenhower's Views on Neutrality*

DWIGHT D. EISENHOWER (1890-   ) served two terms as a popular president of the United States. His professional military career was climaxed by his leadership of the Allied European forces in World War II. He is the author of *Mandate for Change* (1963). The following selection is a White House press release dated June 7, 1956.

The President has authorized the following statement supplementing his informal press conference remarks of yesterday with reference to neutrality.

Questions have been presented to the White House concerning the exact meaning of expressions in the President's press conference yesterday defending the rights of certain nations to a neutral position. He particularly referred to neutrality as a refusal to take sides in any military lineup of world powers.

It is obvious that in some countries of the world there are certain ideological, geographical, or other reasons making military alliances impractical. Such nations may declare themselves to be neutral, hoping thus to secure the support of world opinion against attack from any quarter. Neutrality does not mean either disarmament or immunity from attack. We have had historical examples of this kind of neutrality for many decades.

The President believes in the principle of collective security whereby the nations associate themselves together for each other's protection. This is the modern and enlightened way of obtaining security. The United Nations was designed to provide collective security for all. In view, however, of the veto power in the Security Council it has proved necessary to organize for collective defense under the provisions of article 51 of the charter. The United States has such collective defense arrangements with 42 other nations, and it believes that, under present conditions, these treaties represent the best and most effective means of preserving world order within the framework of the United Nations Charter. Our mutual security program is primarily designed to reinforce that world order. The President does believe that there are special conditions which justify political neutrality but that no nation has the right to be indifferent to the fate of another or, as he put it, to be "neutral as between right and wrong or decency or indecency."

The President does not believe that association for mutual security with the United States will involve any country in added danger but, on the contrary, will provide added security on the basis of mutuality and scrupulous respect for the independence of each. As the President pointed out, [1004/1005] the United States is not going to attack anybody; but some great powers have shown an aggressive disposition, and military association with such a power could lead to difficulties.

---

* "President Eisenhower's Views on Neutrality," *Department of State Bulletin*, XXXIV (June 18, 1956), 1004-1005.

The Cost of Peace*

JOHN FOSTER DULLES (1888-1959) served as secretary of state in the Eisenhower administration during a critical period in American diplomacy. This period saw his management of a peace treaty with Japan, attacks on him at home and abroad for his vigorous role in the Cold War, and (to his admirers) the regaining of American initiative and stature. The following selection is from his commencement address at Iowa State College, Ames, Iowa, June 9, 1956.

Each one of you is going out into a world where you hope to enjoy in peace the blessings of liberty.

That is the kind of a world which United States foreign policy tries to provide.

Today we have peace; no nation is at war with the United States.

Also, we have many blessings. We have good relations with most of the nations of the world. We do not fear them nor do they fear us. We trade with each other and our peoples visit back and forth, all to our mutual profit and enjoyment.

For that peace, and for those blessings that we enjoy, we can be profoundly grateful.

But all of this is not to be had for nothing. Others before you have gone out into the world with eager hopes. But those hopes ended on the field of battle. And those at home were heavy of heart. And the means for economic well-being were dissipated in the wastages of war.

That kind of a price, paid in the coin of war, will always be paid unless men are willing, in time of peace, to pay to preserve peace.

That lesson seems never to be learned. The illusion constantly persists that peace is to be had merely by wanting it. If that were true, war would have been abolished

many centuries ago. The fact is that to keep peace is as hard, indeed harder, than to win a war. Wars have been won. But lasting peace has never yet been won. To win a final victory over war will take planning and action that is farsighted, well calculated, courageous, and at times sacrificial. Such sacrifice will be required under conditions less dramatic and apparently less urgent than those of war. But peace will never be enduring as long as men reserve for war their finest qualities of mind and spirit. Peace, too, has its price.

I want to illustrate that in terms of one phase of the peace effort our Nation is now making. It could be described as a peace insurance policy, and it costs about $40 billion a year.

OUR PEACE INSURANCE POLICY

The basic elements of this peace insurance policy are drawn from early and successful American foreign policy. We go back to the Monroe Doctrine.

In 1823 President Monroe proclaimed to the despotic alliance then headed by Czarist Russia that "we should consider any attempt on their part to extend their system to any portion of this hemisphere

* John Foster Dulles, from "The Cost of Peace," *Department of State Bulletin*, XXXIV (June 18, 1956), 999-1000.

as dangerous to our peace and safety" and that we would not "behold such interposition in any form with indifference."

It was indeed farsighted and bold for our young Nation thus to identify its own self-interest with the fate of freedom thousands of miles away. Yet the pronouncement of that principle, Webster recorded, was greeted with "one general glow of exultation."

That principle has now been extended. Its broadest application is found in the United Nations Charter. But because veto power makes United Nations action undependable, many nations have made with each other treaties which embody the principle of the Monroe Doctrine. Within the last 10 years the United States, always acting in a bipartisan manner, has made such treaties with 42 countries of America, Europe, and Asia.

These treaties abolish, as between the parties, the principle of neutrality, which pretends that a nation can best gain safety for itself by being indifferent to the fate of others. This has increasingly become an obsolete conception, and, except under very exceptional circumstances, it [999/1000] is an immoral and shortsighted conception. The free world today is stronger, and peace is more secure, because so many free nations courageously recognize the now demonstrated fact that their own peace and safety would be endangered by assault on freedom elsewhere.

However, it is not enough under present conditions for the free nations merely to proclaim their purpose to stand together. There is need for forces-in-being to give authority to those words.

At the outset of World War I and World War II, the United States had little military strength in being. In the case of the Korean War, our initial strength was inadequate. But on these past occasions the conditions of warfare gave us time within which to build up our strength.

But since then, man's capacity to destroy has suddenly expanded to a degree that passes comprehension. Today, a single bomb can release destructive power equal to that used in the 5 years of World War II. Potential enemies could destroy so much, so quickly, if initially unopposed, that we dare not gamble on developing military power after an attack has occurred. To deter aggression, to prevent miscalculation, we need not only to warn but to back that warning by forces-in-being which include retaliatory striking power. That is why our peace insurance policy is so expensive.

. . . .

Inaugural Address*

JOHN F. KENNEDY (1917-1963), the thirty-fourth president of the United States, was elected in 1961. His service ended tragically when he was assassinated on November 22, 1963. The withdrawal of Russian missiles from Cuba under American pressure in 1962 and the negotiation of a nuclear test-ban treaty with the Soviet Union are considered among the more outstanding achievements of his presidential career.

. . . .
To those new states whom we welcome to the ranks of the free, we pledge our word that one form of colonial control shall not have passed away merely to be replaced by a far more iron tyranny. We shall not always expect to find them supporting our view. But we shall always hope to find them strongly supporting their own freedom—and to remember that, in the past, those who foolishly sought power by riding the back of the tiger ended up inside.

To those peoples in the huts and villages of half the globe struggling to break the bonds of mass misery, we pledge our best efforts to help them help themselves —not because the communists may be doing it, not because we seek their votes, but because it is right. If a free society cannot help the many who are poor, it cannot save the few who are rich.

To our sister republics south of the border, we offer a special pledge—to convert our good words into good deeds—in a new alliance for progress—to assist free men and free governments in casting off the chains of poverty. But this peaceful revolution of hope cannot become the prey of hostile powers. Let all our neighbors know that we shall join them to oppose aggression or subversion anywhere in the Americas. And let every other power know that this Hemisphere intends to remain the master of its own house. [1]
. . . .

* John F. Kennedy, from "Inaugural Address," *Public Papers of the Presidents of the United States: John F. Kennedy, 1961* (Washington, D.C., 1962), p. 1.

A View of United States Policy in Africa*

ARNOLD RIVKIN (1919-   ) is the economic adviser of the Department of Operations (Africa) in the International Bank for Reconstruction and Development. A former director of the African studies project at the Center for International Studies, Massachusetts Institute of Technology, he was responsible for the legal aspects of Marshall Plan aid for Africa. This selection is from an address to the Nigeria Union of Great Britain and Ireland at the University of London in April 1961.

In order to put into proper perspective the developing policies of the United States toward Africa, it is necessary to consider the nature of the national interest underlying all U.S. policy toward new states and the underdeveloped world generally. Once this is done the nature, the interrelationship, and the likely direction of evolving U.S. policies in Africa becomes discernible.

However, before proceeding to a statement of what I conceive to be the U.S. national interest, I think it might be useful to offer one general observation by way of introduction. The U.S. interest in facilitating the orderly achievement by dependent territories of political independence and self-sustaining economic growth derives from two strands which are and have long been intertwined in American thinking. The first strand, the concept of the U.S. national interest with respect to the large galaxy of new states and the underdeveloped world generally, coincides in broad outline with the national interests of these new states and the underdeveloped countries of the world. It is discussed at length below. The second strand is philosophical, deriving from American ethical values of the rights of man and the comity of nations which first found expression in the Declaration of Independence in 1776 and time and

again thereafter in American state papers. In this century they have found expression in Woodrow Wilson's 14 points, in Franklin Roosevelt's four freedoms, in Harry Truman's Marshall plan and point 4 program, and again in President Kennedy's inaugural address. . . .

Even more recently, in supporting the resolution before the Security Council calling for a U.N. investigation of conditions in Angola, the American representative, Adlai Stevenson, quoted with quiet eloquence the memorable words of Thomas Jefferson:

"We hold these truths to be self-evident, that all men are created equal, that they are endowed by their Creator with certain inalienable rights."

The Liberian delegate to the Security Council said Ambassador Stevenson's words would reverberate throughout Africa and through the world. In fact, the words and the ideas they convey have been reverberating throughout the world since their birth in the American Revolution of 1776. Ambassador Stevenson speaking for the new American administration has given notice to the world in the debate on the Angola resolution that the United States intends to adhere to its philosophical heritage with renewed vigor in international affairs as well as at home.

* Arnold Rivkin, from "A View of United States Policy in Africa," *Congressional Record: House*, 87th Congress, 1st Session, CVII (September 7, 1961), 18597-18599. Reprinted with permission of the author.

I

The U.S. national interest in the under-developed areas of the world is viewed as tripartite and triangular.

First, it is clearly in the U.S. national interest to facilitate the peaceful evolution of independent states with the capacity for orderly political, economic, and social growth without recourse to violence and with a potential for developing viable economics and free institutions. Every independent state that emerges in this image or tends to approximate this image strengthens the kind of world environment in which open and democratic societies can flourish. This concept of the U.S. national interest naturally centers attention on Africa and on the policies which the United States has been evolving with regard to the development of new states in Africa.

Second, it is clearly in the U.S. national interest to facilitate orderly, peaceful and rational accommodation of the developing interests and aspirations of the under-developed areas of the world with the changing interests and aspirations of the relevant European metropolitan countries (e.g., the transformation of the British and French Empires respectively into the Commonwealth and Community) and with the developing interests and aspirations of the free world generally. Such orderly and rational accommodation would serve several purposes. It would prevent strife and violence in areas still evolving toward self-government and independence (e.g., the Federation of Rhodesia and Nyasaland) where conflict could endanger the peace and stability of other large areas. It would minimize the aftermath of colonialism and its attendant bitterness and recrimination in areas which achieve or have achieved independence in the postwar period (e.g., Indonesia, Morocco, and Guinea). In situations where change, too long frustrated, threatens to break all barriers in an uncontrolled rush (e.g., the situation building up in Angola and Mozambique), it

would prevent the recurrence of Congo-type crises. It would preserve and stimulate existing economic relationships which are beneficial to the underdeveloped areas as well as to the former metropoles and which could be increasingly so in conjunction with the development of new complementary relationships with other world states.

Third, there is a long established U.S. national interest in a politically independent and economically expanding Western Europe (as the third side to the United States, Western Europe, and underdeveloped world triangle). This interest requires that every effort be made to prevent Algeria-type situations which not only impose a great economic drain on the metropole but also deflect its energies and resources from important internal political and economic tasks and other free world responsibilities, e.g., the provision of increasing economic and technical assistance to the underdeveloped areas. It embraces the need not only to preserve such existing economic relations as are mutually beneficial to Western Europe and the underdeveloped world but also to create and expand trade and investment opportunities of mutual value. The United States, Western Europe, and the underdeveloped world all stand to benefit from mutually satisfactory economic relations between Europe and the new countries. As the three sides of a series of trade, aid, investment, and other triangular relationships, all three will benefit directly from the peaceful political and economic development of large parts of the globe.

II

What then does this view of the U.S. national interest underlying U.S. policy toward underdeveloped areas mean in specific terms of U.S. policy toward Africa?

(1) The emergence of independent states: The United States has welcomed the increasing accession of African territories to political independence; but until

quite recently it has viewed the political and economic development of the African territories as primarily a matter for the European metropoles and the territories, or in trust areas for the United Nations and the territories. I believe that now and in the future the United States will attach greater priority and sense of urgency to the achievement of rational accommodation between metropoles and territories in order to insure orderly accession of colonial areas to independence. In practice this may mean for the first time intercession by the United States with the metropoles in an attempt to resolve outstanding colonial relationships in a harmonious and peaceful way within a broad multilateral context of free world interest in Africa instead of relying on solutions achieved largely on a bilateral basis between the metropole and the territory. In fact, the United States has already taken a major step in this direction in supporting the resolution [18597/18598] in the Security Council, already alluded to, calling for an inquiry into conditions prevailing in Portuguese Angola. By way of explanation of the vote an official State Department statement declared:

"It was now imperative for Portugal to plan for the political, economic, and social advancement of the people of Angola. The United States was convinced it was the duty of a close and long friend of Portugal honestly to express the belief that such action was necessary."

If the practice envisaged develops, it will imply a coordinated free world approach to the economic and social development of the nascent African States, to the political stability and military defense of Africa, and to triangular economic relationships among Africa, Western Europe, and the United States.

(2) Preparation of dependent territories for independence: The United States has provided a limited amount of technical and economic assistance to dependent territories within the limits set by the colonial context and the accompanying U.S. view that the political and economic development of the territories were primarily the responsibility of the metropoles and the territories. Such aid has been thought of as a contribution to economic growth which would cushion some of the shocks of the passage to self-government and independence. Given a heightened sense of the priority and urgency of change in Africa, we can look, I believe, to an accompanying expansion of U.S. assistance in the preindependence transition period.

(3) Economic and social development of the new states: There has been a steady expansion in the volume, diversity, and techniques of U.S. development assistance flowing to independent African states. President Kennedy's concept that the 1960's are the "decade of development," expounded in his recent special message to Congress on U.S. foreign aid, suggests that his administration will continue this trend. I think that American assistance will not only be enlarged but also will be increasingly coordinated with other free world assistance flowing to Africa. There is likely to be a search for new multilateral aid channels and techniques for development assistance for Africa—both in the free world and within the existing framework of the United Nations and its affiliated agencies. The United States has already taken two initiatives with respect to free world assistance to underdeveloped countries. It has placed aid to the underdeveloped countries as a priority item on the agenda of the new Organization for Economic Cooperation and Development even before it has officially come into being, and it has initiated a series of bilateral talks with principal Western European countries, particularly with the West German Republic, with a view to inducing a considerable expansion of Western European aid flowing to the new states, particularly those in Africa. The recent support given to the U.N. operation in the Congo by both the Eisenhower and Kennedy administrations has carried the suggestion of the overall expansion of U.S. assistance to underdeveloped areas,

particularly those in Africa, channeled through the United Nations and affiliated agencies. This suggestion became explicit in the American proposal, "Africa: U.N. Program for Independence and Development," introduced a few weeks ago by Ambassador Stevenson in the political committee of the U.N. General Assembly.

(4) Neutralism: Irrespective of what U.S. policy may have been elsewhere in the world at an earlier date down through the near present, from the onset of the African independence revolution the United States has not sought the membership in or adhesion to Western military alliances of independent African states. The United States has been loath to provide military assistance to any African state and has as a consequence been criticized by President Bourguiba for not wanting to provide arms to Tunisia and by President Sékou Touré for not providing arms to Guinea. Bourguiba has threatened to go "elsewhere" if the United States refused, and Sékou Touré has gone "elsewhere." The United States has sought persistently to keep the cold war out of the crisis in the Congo Republic. It turned aside the request of Prime Minister Lumumba's government in July 1960 for U.S. military intervention and referred it to the United Nations. The United States has agreed to evacuate by the end of 1963 the air bases it obtained in Morocco during the French protectorate and prior to Moroccan independence. The only other American bases in Africa are an air base in Libya and a communication base in Ethiopia, both freely negotiated with governments of independent states. It is quite likely that in any serious negotiation with the Communist bloc to achieve a truly neutral status for Africa, the United States would be willing to agree to withdraw from these bases as part of a larger agreement to neutralize Africa, guarantee its political independence and territorial integrity from external attack or externally supported subversion, and embargo all arms shipments to Africa outside of the minimum required for maintenance of internal law and order.

There can be no question of American respect for the right of every African state to its own foreign policy. The United States has no intention to urge newly independent African states into military alliances or blocs. It is content to take its chances that politically independent African states, acting in their own best self-interest on critical issues, will more often than not come down on the same side as the United States—for both have common interests in the community of free states. On tactics, specific issues, and even in particular cases on fundamental policies, the oldest friend may differ at times, and so too may individual African states differ among themselves, and with the United States. But the national interest of the newly independent African states—political independence, economic growth and improved standards of living for their people, nation building, and the accession to independence of the remaining colonial territories on the continent by peaceful and orderly processes—coincides in basic terms with that of the United States.

If the application made by independent African states of their national interest to their foreign policy leads some to closer relations with the United States and the West generally than with the Communist bloc, certainly relations with those states will be welcomed. The opposite development will of course be accepted; but it is obvious that U.S. relationships with the various African states will reflect the orientation of these states to the same degree as it might be reflected in relationships elsewhere in the world.

As for the protestations of some African states that they are neutral, neutralist, positive neutrals, nonalined neutrals, uncommitted neutrals, et cetera, the United States is likely to test the protestations in each case in the real world of behavior and action. It seems appropriate to inquire of self-proclaimed neutrals, "Neutral for whom?" and "Neutral against whom?"

If the answer to both questions is "Nobody" then neutralism would seem to be an appropriate description of the foreign policy of those states.

The recent foreign-policy posture, however, of all the self-declared African neutrals in the Congo crisis cannot be meaningfully covered by any acceptable definition of neutrality. They are certainly not neutral toward one another nor toward the various factions in the Congo; and they are not neutral toward the West and the Communist bloc. Given the calculated Soviet introduction of the cold war into the Congo crisis, recognition of and assistance to the Stanleyville regime by African states constitutes at a minimum de facto, if not deliberate, alinement with the Communist bloc on the Congo crisis and, sadly, on the Soviet intrusion of the cold war and its anti-United Nations campaign into the Congo crisis. Recognition of and assistance to the Leopoldville regime also constitutes at a minimum de facto, if not deliberate, alinement with the West on the Congo crisis and, happily, on the West's resistance to the intrusion of the cold war and the Soviet's anti-United Nations campaign into the Congo crisis. Either way, pro-Stanleyville or pro-Leopoldville, neutrality or nonalinement for most, if not all, of the self-proclaimed neutralist states is fiction insofar as the major foreign policy issue in Africa of 1960 and 1961 is concerned. And it is apparently the more transparent fiction for those who have been in the neutralist vanguard than for other self-declared neutralist African states. The Casablanca bloc —the United Arab Republic, Morocco, Mali, Guinea, and Ghana—which has been most vocal in its neutralist protestations, has also been most interventionist in the Congo on the side of the Stanleyville regime.

For practical purposes, then, states which erect a facade of neutrality instead of a structure of neutrality cannot expect to carry the weight they seek to carry in world affairs by reason of being neutrals. United States relations with such states will be based not on their neutralist posture but, as with any other independent African state, on their actions.

As a Senator, President Kennedy said:

"The desire to be independent and free carries with it the desire not to become engaged as a satellite of the Soviet Union or too closely allied to the United States. We have to live with that, and if neutrality is the result of a concentration on internal problems, raising the standard of living of the people and so on, particularly in the underdeveloped countries, I would accept that. It's part of our own history for over a hundred years."

Mr. Kennedy pointed out the true criterion of neutralism—the motivation of a state in adopting a neutralist position in world affairs. When it is to achieve economic development and improved standards of living and national cohesion then such neutralism is fully understandable. When, however, the purpose is to make use of the privileged sanctuary of neutralism to manipulate or interfere in the affairs of other states, or to masquerade a partisan position, it is another matter.

. . . .

The United States Versus Unneutral Neutrality*

WINSTON L. PROUTY (1900-   ) is the junior senator from
Vermont. A "modern" Republican, he is a member of the Senate's Committee
on Commerce and Foreign Affairs. Here he evaluates nonalignment in an
address during Senate consideration of foreign aid.

. . . .

I am tired of our fawning and truckling
to win the allegiance of the uncommitted
nations. We often act "as if we were engaged in a debate with the Communists
in a sort of Oxford Union where the uncommitted or neutral nations act as mod-
erators and award a prize after hearing all
arguments"—"The New Cult of Neutralism," Henry A. Kissinger, page 26, the
Reporter, November 24, 1960.

To avoid offending what is called world
opinion, President Kennedy refused to let
his country resume nuclear testing. I am
sure that this action met with widespread
approval.

Glory was to be ours and shame would
fall upon the Soviet Union when Khrushchev became the first to break the test ban.
This was the theory.

What price glory?

Indeed, what a price for no glory at all.

Assuming the stance of dictator of the
world, Khrushchev did not just take
the lead in resuming nuclear testing—including testing of the most powerful hydrogen bombs the world has ever known.
He started testing above ground—the
method that causes the greatest poisoning
of the earth's atmosphere.

Twenty-four so-called neutral nations
were sitting in the jury box at Belgrade
when the Soviet Union announced its
intention—since carried out—to resume
nuclear explosions.

And what was the verdict of this jury
we have been so assiduously courting?

"Not quite guilty."

Nehru said:

I am not in a position and I suppose no one
else here is in a position to know all the facts
underlying the decision—military, political or
nonpolitical, whatever they may be.

But I know this decision makes the situation
much more dangerous. This is obvious to me.
Therefore, I regret it deeply.

President Tito of Yugoslavia said he
understood why Moscow had decided to
resume nuclear testing; Nasser was simply
shocked. The rest were eloquently silent.

The shrieking shame on you, Russia
hoped for by the White House, turned
out to be a whispered version of "Miss
Otis regrets she is unable to lunch today."

About the only character missing from
the very tragic comedy in Belgrade was
the fictional creation of Lewis Carroll who
said:

I am very brave generally only today I happen
to have a headache.

Joseph Alsop nailed to the wall for all
time the naive code of leading U.S. policy-
makers—the code that lets a synthetic
world opinion—not enlightened self-interest—shape the policies of this Nation.
Alsop said:

If you listen to persons of this school of
thought you might suppose that foreign policy
could be conducted on the principle of Sir Gala-
had—"my strength is as the strength of 10, because my heart is pure."

The truth is, alas, that naked power counts far
more in this sad world than virtuous intentions.

* Winston L. Prouty, from "The United States Versus Unneutral Neutrality," *Congressional Record:
Senate*, 87th Congress, 1st Session, CVII (September 19, 1961), 20226-20238.

Mr. Khrushchev did not give a hoot about world opinion. He was brutally frank about his reason for resuming nuclear weapons tests at this time.

According to the New York Times, Khrushchev told some leftwing British visitors, he is doing it to terrorize the Western Powers into negotiations on Berlin, Germany, and disarmament—on his own terms.

The so-called neutral nations issued a communique summing up their 5-day parley.

The communique called for peace but dealt chiefly with colonialism.

The neutrals saw colonial exploitation in the existence of the U.S. naval base at Guantanamo Bay. The base, they said, "affects the sovereignty and integrity of Cuba."

The neutralists demanded immediate evacuation of French armed forces from Tunisian soil. [20226/20227]

The neutralists also called for immediate freedom for Portugal's African colony of Angola.

No neutralist at Belgrade said anything about the cruel treatment of the citizens of East Berlin, the Chinese occupation of Tibet, or India's refusal to allow a plebiscite in Moslem Kashmir.

There was no sorrow expressed in Belgrade about the enslavement of Hungarians and other Eastern Europeans.

The Soviet Union's breach of the ban on the testing of thermonuclear weapons brought no rebuke—not even a scolding —from the neutralist delegates.

President Sukarno of Indonesia did find time, however, to demand that the West accept the Soviet solution for Berlin and Germany.

Tragic to say, the $6 billion of U.S. aid to the 24 neutralist nations evoked no kind words, no support for the American viewpoint.

Naked power, does, indeed, count for more in this sad world than pureness of heart.

Sukarno has received from the United States since the end of World War II nearly half a billion dollars.

Nehru and Tito, during the same period, got $2 billion apiece in U.S. aid.

Mr. President, it appears that it is now more profitable to oppose us than to appease us.

I have a table, taken from U.S. News & World Report, which breaks down the $6 billion we gave the 24 neutralist nations and I ask unanimous consent that the table be printed in the RECORD at this point.

There being no objection, the table was ordered to be printed in the RECORD, as follows:

SIX BILLION DOLLARS TO THE "NEUTRALS"— WHO GOT HOW MUCH?

Between the end of World War II and March 31, 1961, the United States gave and loaned more than $6 billion to 24 "nonalined" nations, as follows:

[In millions]

	Economic and technical aid	Military aid	Total
Yugoslavia	$1,362	$719	$2,081
India	1,906	0	1,906
Indonesia	458	21	479
United Arab Republic	346	0	346
Cambodia	191	66	257
Morocco	168	0	168
Tunisia	142	0	142
Afghanistan	116	0	116
Lebanon	76	7	83
Ethiopia	44	35	79
Burma	73	0	73
Iraq	20	49	69
Ceylon	63	0	63
Cuba	38	16	54
Sudan	31	0	31
Nepal	27	0	27
Saudi Arabia	27	0	27
Congo Republic	19	0	19
Yemen	10	0	10
Cyprus	7	0	7
Somali Republic	7	0	7
Ghana	5	0	5
Guinea	2	0	2
Mali	(1)	(1)	(1)
Total	5,138	913	6,051

1 Small amount, exact figures not available.

Mr. PROUTY. It is said that what's past is prologue and what is to come may be the formless ruin of oblivion.

If we wish to avoid oblivion, we would do well to look back at the years the locusts have eaten. There are, indeed, traces in the devastation. I shall examine but one of them.

India has left its mark in the United Nations—a mark of support for Moscow or a mark of abstention from any issue that might embarrass the Soviet Union. Here is a part of the record:

Germ warfare, October 21, 1952: India abstained from voting on a motion demanded by the Soviet Union to investigate charges that the United States used germ warfare in Korea. The free world overwhelmingly voted against it.

Red China, October 25, 1952: The General Assembly voted to postpone considering Red China for membership in the United Nations. The Communist bloc voted against postponement. So did India.

U.S. spying, March 26, 1953: When the Communists accused the United States of "spying" behind the Iron Curtain, the resolution was defeated by the votes of the free world. India abstained from voting.

Germ warfare, March 27, 1953: The Communists again demanded a hearing on charges that the United States used germ warfare in Korea. India voted with the Soviet bloc but the proposal was beaten again.

Red China, September 15, 1953: The General Assembly again postponed the question of Red China entering the United Nations. The Soviet bloc opposed delay. So did India.

Korean atrocities, December 3, 1953: When a U.S. resolution was offered in the U.N. Assembly to condemn Red atrocities which had caused 30,000 deaths in Korea, and the resolution was adopted by the free world, India abstained from voting.

Red China, September 21, 1954: The consideration of a U.N. seat for Red China was postponed again. The Russian bloc supported China. So did India.

American prisoners in China, December 10, 1954: When the General Assembly condemned the Red Chinese Government for keeping war prisoners in violation of the Korean truce, the Communist bloc voted against the resolution. Nehru abstained from voting.

Red China, September 20, 1955: The General Assembly again voted to postpone considering Red China's request for a seat in the United Nations. The Communist bloc voted against delay. So did India.

Hungary, November 9, 1956: When the U.N. Assembly passed a resolution denouncing Soviet intervention in Hungary and demanding that Russian troops be withdrawn and free elections held, India was the only non-Communist government in the world to vote against the resolution.

Hungary, November 21, 1956: The General Assembly demanded Soviet troops withdraw, that U.N. observers be permitted to enter Hungary, and that deportations to Russia stop. India supported observers but abstained on the two parts of the resolution relating to troop withdrawal and deportations.

Hungary, December 4, 1956: The General Assembly repeated the demand for Russian troop withdrawal from Hungary and entry of United Nations observers. The Soviet bloc voted against. India again abstained.

Hungary, December 12, 1956: On this day, one of the most important in the history of the U.N., the General Assembly voted to condemn Russian intervention in Hungary and repeated its demand that troops pull out. Communist bloc opposed the resolution and India abstained.

In a speech on November 9, 1956, Nehru justified India's abstention on the November 4 resolution by referring to the military action in Hungary as civil conflict, and the situation as very confusing. In the same remarks, he is reported to have given in detail and without a trace of counterbalance the justification for the Soviet attack that he had received from Bulganin.

How different was Nehru's attitude when he attacked repeatedly and in the harshest terms the Anglo-French invasion of Egypt in the fall of 1956. He sent a vigorous message to Secretary General Hammarskjold, stating that India was profoundly shocked and urging the United Nations to take "strong" measures.

The Hungarian crisis which had been in process since October 1956, called forth no public statement from Nehru until November 5 of that year when he expressed dissatisfaction with the two major world powers.

Nehru's unwillingness to recognize the threat of world communism has been evident even since the Hungarian revolt in 1956.

Two years later we saw the revolt in Tibet, followed in 1959 by the violation of the traditional northern frontier of India by the Red Chinese. In each case Nehru reacted more slowly and more mildly than informed opinion in India.

In his work, "Nehru, Nasser, and Nkrumah on Neutralism," Ernest W. Lefever has this to say:

Nehru's mild response to Peking's harassment of Indians in Tibet drew sharp criticism from some journalists and politicians. The Times of India commented: "Is there no limit to the humiliation we are prepared to accept at China's hands?" One correspondent said that for the first time since 1937 when Nehru became India's foreign affairs expert, "Indian opinion affirmed itself instead of waiting" to hear from Nehru. He added: "Indians are fed up with China and weary of Nehru's wisdom."

When China violated the border of India, Nehru's response was criticized by Parliament and the press. Opposition members charged him with appeasement.

Robert Trumbell, writing in the New York Times on September 5, 1959, said:

A study of leading Indian newspapers suggests that Mr. Nehru has been so far behind public opinion on Communist China in recent months that he may have to run to catch up.

In the General Assembly of 1960 attacks on the West by such leaders as Nehru, Nasser, Sukarno, and Nkrumah, were sharp and direct; those on the Communist bloc blunted, cautious, and ambiguous. [20227/20228]

Henry A. Kissinger characterizes the action of the neutralists as follows:

Almost every speech by these leaders attacked Western imperialism. Not a single reference was made to the unprovoked Soviet threat against Berlin—not to speak of other Soviet policies in Eastern Europe.

Nor did the uncommitted nations that were supposed to have been alienated by Mr. Khrushchev rush to the defense of the Secretary General when he was under the sledge-hammer blows of Kremlin spokesmen.

While Nehru did fail to support the Russian proposal for a change in the U.N. Charter with respect to the Secretary General, he later proposed, as Kissinger suggests, organizational changes whose practical consequence came very close to meeting Mr. Khrushchev's aims.

This persistent pattern was in bold relief last year when the neutralists voted yes with the U.S.S.R. while the United States abstained, on three arms control resolutions.

Indeed, there has never been a time in the history of the United Nations when the so-called uncommitted voted together to challenge or condemn a policy of a Communist nation.

This is the record, Mr. Neutralist.

Nor all your piety nor wit
  Shall lure it back to cancel half a line,
Nor all your tears wash out a word of it.

NEUTRALITY

Neutrality and neutralism each mean different things in different places and at different times. They can even mean different things in the same place and at approximately the same time—see "Neutrality: Varying Tunes." Hamilton Fish Armstrong; Foreign Affairs, October 1956, page 57. Armstrong points out that on June 6, 1956, President Eisenhower defended the right of nations to be neutral and 3 days later Secretary Dulles said that neutrality is "immoral." The President and Mr. Dulles were talking about different things.

The traditional meaning of the term "neutrality" is legal in nature and refers to a state's position of nonparticipation in time of war. Neutrality brings certain legal rights and responsibilities to the neutral state and the states in combat, and international law declares the rules that should govern this relationship.

Neutrality in a specific instance is often termed "ad hoc" neutrality. An example of this type would be the neutrality followed by the United States in the early stages of the First World War.

Another variation of this concept is that of permanent or perpetual neutrality. This type of neutrality, sometimes called "institutionalized" neutrality and exemplified by Switzerland, is frequently recognized in some legal form. A permanently neutral state attempts to be neutral in every war.

In Europe two countries are "neutralized" by international agreement. They are Switzerland and Austria—the former by an agreement of 1815, and the second by international law and international recognition by the United States, Britain, France, and the Soviet Union in 1955.

Finland, under the shadow of the sword of the Soviet Union, has been neutral by law since the end of World War II.

Sweden and Ireland have both been neutral as a matter of policy for a great number of years—the former, since the Napoleonic wars.

In Asia there have been at least two internationally neutralized states. Laos and Cambodia were forbidden by the Geneva Armistice Agreement of 1954 from entering military alliances or allowing foreign military bases on their territory.

Throughout a great part of its history the United States pursued a policy of genuine neutrality, and even acted as the protagonist for the rights of neutrals to carry on activities without hindrance from the parties at war.

NEUTRALISM

The term "neutralism" entered the vocabulary of the cold war about 15 years ago.

Although the dictionaries frequently define neutralism as a synonym for neutrality nothing could be more harmful than to confuse the two as they relate to the present world situation.

At the heart of neutralism, Eugene Lyons suggests, is the intolerable premise that the cold war is simply a conventional conflict between two power-hungry countries, the United States and the U.S.S.R.; that the Soviet bloc of nations and the American bloc are really the same breed of animal—"The Anatomy of Neutralism," Eugene Lyons; National Review, July 18, 1856, [*sic*], page 9.

By explaining away the Kremlin's crimes, said Lyons, and inventing or exaggerating American sin, the neutralist seeks to obliterate the moral gulf that separates the two worlds—Lyons, Eugene, in the work cited, page 10.

Thus, craft and credulity stifle reason and morality.

How has the United States reacted toward neutralism? Let us for a moment turn back the pages of history.

The division of the world in two major armed camps began with Soviet expansion into Eastern Europe at the end of the Second World War.

By 1948, Albania, Bulgaria, Czechoslovakia, East Germany, Hungary, Poland, and Rumania were forced under Soviet control.

In the Far East Communists took over in Outer Mongolia, China, North Korea, and North Vietnam.

Facing the threat of further Soviet advancement, the free nations of Western Europe and the United States and Canada formed the North Atlantic Treaty Organization.

After Communist China became poised for aggression in a second theater, the United States took the lead in bringing about the Southeast Asia Treaty, the Baghdad Pact and other collective security arrangements. These pacts are the backbone of our defense system.

Americans did not express much concern about "neutralism" until the bloody fighting of the Korean war. As lists of American dead and wounded grew larger and larger, many in the United States became bitter toward the countries that failed to assist the United Nations.

American awareness of the neutralist question mounted as the United States joined or encouraged SEATO and other military defense pacts and as neutralists became sharply critical of these pacts.

Consciousness of the question also grew as the Soviet gradually extended its influence into Africa and Asia through aid and trade.

Before the war in Korea was over, the free world community proved itself a myth.

In the words of Arnold Wolfer [*sic*]:

The world had been divided not into two, but into three parts, one of which consisted of nations determined to remain uncommitted to either of what they called the military blocs and to take no share, therefore, in the U.S. collective defense effort.[1]

What motivates newly independent countries to become neutralists? A Library of Congress study gives this answer:

Their strong anti-Western, anticolonial feeling. They are so emotionally antagonistic to those who were only a short time ago their rulers and, in their view, their exploiters, that they find the idea of cooperating with them no [*sic*] emotionally repugnant.[2]

John Foster Dulles drew no real distinction between neutrality and neutralism. He saw in them both a pretense "that a nation can best gain safety for itself by being indifferent to the fate of others. "This," he said, "has increasingly become

an obsolete conception and, except under very exceptional circumstances, it is an immoral and shortsighted conception."

After the death of Dulles, the pendulum began its dramatic swing in another direction. On October 14, 1960, President Eisenhower told 15 African leaders:

You cannot afford to waste your money which is needed to build to [*sic*] hospitals, the schools, the roads that your people need—you cannot afford to put that money into costly armaments.

PAST AND PRESENT ATTITUDES OF THE SOVIET UNION TOWARD NEUTRALISM

The attitude of the Soviet Union is friendly toward neutralism and tries to encourage it. Things were not always thus.

In a recent article, George Ginsburgs shows the zigzag course of Soviet conduct in this area of international diplomacy—"Neutrality and Neutralism and the Tactics of Soviet Diplomacy," George Ginsburgs, The American Slavic and East European Review, December, 1960, pages 531–560.

In 1946, he said, Moscow seemed to think the moment ripe and the Soviet foreign office, apparently counting on the success of its prolonged propaganda [20228/20229] campaign against neutrals in general, and Turkey in particular, presented Ankara, with the demand for a Communist role in the straits of the Dardanelles. Turkey's rejection of the Soviet plan met with the strongest kind of vituperation—Ginsburgs, George, in the work cited, pages 535–536.

Mr. Ginsburgs summarizes Moscow's attitude toward neutrals in the immediate postwar period as follows:

Even those nations which, like Sweden, indicated early in the cold war that they would ad-

---

[1] "Allies, Neutrals and Neutralists in the Context of U.S. Defense Policy." Arnold Wolfers. This article appears in Neutralism, a volume published by the Washington Center of Foreign Policy Research, p. 49.
[2] "The Problem of Neutrality," Foreign Affairs Division, Legislative Reference Service, Library of Congress, p. 11.

here to a policy of neutrality in peace or war, met no encouragement from Moscow and were indiscriminatingly relegated to the camp of imperialism to the destruction of which the USSR declared itself dedicated. Nor did Asian neutralists fare any better at this stage of Soviet diplomacy.[3]

When the growing strength of Western Europe deterred advances there by the Soviet Union, the Kremlin sought consolation in Asia and Africa.

There were practical considerations behind this decision.

By sponsoring neutralist tendencies the Soviet statesmen hope to:

First. Surround the U.S.S.R. with a buffer zone of friendly, or at least uncommitted, nations;

Second. Deny the use of lands bordering on the U.S.S.R. to foreign military installations;

Third. Weaken any Western collective security system by wooing away from it as many candidates for membership therein as possible;

Fourth. Deprive the Western powers of their sources of essential raw materials;

Fifth. Aggravate the struggle by the allied states for fast dwindling world markets by depriving them of colonial outlets and by expanding them in the newly independent areas—Ginsburgs, George, in the work cited, page 555.

In pursuit of these goals, the Soviet Union flatters neutralists about the "positive role" they have played in the interests of peace. It constantly espouses all neutral claims against pro-Western states regardless of their merits. From time to time the Kremlin expresses the view that war is no longer inevitable so long as the so-called Zone of Peace—the Soviet Empire and the friendly neutralists—is adequately strengthened.

Khrushchev continually attempts to identify the interests and policies of the neutralists countries with those of the Communist bloc.

This has been reflected in the United Nations and other organizations. The Soviet Union has been urging a much larger role for neutrals in the composition of the international bodies newly established and has tended to equate neutrals with Communist countries in counting the members of international bodies in order to obtain a kind of equality between East and West. The United States has opposed these attempts to link neutrals with the Communist camp. But many of the neutralist countries have given an impression of supporting the Soviet theory of membership.

When the Communist states boycotted the United Nations Commission on the Peaceful Uses of Space, both the United Arab Republic and India boycotted it also.

The Soviet bloc has also supplied economic, technical, and military aid to many of the uncommitted states. Among these are Yugoslavia, the United Arab Republic, Iraq, Yemen, Ethiopia, Afghanistan, India, Nepal, Burma, Cambodia, Ceylon, and Indonesia.

How long will Moscow's present support of neutrality and neutralism last? Probably until the Soviet Union has overturned the balance of power in its favor.

If that day ever comes, the neutrals will one by one be pinned, wriggling, to the wall like stuck butterflies.

Before the Berlin crisis began to heat up, it was often said that the struggle between the East and West was transferred from the military sphere to the economic and ideological sphere.

This represents the worst kind of wishful thinking. The so-called peaceful competition campaign has a direct connection with military power and policy.

NEUTRALISM VERSUS U.S. DEFENSE POLICY

There are three categories of nations lying between the United States and the Soviet bloc, and changes in the attitudes of any of them could result in a weakening of the U.S. defense position.

[3] Ginsburgs, George, op. cit., p. 536.

The first category consists of allies of the United States, countries bound by agreement or otherwise to support the U.S. collective defense effort; second, are the genuinely neutral countries which neither support the United States nor the Communist camp; and finally, there are the new neutralists whose marked bias against the West brings trouble to American defense policies.

The Communist bloc will be the winner if there is any transfer of U.S. allies to the category of neutrals, of neutrals to the category of neutralists, of neutralists to the category of complete satellites of the Soviet Union or Red China.

The studies of one observer disclose that no country except Cuba and Iraq—the latter never directly allied with the United States—has ever voluntarily changed from alliance to either neutrality or neutralism.

A switch, however, of one of America's major European allies from alliance to neutrality could make NATO unworkable.

In an excellent article, Arnold Wolfers points out that it is not always appreciated abroad why the United States set out to establish a widespread alliance system and why it stands to suffer if additional areas of the world come under neutral rather than allied control.

Wolfers had this to say:

In order to be able to contain the Sino-Soviet bloc inside the Eurasian land mass, the United States must be able to project its military power across the great oceans. It can do so only if given adequate opportunity for the deployment of American forces and facilities overseas and if assured of military cooperation by local allied forces stationed in the Eurasian danger zones. Thanks to its geographic location, the Soviet Union has no similar need—whether for its own protection or that of its allies—of engaging in peacetime deployment of forces beyond the borders of the bloc. This asymmetry of the geographic position of the two great powers gives the Soviet Union a marked propagandistic advantage. It has nothing to fear and much to gain from arousing hostility against military blocs and the stationing of troops on foreign soil.[4]

I do not suggest that the United States would profit if all non-Communist nations were prepared to join our alliance system.

If a country has little attraction, militarily, and is so exposed that an effort to safeguard it exceeds U.S. capabilities, there is a peril that failure to live up to a commitment to defend it may have the much feared "domino" effect of driving other allies into the arms of the Soviets. Furthermore, efforts to protect such a country may be so expensive or provocative that the United States is worse off as a result of the alinement than if the country in question remained uncommitted—Wolfers, Arnold, in the work cited, page 50.

Even though many Americans disapprove of neutrality, it is here to stay and we might as well resign ourselves to it. Certainly genuine neutrality is less harmful to the United States than neutralism or neutralist unneutrality of the type practiced by the newly independent nations.

. . . .

An escapist version of neutralism now endangers the relationships between America and her allies. [**20229/20230**]

The majority of delegates to the 1960 Conference of the British Labor Party went on record in favor of the unilateral nuclear disarmament of Great Britain.

Only a short time ago about 1,300 Britons were arrested for carrying on civil disobedience in support of their "Ban of the Bomb" demonstration.

This attitude does not represent majority thinking in the United Kingdom and probably never will. Official approval of such a view would mean, God forbid, no bases on British soil and quite likely no NATO.

CONCLUSION—WHERE WE ARE AND WHERE WE SHOULD BE GOING

For a time we acted as if the only importance of the new nations was as future military allies; neutrality was scorned as

4 Wolfers, Arnold, op. cit., p. 49.

"immoral." Our policy now goes 180 degrees in the opposite direction.

We do not just encourage neutralism; we exalt it.

In the view of leading U.S. policy makers, our paramount object is to engage in a race to please the uncommitted and to avoid at all costs offending the myth called world opinion.

The worshippers of world opinion prevailed upon the White House to deny air cover to the Cuban rebels and the invasion was a flop.

The worshippers of world opinion envisioned a great victory if the Communists broke the nuclear test ban and they saw their victory turn into a handful of dust—radioactive dust.

As Hans J. Morgenthau, writing for the New York Times has so wisely said:

> It will avail the United States little to try to curry favor with the neutralists by trimming its policies to their preferences; neutralism feeds on this kind of weakness. Rather, we must pursue clearly defined, strongly executed and ably presented policies to a successful conclusion, thereby demonstrating to all concerned that we know what we are about and that it does not pay to cross us.

Tragic to say, there are some in high places in this country who have not turned deaf ears to those who would have us pursue the cult of world opinion rather than enlightened self-interest.

Our situation calls to mind the story that is told of a man in Paris during the upheaval in 1848, who saw a friend marching after a crowd toward the barricades. Warning him that they could not be held against the troops, that he had better keep away, and asking why he followed those people, he received the reply, "I must follow them. I am their leader."

It is possible, as Kissinger suggests, to accept the desire of a new nation to remain neutral without transforming that acceptance into "an exaltation of noncommitment."

We ought at least to acknowledge that some of the new countries are in need of a time of peace and unentanglement to put their domestic house in order.

Moreover, we should harbor no illusions about pushing our precise form of government on peoples who do not yet have the sophistication to operate it.

Our Anglo-Saxon concepts of liberty and our American values evolved and have been refined over a number of centuries.

We cannot expect the newest of the emerging societies to gain a full appreciation of them overnight.

Let it be said also that as a nation we welcome the aspirations of the new countries for a better life for their people.

If the time ever comes when we can have arms reduction under a realistic, enforceable agreement, the United States and all the Western Powers will have at hand resources which can be used to further these aspirations. [20230/20231]
. . . .

The words I have spoken today do not come easily from the throat of one who has given his voice and his vote to measures which would aid the underdeveloped nations.

The world has revolved a number of times since I first gave my wholehearted support to our aid program. I have tried to understand the misjudgments and indeed the folly of the infant and more advanced emerging societies.

Now, however, we are but minutes away from the hour of vital decision when all may be won or lost.

Let us talk dollars to the neutralists only when they talk sense to us.

Parties and Politics in Contemporary Japan*

ROBERT A. SCALAPINO (1919-   ) is professor of political science at the University of California at Berkeley and a specialist on Japan and East Asia.
JUNNOSUKE MASUMI (1926-   ) is associate professor of political science at Tokyo Metropolitan University.

. . . .
The policy of military alliance with the United States probably has positive support from about one third of the Japanese people, with an additional third being uncertain or indifferent. However, polls on certain issues or at certain times would appreciably raise or lower that number. For example, it appears that a considerable number of Japanese now support limited rearmament for defense purposes only. It is the issue of American bases in Japan and, thus, the direct connection with American military strategy pertaining to Asia, that seems to raise the most serious doubts. While the military aspects of the American-Japanese alliance remain vulnerable, a certain counterbalance is provided by the high degree of support given the economic and cultural aspects of the alliance.

Despite the various arguments advanced for the alliance, however, public opinion polls would indicate that neutralism has had a positive appeal to at least one third of the Japanese. . . . Many of the reasons are obvious. The disaster of World [129/130] War II has not been forgotten, nor will it be forgotten soon—230,000 Japanese still suffer from radioactive diseases as a result of the Hiroshima and Nagasaki bombings, and many thousands of other victims of the fire raids or of combat injuries serve as living reminders that the last war did not pay. There is an acute awareness of the vulnerability of Japan in this age of nuclear war. Her densely packed cities are now only minutes away from Soviet or Chinese bases. Her population, approaching 93,000,000 at present, lives in an area approximately the size of California. Foreign trade is indispensable to survival. Japan must import 80 per cent of her industrial raw materials and 20 per cent of her foodstuffs. The difficulties of supply in the event of war seem enormous. There is [130/131] the additional problem of trade expansion in time of peace, with the argument that neutralism would open new markets without losing old ones.

We remarked earlier that neutralism is also an expression of nationalism in foreign policy. After an era of intensive occupation, perhaps the remarkable thing is that personal relations between Japanese and Americans have remained generally good. The United States has done well in "popularity" polls, and personal anti-Americanism has not shown any appreciable increase despite the rising nationalist sentiment and the dissatisfaction with cer-

* Robert A. Scalapino and Junnosuke Masumi, from *Parties and Politics in Contemporary Japan* (Berkeley: University of California Press, 1962), pp. 129-132. Reprinted with permission of the University of California Press.

tain American policies.[3] Sharper reactions might have been expected, given the historic Japanese tradition of isolation, xenophobia, and extreme national and individual sensitivity. In spite of the relatively moderate reaction to the Occupation era, however, the demand for "full independence" has been a strong one. In politics, the socialists have kept up a drumfire attack upon conservative foreign policy as subservient to the United States. They have denounced foreign bases not merely as dangerous, but also as symbols of the fact that the Occupation has not been completely liquidated. They have insisted that only through a neutralist policy can Japan assert her independence and her proper identity as an Asian state.

For many Japanese socialists, neutralism, in addition to its other virtues, is also an article of political faith. Pacifism and Marxism have both had a deep influence on the Japanese socialist movement. Each of these now lends its weight to the neutralist [131/132] cause. This may seem strange as applied to Marxism. It is true that Marxist-oriented Japanese socialists may *sound* as if they belonged to the Soviet camp. It is also true that some of them act that way. The combination of having the United States as the immediate, close-at-hand object of attack and of being trained only in Marxist terminology and methods of attack is conducive to a conscious or unconscious Communist bias.

But there is another important side to this picture. It is connected with the intricate history of Japanese socialism. The great majority of Marxists and quasi-Marxists within the Japanese socialist movement long ago broke away from the discipline of Moscow. Subsequently, the recriminations have often been bitter on both sides. Thus the postwar Japanese Socialist party, while increasingly dominated by its left wing, has not sought a broad popular front with the Communists. At home, as abroad, it has opted for neutralism. The majority of socialists continue to maintain a relatively orthodox Marxist position on many economic and political issues. This separates them decisively from the West, especially the United States. But their own experiences as well as their political instincts have caused them to seek identification with Nehru and the other Afro-Asian neutralists rather than with Khrushchev. Mao, as an Asian and a Chinese, has had somewhat more personal and political appeal, it must be admitted, but it is the traditional Nehru line that has constituted the basic socialist approach to world politics.

. . . .

[3] For example, in response to a Newspaper Public Opinion Survey League national poll in December, 1954, asking the question "Which country do you like?" 33.3 per cent answered, "the United States"; 26.3, "Great Britain"; 22.5, "Switzerland"; 22.3, "France"; and 11.9, "Communist China." "What country do you dislike?" got the following answers: 37.3 per cent answered, "the Soviet Union"; 30.3, "Korea"; 21.3, "Communist China"; and 10.6 "United States." (*Ibid.*, 1956, p. 320.)

Another national poll on the same subject, in November, 1957, produced the following results: "Which country do you like?"—26.5 per cent, "the United States," and 5.6, "India"; "Which country do you dislike?"—30.5 per cent, "the Soviet Union"; 4.0, "the United States"; and 3.7, "Communist China." (*Ibid.*, 1959, p. 158.)

The Influence of Titoism Abroad*

FRED WARNER NEAL (1915-   ) is professor of international relations and government at the Claremont Graduate School and the author of *Titoism in Action: Reforms in Yugoslavia, 1949-1954* (1958).
GEORGE W. HOFFMAN (1914-   ) is professor of geography at the University of Texas and the author of several books.

· · · · · · · · · · · · · · · · ·
Titoism may be having a significant impact on the new, underdeveloped nations of Asia and Africa. For both political and economic reasons, the Yugoslavs have sought to extend their influence to these areas, and also, more recently, to Latin America.[2] They have succeeded in establishing par- [471/472] ticularly close relations with India, Egypt, Indonesia and Burma. Since these countries had begun to follow a foreign policy of nonalignment on their own initiative, they had a natural affinity with Yugoslavia, which encourages them by example and advice.

Furthermore, these and other underdeveloped countries have demonstrated socialist tendencies in varying degrees, while showing opposition to Soviet-type Communism. The Yugoslavs, again by advice and example, have helped strengthen these tendencies. Tito has made two extensive tours of the underdeveloped countries of Asia and Africa, and the leaders of many of them have come to Yugoslavia.[1] Hardly a week goes by without at least a Yugoslav mission of some sort in some of the underdeveloped nations and without a delegation from one or more of them in Yugoslavia. Vice President Kardelj was invited to Egypt in 1960 to advise the Nasser government on its economic and social problems. At the same time, the Federal Executive Council loaned Leon Geršković, one of its top administrative experts, as an advisor to the government of Ethiopia. In Ghana on a trade union mission, Vukmanović-Tempo signed a declaration stating that "the road toward social progress and happiness that leads to lasting peace can be secured only by means of a Marxist, Socialist policy adapted to the concrete needs of a country."[2]

Probably the strongest Yugoslav influence is noticeable in India and Egypt. Despite their different personalities and backgrounds, Tito and Nehru get along well, and the latter has displayed great interest in Yugoslav political and eco-

[2] The meeting in Belgrade in the late summer of 1961 of representatives of twenty-seven nations for a "Conference of Non-Aligned Countries," called largely on Yugoslav initiative, was an impressive example of Titoist activity of this sort.
[1] Tito's propensity for travel is the target of some amusement among the Yugoslav people. A story often told concerns one Yugoslav who asked another if he thought the moon were inhabited. "Positively not," said the second Yugoslav. Asked how he could be so sure, he said: "If there were people on the moon, certainly President Tito would have traveled there."
[2] *New York Times*, November 27, 1960, p. 25.

* Fred Warner Neal and George W. Hoffman, from "The Influence of Titoism Abroad," *Yugoslavia and the New Communism* (New York: The Twentieth Century Fund, 1962), pp. 471-474. Reprinted with the permission of The Twentieth Century Fund.

nomic developments. Tito regularly gives Nehru informal advice on Soviet and Eastern European affairs, and some observers credit Tito and Kardelj with having persuaded Nehru to commit his Congress party formally to socialism. At the same time, Yugoslavs believe that Titoism has also had an influence on the confused Indian Communist Party, which, traditionally, has contained some "moderate" and "nationalist" elements.

Associations with Egypt have been furthered not only by similarity in foreign policies and a close personal relationship between Tito and Nasser but also by the efforts of the Yugoslav Moslem community. The Yugoslavs feel that they have had a moderating effect on Nasser's tendency to extreme action and have helped him avoid getting too ensnared in his dealings with Moscow.[3] Nasser visited Yugoslavia four times, three times to meet with Tito and Nehru [472/473] and once, in 1958, alone on a state visit; and Tito made three trips to Egypt. Each apparently tried to outdo the other in extending a warm welcome. When Tito was in Cairo in 1959, the foreign editor of *Borba* reported that the spectacle of hundreds of thousands of people chanting "Ti-to, Ti-to" gave him the feeling of being at a mass meeting at home. Present at another occasion, when Nasser initiated a land reform in Damascus, Tito declared that "this great and significant act . . . leads to social democracy."[1] Thousands of copies of the Program of the League of Communists in Arabic were distributed in the United Arab Republic, and in honor of Tito's 1959 visit Nasser's information office published a book entitled *Yugoslavia and Positive Neutrality.*

Sukarno of Indonesia and U Nu of Burma have also been intrigued by Yugoslav ideas. Although the Yugoslavs have claimed no special credit, it was after his visit to Yugoslavia that Sukarno embarked on a program of "guided democracy," a term not altogether inapplicable to Titoism.

It should be noted that not all the Yugoslavs' interest in courting the underdeveloped countries is political. They also see them as customers for their increasing production of industrial goods. Although such trade is limited by the fact that new nations often do not have what Belgrade needs most, Yugoslavia is in the market for things like cotton and other fibers, coffee, sugar, cocoa and tropical fruits. Yugoslav trade interest in Asia and Africa is stimulated by fears that economic integration in Western Europe increases the difficulties of breaking into that market.

At the same time, like good materialists, the Yugoslavs feel that close economic relations bring close political relations. In Latin America, for example, only Mexico, Brazil, Argentina, Uruguay and Chile had official diplomatic ties with Yugoslavia in 1959. New trade relations were expected to bring a further exchange of ambassadors. Interestingly enough, Foreign Minister Popović, and also a Yugoslav trade group, visited Castro's Cuba in 1960, several months ahead of Anastas Mikoyan, and discussed long-term economic and technical cooperation. Earlier, a Cuban goodwill mission came to Belgrade, issuing a statement praising Yugoslavia's "deep sympathy" for the Cuban revolution.[2]

The Yugoslavs, like the Russians, are convinced that all roads lead to socialism in some form or other. They are hopeful that their independent and more moderate brand of Communism will show the new nations that nationalism and Marxism can mix. To the extent that they are right, some in the West profess to see in Tito's influence more of a menace than in the [473/474] Soviet influence. Others, however, who see the great underdeveloped parts of the world gripped by revolutionary nationalism with socialist over-

[3] The Yugoslavs repeatedly advised the United States informally that Nasser would be a bulwark against Soviet penetration of the Arab world if only he were not forced into the Kremlin's arms by Western policies.
[1] *Borba*, February 25, 1959.
[2] *New York Times*, August 22, 1959, p. 3.

tones regardless of anybody's influence, hope that Tito's impact will be greater than Moscow's[1] and should, even, be encouraged rather than discouraged.

[1] Whether it will be or not, Tito's interest in the underdeveloped countries has not made the Kremlin happy, and on at least one occasion it has been sharply attacked by a member of the Presidium of the Central Committee of the Soviet Communist Party. (See *Borba*, February 6, 1959.) Even before this, Yugoslavia had been attacked by the Communist Party of Syria and Lebanon. Pinning the responsibility on Moscow, the Yugoslavs retorted that "such immoral acts . . . cannot compromise anyone but their perpetrators." Cf. Dragon Stojilković, "A Foredoomed Venture," *Review of International Affairs*, October 15, 1958, pp. 5-7.

Trans-Himalayan Confrontation*

NORMAN D. PALMER (1909-   ) is professor of political science at the University of Pennsylvania. He is the author of *The Indian Political System* (1962) and *International Relations* (1954) with Howard C. Perkins.

On October 20, 1962, the Chinese launched a major offensive against India in the North-East Frontier Agency (NEFA) and Ladakh. This unexpected attack, as A. M. Rosenthal has pointed out, "has brought about a great confrontation that Asia had not expected for years and perhaps decades to come."[1] Why has China precipitated this confrontation? Above all, why has it chosen to clash head-on with India?

For several years, in the mid-1950's, Communist China wooed the "neutral" states of South and Southeast Asia, and it seemed to be making a deep impression by its policies of moderation and "sweet reasonableness." In the Sino-Indian treaty regarding Tibet in April 1954, it endorsed the famous "Five Principles of Peaceful Coexistence"—the *Panch Shila* or *Panchsheel*—and at the Bandung Conference a year later its Prime Minister, Chou En-lai, blandly subscribed to these principles and to several more besides.

About 1957, however, the Chinese line rather abruptly hardened, and the "neutral" Asian states discovered that they had been concentrating so intently on the silver lining that they had almost overlooked the dark cloud behind it. In 1959 China deliberately precipitated a crisis with its greatest Asian neighbor, India, by its ruthless suppression of the uprising in Tibet and its more serious intrusions into territory south of the McMahon Line in the North-East Frontier Agency and into Ladakh. These actions led to an abrupt change in Sino-Indian relations which, as a result of the major Chinese offensive

since last October 20th, has developed into an undeclared war of unpredictable duration, dimensions and consequences. Speaking to the Indian people over All-India Radio on October 22nd, Prime Minister Nehru described the crisis as the "greatest menace that has come to us since we became independent." Two weeks later he called it a "turning point in India's history."

To most Indians the Chinese actions since 1959 are as incomprehensible as they are alarming. Indian spokesmen and Indian newspaper editorials often refer to the "Chinese puzzle." Expres- [513/514] sions such as "We did not expect the Chinese to behave that way," "We thought we could trust the Chinese," or "We thought China was our friend," are in common currency inside India. Indians found it hard to understand why China should deliberately forfeit the friendship of a country which had been China's leading champion among the noncommunist states. At a meeting organized by the Delhi Citizens Committee for Disarmament and against Nuclear Arms and for National Integration, held in New Delhi on October 2, 1962, Mahatma Gandhi's birthday, Nehru expressed his own feelings of bewilderment regarding the aims and motives of the Chinese communists:

We had a very friendly attitude towards the Chinese but they attacked us. This was completely a meaningless thing which one would not understand. Many other people ask me, "Why did China attack India and lose the valuable

[1] "Battle Between India and China Has Wide Impact," *New York Times*, November 4, 1962.

* Norman D. Palmer, from "Trans-Himalayan Confrontation," *Orbis*, VI (Winter, 1963), 513-527. Reprinted with permission of *Orbis* published by the Foreign Policy Research Institute of the University of Pennsylvania.

friendship of India?" What reply can I give them? I feel helpless. I can, of course, say many things to explain the reasons for the Chinese aggression. But I do not understand why they have destroyed the valuable friendship of thousands of years existing between us by attacking us.

I

The motives and aims of the leaders of Chinese communism with reference to particular situations are even less clear than those of the leaders of Soviet communism, although uncertainty about immediate motivations should not blind noncommunist states and peoples to the clarity of ultimate communist aims and to the remorseless persistency with which these aims are pursued. While one can understand Nehru's feelings of bewilderment and even of helplessness, he can hardly agree that the Chinese actions against India since 1959 are "completely a meaningless thing." Whatever their limitations, communists seldom act in a "meaningless" way. Acts which may seem meaningless to noncommunists all too often turn out to have a distinct meaning and significance from the point of view of the communist planners. The Chinese communist leaders must have recognized clearly that their behavior and actions in 1959 and subsequently would cost them the friendship and confidence of India, and would substantially drain the reservoir of goodwill which they had built up in the noncommunist Asian countries by moderate policies and careful diplomacy over a period of several years. We must assume, therefore, that in their sudden change-over to a hard policy toward India they felt that their gains would outweigh their losses. [**514/515**]

Until the fall of 1962, at least, it was still possible to make a fairly logical case for the Chinese behavior on grounds of limited objectives and the pursuit of traditional Chinese claims. The immediate source of the Sino-Indian controversy was Tibet. In retrospect, the current troubles between the two Asian giants may be traced to the Chinese decision to establish direct control over the "Tibet region," to the Indian acquiescence in that decision in spite of apprehensions about its consequences, and at the same time to Indian protests against, first, the consolidation of Chinese control at the expense of Tibetan autonomy, and then against the brutal suppression of the uprising in Tibet in March 1959. [**515/517**]

. . . .

As Chinese nationalism became a fairly strong force in the twentieth century, whether under Sun Yat-sen or Chiang Kai-shek or Mao Tse-tung, ancient historical precedents and claims were occasionally revived; but until the rise to power of the Chinese communists no Chinese regime had a strong base for operations and control in the Himalayan regions. "China's main motive," in the opinion of Guy Wint, "is to take back what she believes is her own. The communist revolution has restored her sense of strength, and she is determined to right the wrongs which she considers were done against her in the past. She wants to regain her old frontiers to the utmost extent."[4]

It is worthy of note that the Chinese Nationalists have agreed completely with their communist rivals in China that Tibet is legally a part of China and even that China has some rightful [**517/518**] historical claims to territories which India claims on the basis of custom, tradition and usage, and to some extent of treaty rights, as the legitimate boundary between India and Sinkiang and Tibet. The Chinese Nationalists, like the communists, have refused to accept the legitimacy of the so-called McMahon Line; they have not protested the intrusions of the Chinese communists into territory in the Himalayan regions which India regarded as no longer being in dispute, although they have criticized the forceful methods which the Chinese communists have employed against India. Hence it is possible to explain China's recent aggressive actions in the Himalayas as being motivated, to

[4] "India and China," *The Radical Humanist*, XXIV (January 17, 1960), p. 28.

use the words of an American specialist on China, "by an uncompromising commitment to the reestablishment of China as it existed in the Chinese Empire,"[5] and/or by a militant nationalism that is now backed by formidable power and "revolutionary zeal."

The element of "revolutionary zeal," however, stems from the stage of communist militancy in which China now seems to be engrossed, and therefore adds a new and major dimension to the danger and threat of Chinese expansionism. As the stronghold of communist orthodoxy, China seems to regard itself as the true defender of the faith, and it has taken an uncompromising stand in opposition to deviation from the more inflexible tenets of Marxism-Leninism, with a strong flavor of Stalinism as an added ingredient. This orthodoxy and inflexibility have been manifest in many ways, inside and outside the communist bloc, most notably by the reassertion of Marxist-Leninist principles against Khrushchev's "pragmatism," by the rejection of Khrushchev's thesis of the possibility of a peaceful transition to socialism, by many other disagreements with the Soviet Union, by the reversion to a harder line in dealings with noncommunist countries, and by an apparent drive to strengthen China's influence in the communist fold and elsewhere.

This mixture, in unknown degrees, of ancient Chinese imperialism, militant nationalism and the "revolutionary zeal" of militant communism is potentially an explosive one, and may explain in large measure recent Chinese intransigence and expansionism. In the heyday of their great disillusionment and new alarm over China, many Indians are now warning the world that almost anything should be expected from the present rulers [518/519] of China. As one Indian student has observed: "The destinies of no great country have in recent times fallen into the hands of more dogmatic, ruthless, irrational and irresponsible leadership as China. The dangers to the world inherent

in such a situation are obvious."[6] Unfortunately, most Indians discovered only at a late hour the real nature of the communist leaders of China and the danger which they pose to India and to the world.

Other explanations for China's recent behavior and actions have also been advanced. Foremost among these are the beliefs that Chinese pressures on India were prompted by internal problems and pressures, and that they are a by-product of differences between China and the Soviet Union. [519/520]

. . . .

. . . One of the results of the major Chinese military moves in the fall of 1962 was that the Soviet Union was forced to abandon its position of affected "neutrality" in the dispute and side openly with its fellow-communist state, against India. It was apparently not happy with the Chinese moves against India—in 1959 Khrushchev was reported as saying that the border dispute was "a sad and stupid affair"—and until late 1962 it led India to believe [520/521] that it could be counted upon to restrain China and, if called upon, to mediate in the Sino-Indian dispute. Its abandonment of that role in October 1962 convinced many observers that, however unhappy it may have been with Chinese expansionism in Asia and about antagonizing India, it would in any showdown join with its great communist neighbor. Indeed, there is always the possibility that the differences and disagreements between the Soviet Union and Communist China have not been as serious as they would appear to be, or even that they are largely feigned to allay suspicions of noncommunist countries and to foster a spirit of complacency and a lack of preparedness in intended victims. In a book published in 1960, an Indian journalist stated flatly: "The conclusion seems to be irresistible that the activities of the Chinese authorities in Tibet, in-

[5] Allyn W. Rickett, interview in *The Daily Pennsylvanian*, November 1, 1962.
[6] C. Satyapalan, "Sino-Indian Relations: 1954-59," p. 11 (unpublished manuscript).

cursions into India and the policies of the Soviet Government and Communist Party of India have to be viewed as parts of an over-all plan, which is to subvert democracy in favour of 'people's democracy' in India."[8] When these words were published few Indians would have been impressed with this warning; but after the events of late 1962 it seemed to have greater relevance. [521/522]

. . . .

Soviet-Chinese rivalry seems to be especially focused on Asia. The Soviet Union has been remarkably successful in overshadowing the Chinese in places as close to China as Laos and Indonesia; its hold on most of the communist parties in non-communist states seems to be far greater than that of China, although some of these parties, as in India, seem to be split into pro-Russian and pro-Chinese and other factions. But Chinese influence in communist circles in Asia is increasing, and China seems to be deliberately engaged in the process of undermining or curbing Soviet power and influence in Asia, as it is in humiliating and weakening India. Some Western, and a few Indian, commentators have speculated on the possibility that the Soviet Union may become so concerned over expanding Chinese power and influence that it may even be willing to join with noncommunist states in curbing China. Walter Lippmann, for example, has referred to "the change in the Soviet position in Asia," and has argued that "Chinese aggression is a peril not only to the political influence of Moscow, but also to the vital interests of Russia from the Urals to the Pacific."[9] Mr. Lippmann advanced this view even after the Soviet Union had refused to support India in its dispute with China, and instead had indicated that it was forced to side with China, had informed the Indian government that it would be obliged to "postpone" the delivery of the MIG-21 jet fighters that had been promised, and had advised India to accept China's terms for a peaceful resolution of the border conflict. Yet up to October

1962, and to a lesser extent since that date, Moscow and Peking seemed to be following different policies toward India. One of China's aims in abandoning its pretense of friendship with India may have been to strengthen its position in the Himalayan regions and in the Indian subcontinent vis-à-vis the Soviet Union.

IV

India and China have often been described as inevitable rivals in Asia, and much depends on their relative progress or lack of progress. Each country is trying to deal with fundamentally similar problems in fundamentally different ways. India is an open and China is a closed society. India has deliberately chosen the democratic way, whereas China has come under the control of some of the most fanatically devoted communists in the world. Thus India and China are inescapably involved in a [522/523] test of strength and perhaps of will, in a competition between different methods of political, economic and social organization. If China makes much more rapid progress than India, this will have a profound influence on other developing countries, regardless of the cost of this progress in human terms. If, on the other hand, it becomes apparent that communism has brought to the Chinese people not only totalitarianism but economic misery and greater human suffering, while India manages to move slowly toward a better deal for its growing millions, the power of example may be compelling. In any event, if China wants to promote the spread of communism in Asia or even to extend its own physical presence and power, India stands squarely athwart its path. This rivalry is not occasioned by any conscious desire or plan on India's part—indeed, until recently Indians dismissed

[8] Girilal Jain, *Panchsheela and After: A Reappraisal of Sino-Indian Relations in the Context of the Tibetan Insurrection* (New York: Asia Publishing House, 1960), p. 216.

[9] Column in *The Philadelphia Inquirer*, November 1, 1962.

the idea of Sino-Indian rivalry and preferred to emphasize the things they thought India and China had in common. It is rather occasioned by the "facts of life" and by the expansionist aims and intolerance of a militant Chinese communism.

China's basic aim, therefore, may be to weaken and humiliate India, to gain strategic superiority over its Asian rival, to lessen Indian power and influence generally, especially in Southeast Asia, and to hamper India's economic progress. If it could slow up the already painfully slow rate of India's economic development, it would score several gains at one and the same time: it would weaken India greatly, and therefore would give China an even greater edge in the test of strength; it would weaken parliamentary democracy in India, and might lead to a shift to extra-democratic and eventually anti-democratic forms and processes; it might create a chaotic condition which would pave the way for a communist take-over; and at the minimum it would make India a less formidable competitor in Asia.

The full implications of the Sino-Indian dispute cannot be properly assessed at this stage. It will probably have greater effects on India than on China, although China too is bound to be affected by the many changes to which this dispute will inevitably lead. On India its impact is already profound. It has forced the Indian government and the Indian people to reassess their domestic and foreign policies, their basic convictions and their most cherished ideals, their images of themselves and of the rest of the world. Speaking in the Indian Parliament in October 1962, after Chinese troops had launched major thrusts deep inside Indian territory, Prime Minister Nehru confessed: "I want [523/524] you all to realize the shock we suffered during the last week or so. We were getting out of touch with the realities of the modern world. We were living in an artificial atmosphere of our own creation, and we have been shocked out of it." Thus it is

no exaggeration to say that after the shocks administered by China, after the events of 1959 and especially of October 1962, India will never be the same again. As an astute Indian student of foreign affairs wrote in late October, in a personal letter: "It is a new India to which we all shall belong; and who can be certain that it will be as pleasant as before! The Chinese have succeeded in their primary objective; they have brought about fundamental changes in the nature of India and it is now a different confrontation that they will have."

By forfeiting India's friendship and trust, by cynically violating the *Panchsheel*, to which its leaders had devoutly and frequently subscribed, and by launching a major military offensive against India itself, China struck at the roots of India's policy of nonalignment in foreign affairs. Because India's arms and equipment were demonstrably inadequate and outmoded, and quite unsuited for the needs of mountain warfare against a more numerous and better armed foe, India did not allow a rigid adherence to the principles of nonalignment to prevent it from asking for arms and military equipment from friendly Western countries which were able and willing to respond promptly to its emergency appeals; nor did these countries hold back military aid because India was not a military ally. If the Chinese push develops into a major threat to the independence and survival of free India, that beleaguered nation would almost certainly have to rely on outside support in resisting the Chinese invader. There can be little doubt that such support would be forthcoming. Thus the limitations of nonalignment are now more clearly understood in India, and Western powers which have placed a heavy emphasis on military allies and alliances have been brought to redefine the nature and purposes of their alliances. A different kind of alliance seems to have developed between India and the Western nations which have come to its aid in an economic and more recently in a military way. It is an alliance without formal ties, an alliance which is compatible with both alignment and nonalignment, an alliance springing from an emergency but based perhaps on a greater awareness of "the realities of the modern world" and the steps that free peoples must take to protect their freedoms and ensure their survival. [524/525]

In territorial terms China's immediate objectives may have been quite limited. If this is the case, Peking is probably reviving ancient Chinese claims in the Himalayan border areas and intruding into territory which India regards as its own to compel India to agree to some minor rectifications of the frontiers in the North-East Frontier Agency and to some rather important territorial concessions in Ladakh. If it has limited objectives, of a territorial nature, these probably concern Ladakh more than NEFA. Chou En-lai's offer in April 1960, to accept the Indian position in NEFA if India would accept the Chinese position in Ladakh, suggested that China attached greater importance to Ladakh than to NEFA. The same implication could be drawn from the dramatic Chinese announcement of November 20, 1962, of a unilateral cease-fire as of midnight on the following day and a withdrawal of Chinese troops, beginning on December 1st, twenty kilometers "behind the line of actual control" on November 7, 1959.

China might settle for much less than the 15,000 square miles which it has claimed in Ladakh, but it would certainly insist on retaining all or most of the Aksai Chin region, through which passes a portion of a vital highway between Sinkiang and Tibet. It would of course be difficult for India to accept this kind of proposition, for it would simply mean that it would give up territory which it has consistently regarded as belonging to it in return for a Chinese acceptance of the McMahon Line, without a recognition of its legality. On the other hand, it will be very difficult for India to drive the Chinese out of any positions which they may choose to defend in NEFA and Ladakh. Thus India may have to endure the frustrations and dangers of a situation which it officially rejects but which it is unable to change either by diplomatic or military means.

The threat to India itself lies in NEFA, and in other relatively accessible border areas in Nepal, Sikkim and Bhutan, rather than in distant Ladakh, separated from India proper by formidable mountain ranges and difficult terrain. If China's objectives are unlimited, it can more easily push across the Himalayan passes and into northern India through the most direct and accessible routes. If it establishes a foothold in North India, south of the Himalayas, and if it can maintain that foothold against Indian attacks, it will then be in a strategic position to exert all kinds of pressures and influence, not only on India [525/526] but on all of South and Southeast Asia. Soon after the "liberation" of Tibet in 1950—the event which triggered the Sino-Indian crisis—the Chinese indicated that they intended to "liberate" Ladakh, Nepal, Sikkim and Bhutan as well, which they described as "the four teeth with which the Chinese will grind their way to the Southern Seas."[10] Unfortunately, the crisis in India's relations with China since 1959 has coincided with a worsening of its relations with Nepal, so that Nepal is a particular source of weakness as far as India is concerned. Moreover, the recent engagements into which King Mahendra has entered with the Chinese communists, including an agreement to accept Chinese aid in building a motorable road from Kathmandu to the Tibetan borders, suggest that the King is playing a dangerous Himalayan balance of power game which creates additional political and strategic problems for India. In Bhutan and Sikkim Chinese pressures are less direct, but these areas offer fertile opportunities for Chinese infiltration and penetration.

[10] Quoted in P. C. Chakravarti, *India's China Policy* (Bloomington: Indiana University Press, 1962), p. 148.

The intricacies and complexities of the political situation in the Himalayan border states provide Peking with numerous opportunities for advantageous and comparatively safe meddling. . . . Tactically, Peking may be merely attempting to shift the main arena of Sino-Indian rivalry away from Tibet and into areas under a tenuous Indian hegemony. . . . On the other extreme, we may be witnessing the preliminary phase of a long-range campaign devised to undermine Indian prestige and influence in the entire Himalayan region with the ultimate intention of extending Chinese control over this area.[11]

Thus Tibet may have been but the first step in what Professor P. C. Chakravarti has called "China's *drang nach süden.*"[12] Even if it was not, the threat of this kind of southern push cannot be disregarded so long as the Chinese are active either by military operations or by infiltration and other clandestine means to the south of the high Himalayas. As long as they remain in Tibet and maintain formidable military strength and air bases there, they will be an ever-present threat; but if they can be kept north of the Himalayas the threat will be less formidable and, now that India and other noncommunist nations are more fully alert to the Chinese peril, the chances of successful resistance to any further Chinese moves, whether overt or covert, will be brighter. In the meantime India, with the help of some of its noncom- [526/527] munist friends, must deal with present dangers and must readjust its thinking and its policies to conform more closely to "the realities of the modern world" without abandoning its basic ideals and objectives and without losing sight of the equally basic objective of developing the kind of political, economic and social structure which will be worth defending.

In the postwar era the communists, by their relentless and persistent pressures, have involved all the world in a protracted conflict of gigantic proportions. "For the Communists, protracted conflict brackets all possible relationships between states and groups—political, economic and cultural—and some that, from our point of view, signify the exact opposite of con-

flict."[13] Most Indians have been reluctant to recognize the fact of protracted conflict, and to the extent that they have recognized it they have been inclined to ascribe it as much to the policies and intentions of the Western powers, with the United States in a leading role, as to the Soviet Union and international communism. South Asia has in fact been a prime target of communist interest and activity for many years. Indians have been remarkably unconcerned about the dangers from communists within their country, and even less concerned about the dangers from communist states to the north.

By their brutal and unexpected behavior since 1959, however, the Chinese communists have taught Indians a lesson they will not soon forget. While it is true, as most Indians are now ready to admit, that India should not have assumed that the Chinese would act in accordance with the principles of *Panchsheel,* for a long time neither the Indian government nor the Indian people could conceive that China might turn into a hostile neighbor. Now they are aware that they are engaged in a protracted conflict with China—a conflict that will take many forms and that will have profound repercussions on the balance of forces inside India, in South Asia generally, in Asia, and in the world as a whole.

India is therefore faced with a situation of great peril, which it did not anticipate and which it is ill-prepared to meet. This new crisis may be disastrous for India's future. On the other hand, it may bring out the best in Indian character and traditions, and the Indian nation may emerge from the test with greater unity and vigor. Unhappily India, like all nations, is a participant and not a spectator in the protracted conflict of our times; but in this conflict, as it now seems to realize, it is not alone.

[11] Leo E. Rose, "Sino-Indian Rivalry and the Himalayan Border States," ORBIS, Summer 1961, pp. 214-215.
[12] Chakravarti, *op. cit.,* p. 148.
[13] Robert Strausz-Hupé, William R. Kintner, James E. Dougherty and Alvin J. Cottrell, *Protracted Conflict* (New York: Harper, 1959), p. 2.

PART FOUR

EVALUATION—NEUTRALISM AND DISENGAGEMENT

IN THE DEVELOPED NATIONS

Isolationists and Neutralists*

MCGEORGE BUNDY (1919-   ) is special assistant to President Johnson for national security affairs. A Kennedy appointee, he is a former dean of Harvard's Faculty of Arts and Sciences and co-author of *On Active Service in Peace and War* (1947), a biography of Henry L. Stimson.

Strange bedfellows ordinarily resent their companionship even when it is the result of their own free choice. There is, therefore, a certain danger in undertaking to point out similarities between the opinions and attitudes of two groups which thoroughly disapprove of each other—the American isolationists and the European neutralists. If, nevertheless, I do so, it is not to engage in the somewhat facile and condescending task of demonstrating how wrong these groups have been, but rather to make a much more fundamental point. I propose to argue that the most important similarity between neutralists and isolationists lies in the manner in which their very great qualities are stultified by a refusal to face reality, and that this act of voluntary withdrawal tends to aid the very forces they most energetically and properly hate.

I

For one who has often engaged in discussion with both isolationists and neutralists, the most obvious (and most superficial) likeness is in their arguments. America in 1939, as Europe today, was divided by the question whether there existed a major threat of aggression against which it was proper to combine and rearm with energy. The isolationist of the thirties insisted that collective security and rearma- **[70/71]** ment would bring war, not peace; he maintained that the danger was wildly exaggerated and, in any case, was not aimed specifically at Americans. He pointed out that although the Nazis were perhaps not very attractive, the England of Chamberlain and the France of Blum also had their faults—indeed he gloried in emphasizing their follies, crimes, and weaknesses. In some extreme cases, he tended to make excuses for Hitler. He inclined to the view that the tension in the world was the result of a power struggle from which America could and should stand aside, and he felt that only a war-monger could gain from taking sides. For war the isolationist had a deep and passionate hatred, born of experience with its futility (though not, perhaps, with its full fury). And he emphasized that the whole course of armament and alliance must inevitably destroy his vision of a quiet, prosperous, and spiritually self-sufficient homeland.

I will not labor the point that similar arguments can be heard again today from the earnest men who stand, in one way or another, for neutralism in Europe. They, too, insist that the danger of war is exaggerated and that it is used by sinister forces for their own ends. In Bevan's restatement of Senator Nye's familiar attack on the deviously plotting munition makers, rearmament has become a conspiracy to deprive the workers of social gains hardly achieved. Or, as the symptoms of danger mount, neutralists may have recourse to *special information.* Just as Senator Borah in 1939 reinforced his isolationism by stating bluntly in the early summer that he knew by special informa-

* McGeorge Bundy, "Isolationists and Neutralists," *Confluence*, I (June, 1952), 70-78. Reprinted with the permission of McGeorge Bundy.

tion that there would be no war that year, so Mr. Domenach's journal *Esprit* has recently informed us that *certains renseignements* permit the conclusion that Stalin's armed forces are only one-fifth as strong as most authorities believe. There exists the same tendency to view the tension as a power struggle; but Wall Street has replaced the City of London as the chief villain. And the American isolationist who tended to consider the very existence of tension as a symptom of European decadence finds his counterpart in the European neutralist who inveighs against America's cultural barrenness. Finally we find a version of neutralism based on tactical considerations of policy and deriving its strength from a criticism of [71/72] the specific means used to contain the aggressor. Isolationists in 1939 would point to Munich, and neutralists today often invoke Yalta or—as with Beuve-Méry—the "adventuresome" policy which invited an attack on Korea without adequately providing for its defense.

It would be possible to point out that this last argument in particular grants the fundamental issue, the existence of a threat of aggression, and that it hardly seems to call for neutralism or isolationism. It would also be possible to press the comparison much more closely. But such pressure might prove more irritating than persuasive, and it is a real question whether it would mean very much standing alone. Let me suggest, then, that behind the arguments in both cases there has been a similar basic motivation and a set of important insights which opponents of the two groups ignore at their peril. I shall emphasize the American experience because European readers might justly resent my version of their motives. I will leave it for them to decide how far my analogy is valid.

II

Nowadays in America no one has a good word for the isolationist. Even Senator Taft, who really loves him still, thinks it wisest not to defend him and to dispose of him by announcing his death. There is a school of so-called historians who delight in blackening the memory of those who *opposed* isolationism, but even these writers do not ordinarily bother with the resuscitation of the isolationist. This neglect is not only unkind; it is unwise. For the great rush of opinion which made isolationism our dominant dogma in the middle 1930's was not all blind or rooted in error. Much of its motivation was generous and clear-sighted, and neither its eventual frustration and bitterness nor its basic and desperate error should obscure the qualities which gave the movement its impetus. We should not let the raging Wheeler or the corroded Beard stand in our memories as the symbols of isolationism; we should choose, instead, any one of the hundreds of thousands of younger men, who were more to be hon- [72/73] ored in their error than many of those who chose the other side. It is they who seem to me to stand in sympathetic connection with the modern European neutralist.

America in the 1930's was dominated by the Depression; the question of war and peace was secondary and, in a sense, intrusive. The Depression represented the most powerful and distressing challenge ever issued against the American "way of life." It was a challenge not in rhetoric or vague possibility, but in the immediate and enormously painful reality of lost jobs, narrowed opportunity, wounded self-confidence, and the slow, hope-destroying process of scratching out a living against the will of the business cycle. Many who lived through this experience made a half-conscious vow that in the future they would protect themselves, at almost any cost, against such hammer-blows. This they would do by redoubling their effort to assert and maintain their autonomy as individuals. Those who were entangled in this struggle, and also those whose conduct was influenced by fear of such entanglement, had little time or sympathy to spare for foreign dangers or the larger questions of freedom *versus* tyranny. They were the elder cousins of the existentialists of post-war Europe.

Others, in a different current, yet driven by similar forces, turned their attention to the reform of American domestic life. These were the years of the great political awakening of intellectual America, a characteristic aspect of which was the revival of attention and attachment to the specifically American inheritance of our society. Interest in European ideas continued, of course, but the true fervor was reserved for rediscovered American forebears of the New Deal. In this period many of the expatriates came home and the fashionable figure was no longer Gertrude Stein, but John Steinbeck.

In opposite ways, then, but in both cases with great energy and singleness of mind, two large groups of Americans were driven by the Great Depression and its aftermath into a mood of preoccupation. In this mood, they often looked with suspicion on all that did not fit in with their personal plan and purpose; and particularly they tended to resist the suggestion that there might be a need to arm, [73/74] to act with others, and perhaps in the end to fight. No one who respects the achievements of the New Deal or the American tradition of self-reliance can avoid the recognition that the forces which created this attitude were honorable and productive.

Not all of the isolationist's objection to foreign entanglement was the result merely of his concern with home affairs. He was also moved by a deep and genuine hatred of war, coupled with a conviction that in the twentieth century wars settle nothing, or at least create new problems even more dangerous and pervasive. This seemed particularly true of the First World War, all the more so because in its pretensions it had been a final crusade against evil. When the first alarms at the rise of Hitler were couched in similar terms, they seemed only too reminiscent of the old and discredited refrain about the Kaiser.

As opinion began to shift under the impact of Hitler's lengthening record, it was often the most devoted, the bravest, and the most independent who held to their original conviction as it became less popular. It is not surprising that for such men there was a special comfort in contemplation of the mistakes and weaknesses of Hitler's enemies. Never noticing that to denounce Chamberlain was also, by inference, to denounce Hitler, they reinforced their belief in American inaction by pointing with a kind of perverse pride to non-American errors. It was not logic, perhaps, but it was most human.

I will not attempt, at a distance of three thousand miles, to tell the neutralist what his real motives are. I may be permitted, however, to raise in all humility a number of questions based on this sketch of the sources of American isolationism: Are there not, among the neutralists, many who came to the end of the last war with a conviction that the great and central task was to rebuild their national societies? And do not some of these men react to talk of foreign danger like men who are interrupted by something which they try to ignore simply because it is unpleasant? Are there not among them men so exhausted by foreign occupations barely surmounted that talk of a danger which might mean another occupa- [74/75] tion merely leads them to an angry denial that such a danger exists? May we not suggest that what the Great Depression was for so many Americans, the Second World War has been for many in Europe—a mountainous shock followed by a will to reconstruct in some cases, and a will simply to survive in others, with both desires operating to reduce one's interest in foreign dangers? And as the danger grows more real, do not many of these men take comfort in a close examination of the errors and weaknesses of the Americans, who choose to face the danger? I will add only that if, in fact, my comparison holds, we may expect to find among the persistent neutralists today many of the best minds and hearts of Europe.

My whole argument assumes, of course, that there is a danger now as there was in 1939. I am not claiming—and I do not believe—that Stalin is a precise replica of Hitler. I claim only that there exists today a major danger against which the West must defend itself by alliance and rearmament, and that neutrality for Germany, for France, and for Great Britain is absurd, just as absurd as neutrality for America in 1939. In a way, it is illogical that I should take for granted the very point which is fundamentally denied by the neutralist to whom I address myself. But I cannot believe that a hopeful estimate of Stalin's intentions is the cause of neutralism; it is rather, in my view, a result. The true causes of the neutralist reaction are the same kind of honorable preoccupation with other matters, the same honorable hatred of war and power politics which characterized the best of American isolationists. In honesty I should add that I suppose some men are neutralists simply because they are cowards—but some men have joined in rearmament for the same reason.

III

I have sketched similarities in argument and similarities in attitude. I have asserted a basic similarity in the situations. I come now to the larger claim that the isolationist, in the end, betrayed his own most important convictions, and that the neutralist is in danger of [75/76] doing the same thing. The reverse of this proposition is, evidently, that both groups have had it in them to contribute greatly to the policy and action of their nations— and in the case of the neutralist this opportunity is still open.

In their concern for domestic reform, individual self-reliance, and many other fundamental purposes, the isolationists were right. In their hatred of war and in their fear that international politics might

be a dirty and destructive business they were right again. Very many of them had a clarity of mind and a quality of conscience that could not well be spared from American life. Yet, in a most fundamental and inevitable way, their isolationism, while it lasted, cut them off from the reality of life and politics. In spite of their best pretensions, there was no escape from the reality of Hitlerite Germany and Imperial Japan. We need not claim that these dangers were dealt with by the wisest of men in the best of all possible ways. It is enough to note that they had to be dealt with, not ignored, and that on this single, fundamental fact the whole case for isolationism was shattered.

Worse yet, by turning the discussion into an argument between those who recognized the facts of life and those who believed in never-never land, the isolationists distracted attention from the very matters which most deeply and properly concerned them. If you assert that the right course is not to face the danger at all, you cease to have much of a voice in the *way* in which the danger is faced; if you insist merely that war is wicked, you lose your chance to moderate its wickedness—and in particular you lose your chance to prevent it by a timely show of will and strength. Throughout the years between 1937 and 1941, the isolationists kept the national mind focused narrowly on a single, unreal issue. Nothing could have been a greater disservice to their own aspirations for tranquillity, prosperity, and eventual peace. And, of course, it is self-evident that a real aggressor gains from being described as non-existent.

I must reluctantly note one further charge against isolationism—the human cost in isolationists corrupted by the violence of their own self-deception. In some cases, of course, it was the corrosion that led [76/77] to the isolationism, but these cases are not of present interest. After all, whom shall I convert by comparing him with Colonel McCormick? Consider, rather, such a man as Charles A. Beard.

Is there any other explanation for the collapse of this distinguished scholar's conscience than the violent frustration he incurred in his pursuit of objectives which at last he had to recognize, perhaps unconsciously, as quite unreal? Or examine the first great step in the prolonged and embittered self-deception of Senator Robert A. Taft. Here there was no recognition of the reality, but rather a deepening belief that its effects must instead be caused by some hideous conspiracy. Thus, when Mr. Taft was denied the nomination for the Presidency in 1940, it could not be, in his mind, because people did not trust him to deal with a world crisis, for in his view there was no such world crisis, at least for America. So he laid the blame on wicked Eastern internationalist plotters. And corrosion of the intellect set in.

These are fearful costs. Because I have only assumed, and not demonstrated, the reality of my comparison between the dangers then and now, it would perhaps be unwise to press any claim that similar effects must come from neutralism. So I make no such claim; it is enough to indicate a possibility, and to suggest that some distinguished men in Europe give good reason for fear that the possibility may become real. But we are talking of a matter still unfinished, and there is still time for change; there are signs, indeed, that neutralism may eventually be transmuted into a kind of cautious and corrective participation. Let me turn, then, to my last and most important claim about the nature of isolationism: that the men who turned away from it in general contributed great weight and wisdom to a world which sorely needed it—and their impact proved all the greater for their having traversed the valley of doubt.

The most famous case of conversion is, of course, the case of Senator Vandenberg. This conversion was no abandonment of his basic purposes, as his *Private Papers* plainly show. It was rather a gradual and generous acceptance of the basic fact that isolation was impossible. This acceptance multiplied his power without changing his basic objectives in the slightest. His homely national pride, his mis- [**77/78**] trust of totalitarianism, his belief in the vitality of a business economy—all these became important and influential; they began to affect events. It is not important, at the moment, whether Vandenberg's basic attitudes were good or bad—though on the whole I think they were good. The point here is more limited; it is that recognition of reality was, in his case, the gateway to enormously increased effectiveness as a servant of his own beliefs.

Vandenberg was an unusual man in an unusually strategic position, and, no doubt, much of his multiplied power resulted from these special conditions. Yet he is only the most famous of a multitude who somewhere between 1941 and 1951 have preferred conversion to corrosion. Over and over, such converts have brought from their errors the same powerful abilities and insights that had so much to do with their original rejection of an activism which, after all, was often fuzzy in its thinking and undistinguished in its motives. Some of the ablest Americans in the great Marshall Plan experiment have been men who were converted from isolationism, and in their new recognition of reality they have not lost the clearheadedness and the impatience of thin sloganeering which played so large a role in their earlier alignment.

No one who keeps a watch on American foreign policy in 1952 can suppose that it is without error; no one who keeps track of the American temper can suppose that it is wholly calm or generous in its estimate of the world situation. No one can find perfection in American society. Very much of what the neutralist says about us is true—or partly true. And very many of the neutralist's values and insights are insufficiently known and shared among those on both sides of the Atlantic who are committed to collective self-defense. Yet I cannot avoid a double conclusion. First, as long as the neutralist tries to stand aside, he can only increase the very dangers which he rightly fears. Second, if he could only face reality and take the great step of admitting that we must all live or die together, he would find himself set free for a great and badly needed contribution both to his own best purposes and to the general freedom.

Neutralism*

ALDO GAROSCI (1907-   ) is an Italian publicist and lecturer. An antifascist during the Mussolini period, he was a director of the newspaper *Italia Socialista* following World War II.

. . . .

An understanding of the vicissitudes of the interwar period [1919–1939] is essential in order to understand present-day French neutralism, as well as that of the other European countries. In Germany, neutralism did not take root. Having been defeated and having lost both the hope for world hegemony and its key position on the Continent, there could not be such radical rejection of war. The Germans believed that a less foolish and more energetic policy than that followed by William II and his cabinet could obtain results and regain some of the ground lost with World War I. Domination of Europe seemed to have been missed, not because of lack of potentials, but because of remediable errors, or even because of betrayal. In fact, the Reich had reached or forged for itself a position somewhere between that of a world power, a goal that could be achieved, and that of a medium-sized state satisfied with its position and hence conservative. From this originated the varied reactions which were to explode in a second attempt at world conquest. The neutralist alternative never existed, it was only a choice of internal politics.

We have already spoken about Italy. Paradoxically enough, Italy had fulfilled, through the war, her primary objectives. Not only had she acquired the Irredentist provinces, but she also had gained an [203/204] important position in the Adriatic. There were no great powers pressing at her own borders, save France, again too involved in Central Europe to be a cause for worry; she had no obligations and her hands were free. Moreover, she had proved her ability to participate in a coalition war, and she was not to be overlooked as an element in the European military equilibrium. But due to her well-known lack of raw materials, to the precarious state of her industries, to the wartime loss of wealth and markets, and above all to the internal turmoils that plagued her—consequences of the efforts necessary not only to wage and win the war, but also to bring about her intervention in it— Italy was paying a great deal more than other nations for the dire consequences that unbound nationalism had spread in Europe. The Fascists cleverly exploited this sense of frustration of the Italian people by insisting that the war was not really won because the victory was not properly utilized, thus creating the myth of the mutilated victory. Italy, they began to say, could become a great power, even an empire, but it was necessary to keep alive an aggressive spirit of intervention, suppressing once and for all neutralists and pacifists. In doing this Fascism exploited an uneasiness that was real, the sum and substance of which was that Italy had become a European power in her own right at a time when the other great powers were on the road to decline; and now it became necessary to risk national existence once more in order to reach—

* Aldo Garosci, from "Neutralism," *European Integration*, ed. C. Grove Haines (Baltimore: Johns Hopkins Press, 1957), pp. 203-208. Reprinted with the permission of the Johns Hopkins Press.

artificial and indeed unobtainable aim—
the status of a super-power.

In reality, as with everything that is
untimely, it was one thing for the dictator
and his propaganda organs to pay lip
service to these assertions and another to
expect the nation to make them its own.
Thus in 1940, when the decision had to
be made as to whether or not to enter the
war, neutralist points of view were quite
strong, even among Fascist leaders. The
deadlock was broken only by the spreading of the fiction that Italy would not be
involved seriously in the war, but was preparing only to sit at the peace table, and
finally by the personal decision of the
dictator. But there was none of the emo-
tion and enthusiasm that accompanied
intervention in World War I.

In Great Britain neutralism seemed to
characterize a situation in which the country appeared to have lost sight of her
European role; however, except among
some extreme Labourites, it never took
the [204/205] form of an unconditional
renunciation of participation in foreign
affairs. For some time, the disillusionment
of World War I led the British ruling
class, and public opinion as well, to seek
a haven in the League of Nations. Actually, the collapse of the British willingness
to maintain an international political
position and to bear all the risks entailed
in it occurred, for a brief, but decisive
moment, at Munich. However, because of
the difference between the crisis of the
British state, which was the crisis of a
great empire, still remaining a world
power and first-rank member of international society, and those crises taking place
in other European countries, British neutralism was tempered and never absolute.
On one side Britain, through Henderson
and Lansbury, paid lip service to pacifism,
while on the other, with the Ottawa
policy, she seemed to embody the will for
imperial self-sufficiency. This never for an
instant, however, implied a complete lack
of faith in its own body politics, or even
indicated a tendency to abrogate its own
political responsibilities.

If we now pass from the study of neutralism in World War I to that in World
War II, it is easy to discern in this the
result of that state of mind which had
characterized France and Italy after World
War I. It should be remembered, however,
that both Italians and Frenchmen fought,
though in different ways and by different
means, but always with great enthusiasm,
to end World War II and to destroy nazi-
ism and indigenous fascism. No doubt
they were also animated by the desire, in
so doing, to save their own existence as
nations. In a certain sense, the Italian
fatherland had never been so popular as
during World War II, when the partisan
war had the active co-operation of the
peasants. But if the people rebelled, in
self-defense, against the Nazi occupation,
which stood as an obstacle to a return to
peace and liberty—a miracle which had
seemed a reality on July 25, 1943—it never
occurred to them that they were fighting
to restore the Italian state as a power or
as an international political entity. The
Resistance, an act of faith in the worth
of one's country—later equated with a
political idea—was also a loud assertion of
the insufficiency of the old political order.
These people who had greeted the end of
the war with tumultuous joy, even though
defeated, took up arms again for liberty
outside the bounds of the state.

The states which were reborn through
the Resistance found them- [205/206]
selves as much in a state of contradiction
and weakness as had their predecessors;
just because the Italian or French flag was
flying again atop the public buildings did
not mean that confidence was restored in
the state as the safeguard of national interests at home and abroad. Following World
War I it was said that the aims of the war
effort had not been achieved; the same
could not be said after World War II,
when at least the invaders had been forced
to flee, and freedom had been restored.
But in reality the political situation had
become worse even than the precarious
state of affairs which had preceded the
war. France had lost her role as a colonial

power, a loss more apparent than real at the time, but one which caused her to wage another war, thus intensifying the disillusionment in the ability of the state to fulfill its mission. France did have "status" and ranked among the great powers in the United Nations, but in reality her position as a power was a fiction not commensurate at all with the reality of the situation, with the practical effect of only aggravating the people's sense of mistrust toward the state and toward any policy which it would choose to follow.

I already have spoken of Italy. Although, as was said, she had fallen, she was better off and even more prosperous, since she had been forced to abandon the burdens of her imperial dreams, and there was a growing mistrust of military action as a means to gain success. To this it should be added that the division of the world into two blocs had repercussions in Italian internal politics, even more than in other countries. Italian states, since surviving the catastrophe of the Renaissance, had grown used to taking the part of France and Spain, making it almost natural in Italy to be open to the influence of foreign domination. As a result, the citizens did not feel obligated, on principle, to follow the orientation of the Italian state toward this or that power.

Neutralism also had arrived in Germany, chiefly because the second attempt to dominate the world had been more disastrous than the first, causing collapse of the state, destruction of a great part of German territory, uprooting of citizens, and, more important this time, charges of the perpetration of crimes against humanity. This great moral bankruptcy seemed to imply the failure of all German history, of all the efforts of the German people to band together as a national state, and, at the least, failure of the state as a military organization. *"Ohne mich, ohne uns"* was the [206/207] spontaneous reaction to the first attempts to bring the German people back within a framework of politico-military obligations. Was not

the loss of her "status" due to her having pursued too persistently the phantom of power? And now the other states were asking her to return to this road.

This profound sense of neutralism spread throughout Europe following the last war. It is deep-rooted and very strongly felt, and it defies any attempt at utilization for any purpose of state policy. It would be a grave error to neglect this as a factor in European politics, even if it has been possible on occasion for a state to adhere to this or that treaty, to this or that alliance. One should never forget that Europeans, with all the best intentions in the world of fulfilling loyally these accords, *have little faith in the capacity and ability of their states to operate in the field of foreign policy.* This does not mean that Europeans are not attached to their liberties or that they are not prepared to defend them. I am not sure that, in the event of an invasion, the large vote given today to the Italian and French Communist parties would necessarily mean that the vast majority of these populations would not take arms against the invaders. The dilemma, however, would not be so clear-cut, as it was in the case of France in 1939, if it were a question not simply of defending one's frontiers, but of having to fight for a political position, a principle, or something beyond one's borders. It seems a paradox, and indeed it is, that the loss of trust in the political capacity of one's state takes almost the form of a nationalistic revival or, at least, a return to national positions. European people are averse to supporting policies that go beyond the defense of their own frontiers, because alliances imply a policy of action and also the belief that through alliances it is possible to achieve some practical goals and the fruition of some common ideals. This cannot be guaranteed by the states which, after two great wars, whether won or lost, have shown their inability to carry through their policies of action and expansion. Hence they believe that the sacrifices needed to support these policies are wasted.

Here we have neutralism at its elemental stage, alive even though not expressed. In France political neutralism has found a voice in periodicals, in great organs of public opinion, even outside Communist circles. Certainly the gentlemen of *Le Monde, Esprit, Temps Modernes,* and *La Vie Intellectuelle,* even if their reasoning may be [207/208] obnoxious, do not all reflect Communist influence. In Italy, this has not happened, or if it has, it has gained a voice only after the failure of the EDC [European Defense Community]. But does this mean that the basic elements of neutralism are less widespread in Italy than in France? If by neutralism we mean essentially a mistrust of the ruling class of a country and of its capacity to conduct an efficient foreign policy, then we can observe neutralist influence in the difficulty which its enemies encounter in

having the population accept what, under normal circumstances, are the basic attributes of a state, i.e., the conduct of foreign policy. To understand how much the supporters of the Atlantic Pact feared the effects of neutralism, it is enough to note the many efforts which have been necessary in Italy, France, and Germany since the war for the conclusion of this and other alliances.[5]

. . . .

[5] A lively example of this widespread feeling is illustrated by Alberto Tarchiani, former Italian Ambassador in Washington: "The meeting with Saragat was very enjoyable, especially since he had been described to me as the leader of the friendly neutralists. Actually he is clearly on the side of the United States, but he could not say so in public, and he would have denied it if I had quoted him, because many would have misunderstood his reasoning . . . but he remained decidedly and clearly on the side of the United States." Alberto Tarchiani, *Dieci Anni tra Roma e Washington* (Milano: Mondadori, 1955), p. 51. See also p. 169.

[Limitations of the Rapacki Plan]*

The revised Rapacki Plan (see pp. 62-64) produced Western criticisms of its proposals for a Central European denuclearized zone. The following selection represents an official American evaluation as of 1958, but it is also typical of subsequent views of the United States. The communication was addressed to Foreign Minister Adam Rapacki of Poland by Ambassador Jacob Beam.

. . . .
Recognizing that the initiative of the Polish Government stems from a desire to contribute to the attainment of a stable and durable peace, my Government has given these proposals serious and careful consideration. On the basis of this study it has concluded that they are too limited in scope to reduce the danger of nuclear war or provide a dependable basis for the security of Europe. They neither deal with the essential question of the continued production of nuclear weapons by the present nuclear powers nor take into account the fact that present scientific techniques are not adequate to detect existing nuclear weapons. The proposed plan does not affect the central sources of power capable of launching a nuclear attack, and thus its effectiveness would be dependent on the good intentions of countries outside the area. The proposals overlook the central problems of European security because they provide no method for balanced and equitable limitations of military capabilities and would perpetuate the basic cause of tension in Europe by accepting the continuation of the division of Germany.

An agreement limited to the exclusion of nuclear weapons from the territory indicated by your Government without other types of limitation would, even if it were capable of being inspected, endanger the security of the Western European countries in view of the large and widely deployed military forces of the Soviet Union. Unless equipped with nuclear weapons, Western forces in Germany would find themselves under present circumstances at a great disadvantage to the numerically greater mass of Soviet troops stationed within easy distance of Western Europe which are, as the Soviet leaders made clear, being equipped with the most modern and destructive weapons, including missiles of all kinds.

The considerations outlined above have caused the United States in association with other Western Powers to propose that nations stop producing material for nuclear weapons, cease testing such weapons and begin to reduce present stockpiles. The United States has further proposed broader areas of inspection against surprise attack, including an area in Europe, roughly from the United Kingdom to the Ural mountains. We remain willing to do this. You will recall, moreover, that the Western nations offered at the London disarmament negotiations to discuss a more limited zone in Europe. With regard to missiles you will recall that over a year and a half ago the United States proposed that we begin to study the inspection and control needed to assure the exclusive peaceful use of outer space now threatened by the development of such devices

* From "U.S. Note of May 3," Department of State Bulletin, XXXVIII (May 19, 1958), 821-822.

as intercontinental and intermediate range ballistic missiles.

The United States, in association with other Western Powers, has also proposed that a comprehensive and effective European security arrangement be established in conjunction with the reunification of Germany. The proposed arrangements would provide for limitations on both forces and armaments, measures for the prevention of surprise attack in the area, and assurances of reaction in the event of aggression.

Your note speaks of the existence of opposing military groupings in Central Europe as being responsible for tensions in the area. It should not be necessary for me to recall that the present division of Europe stems primarily from the decision of the Soviet Union not to permit Eastern European nations to participate in the European Recovery Plan. Nor need I repeat the many assurances given as to the defensive character of the North Atlantic Treaty Organization which is reflected in its entire organizational and command structure. The entire history of its creation and development testify to this, though persistent efforts are made in some quarters to portray it otherwise. [**821/822**]

In the absence of effective arrangements either general or regional in character which would promote real security and in view of the present policies and armaments of the Soviet Union, the countries of Western Europe along with Canada and ourselves, joined in alliance with them, have no other recourse than to develop the required pattern of integrated NATO military strength and to utilize for defensive purposes modern developments in weapons and techniques.

The views which I have presented above on behalf of my Government point out the basic reasons why the United States considers that the Polish Government's proposals for establishing a denuclearized zone in Central Europe would not serve to advance their expressed objectives. Nevertheless, the United States appreciates the initiative of the Polish Government in seeking a solution to these problems. It hopes that this exchange of correspondence will enable the Polish Government better to understand American proposals in the fields of European security and disarmament. I trust that the improved relations between Poland and the United States will serve as a basis for a better understanding between our two countries on these problems, as well as on other matters.

Declaration of the Warsaw Treaty States*

THE WARSAW TREATY ORGANIZATION, a Communist defense bloc, was formed in 1955 as a response to the North Atlantic Treaty community. In May, 1958, the Political Consultative Committee of this organization met in Warsaw to consider internal and external problems. The Warsaw pact nations—Albania, Bulgaria, Hungary, East Germany, Poland, Czechoslovakia, Rumania, and the Soviet Union—issued the final declaration of the conference on May 27. The complete declaration was originally published in *Pravda* (May 27, 1958).

. . . .
The unceasing efforts of the countries of the socialist camp to develop international cooperation on the basis of peaceful co-existence among states with differing social systems, to settle disputes through negotiations between states and to put an end to the arms race and eliminate the threat of atomic war exert an ever-greater influence on the state of affairs in the world.

Participants at the conference noted with satisfaction that not only the socialist countries but also the majority of the countries of Asia and Africa that have freed themselves from age-old colonial dependence are acting in the interests of strengthening peace. Popular masses, influential public circles, many parties and trade unions that heed the demands of the working people, scientists, cultural figures, clergymen, and people of various political views in the countries of Western Europe, America and other continents are also taking a stand on the side of peace. The states which conduct a policy of neutrality are also making a positive contribution to the struggle for peace.

The course of international events shows again and again that the Warsaw Treaty of Friendship, Cooperation and Mutual Aid, which was signed three years ago, not only affords reliable protection to the security and independence of the peoples of these states, but also acts as a powerful deterrent to the activities—inimical to the cause of peace—of the military alignments of the Western powers, particularly the North Atlantic bloc. . . .

At present, NATO military agencies are drawing up new plans for increasing the armed forces and military expenditures of these countries, and the NATO Defense Ministers' conference in April, 1958, discussed the question of doubling the armed forces under the American Supreme Commander of NATO. It is further known that on May 1, 1958, the permanent NATO Council adopted a decision on supplying atomic weapons to those members of the North Atlantic bloc that do not have such weapons at present. The governments of a number of NATO countries—Britain, France, Italy, Turkey and others—made land available for American launching sites for atomic-armed missiles and for atomic weapons depots, despite the vigorous protests of the peoples of these countries.

* From "Declaration of the Warsaw Treaty States," *The Current Digest of the Soviet Press,* X (July 2, 1958), 16-17. Reprinted by permission of *The Current Digest of the Soviet Press,* published weekly at Columbia University by the Joint Committee on Slavic Studies, appointed by the American Council of Learned Societies and the Social Science Research Council. Copyright 1958, the Joint Committee on Slavic Studies.

Military preparations in the Federal German Republic, whose Bundestag passed a resolution authorizing the F.G.R. government to equip the West German armed forces with nuclear weapons and missiles, are becoming particularly dangerous. Thus, the most dangerous types of weapons are being placed in the hands of militarist and revanchist circles making territorial claims on other states.

By supporting the policy of arming the F.G.R. and undertaking to supply West Germany with nuclear weapons and missiles, the U.S. government is in fact encouraging these circles to pursue a policy jeopardizing peace and involving disastrous consequences for the German people themselves. At the same time, measures are being taken to enlist West Germany in the production and development of the latest types of weapons; one such measure is the tripartite agreement between France, Italy and the F.G.R. on cooperation in military research and arms production—an agreement that has been quite widely publicized.

These military preparations are provoking grave apprehension in West Germany itself and are encountering constantly increasing popular resistance there. . . .

One cannot but note with satisfaction that certain NATO member-states, aware of the consequences of a policy of preparing for atomic war and juggling atomic weapons—a policy pursued by the leading powers in the alignment—are taking a more sober stand, a stand that cannot but be a definite positive contribution to the easing of international tension, especially in Europe. This demonstrates that, despite aggressive military alignments and the commitments that the initiators of such alignments have imposed on the other members, there are still untapped possibilities for achieving a detente in Europe and for reducing international tension. . . .

The participants in the conference express deep concern over the continuing attempts of the governments of the U.S.A., Britain, France and other colonial powers to interfere in the affairs of the countries of Asia and Africa and to set up regimes and governments in these areas that are alien to the people and that are prepared once again to sell out to the colonizers countries that have only recently embarked on the road of national independence. If guns are roaring and the blood of patriots is being spilled in Indonesia, Algeria, Lebanon, Yemen and Oman, the responsible parties are those selfsame imperialist circles whose policy is being carried out by NATO, SEATO and the Baghdad Pact and who are attempting to grab up the natural riches of these countries and throttle the national liberation movement of the peoples of Asia and Africa through pressure and gross interference in the internal affairs of other states. Just as in the summer of 1957 storm clouds gathered over Syria, so today dangerous plots are being hatched against Lebanon, but this time the U.S.A., citing the notorious "Dulles-Eisenhower doctrine," which has been rejected by the Arab peoples, is preparing to send its armed forces into action against a people that wants only to be master of its own house and free from foreign dictation. [16/17]

. . . .

The Warsaw Treaty member-states have nothing to fear from a reduction in international tensions; they are united not by the "cold war" atmosphere and not by the state of war hysteria in which the advocates of military preparations want to keep the world, but by a community of ideals and aims for building a new socialist society and strengthening peace among all peoples. . . .

The countries signatory to the Warsaw Pact resolutely condemn the policy of exacerbating international tension and preparing for atomic war which has been pursued in NATO by the leading states of that aggressive alignment. They call upon the governments of the countries of the North Atlantic alliance to take no steps at the present crucial moment that might increase the already tense situation in Europe and certain other parts of the world. In order to decrease the danger of war rather than increase it and to replace mistrust and suspicion between states with confidence and businesslike cooperation, it is necessary above all to refrain from such senseless actions as those engaged in by the American Air Force or as the decision to equip West Germany with atomic weapons, which amounts to a challenge to all the peoples of Europe.

The socialist countries of Europe and Asia have given many proofs of their good will and desire for cooperation with other states in the interests of strengthening peace among all peoples. All the Warsaw Treaty member-states have frequently made unilateral reductions in their armed forces. These forces have been reduced by a total of 2,477,000 men since 1955. These countries' armaments, military facilities and equipment and expenditures for defense were correspondingly reduced. During the same period the armed forces of the Soviet Union were reduced by 2,140,000 men, of the Polish People's Republic by 141,500 men, of the Czechoslovak Republic by 44,000 men, of the German Democratic Republic by 30,000 men, of the Rumanian People's Republic by 60,000 men, of the Bulgarian People's Republic by 18,000 men, of the Hungarian People's Republic by 35,000 men and of the Albanian People's Republic by 9000 men.

No one can deny that states that make such large cuts in their armed forces are preparing for peaceful cooperation, not for war. And conversely, when states increase their armaments and the size of their armed forces, this is a sure sign that they—or, more accurately, those who determine their policy—are thinking not of peace, but of war.

Thus, one sees that the NATO countries are responding to the Warsaw Treaty states' reduction of armed forces and of armaments expenditures by increasing their armed forces, expanding their military budgets and building up their armaments. Through conducting such a policy the leaders of NATO would like to block

any reduction in international tension or the attainment of any agreement among states that would assure peaceful coexistence, and thus force the Warsaw Treaty member-states to participate in the arms race and "cold war" in order to slow down peaceful construction and delay a rise in the living standards of the peoples of the socialist countries. All this compels peoples to be on the alert and to take a more active part in the struggle against forces that are preparing for war. . . .

The conference participants declare that the peoples of the countries they represent, peoples determined to use every means to strengthen peace and avert a new world-wide war conflagration, are interested in establishing a zone free of atomic, hydrogen and rocket weapons in Central Europe, in an area including both German states—the G.D.R. and the F.G.R.—as well as Poland and Czechoslovakia.

In supporting the proposal of the Polish People's Republic to create a zone free of nuclear weapons and missiles, the participants seek no military advantages whatsoever for themselves.

If comparison is made of the size of the territories of the states that would be included in the atom-free zone, it is seen that the area comprising the G.D.R., Czechoslovakia and Poland is more than twice as large as that of the fourth participant in this zone, West Germany. Moreover, the size of the population of the states to be included in this zone from among the Warsaw Treaty member-states also exceeds the size of the population of the NATO state to be included in this zone.

As for the production of nuclear weapons, as is known, neither the G.D.R., Czechoslovakia, Poland nor the F.G.R. would produce such weapons. What is more, the government of the F.G.R. at one time assumed an international commitment not to produce such weapons. All this shows that there is no reason to assume that the creation of an atom-free zone represents some sort of one-sided military gain for the countries of the Warsaw

Treaty to the detriment of the interests of the NATO states. On the contrary, the realism of the proposal to create an atom-free zone in Europe lies precisely in the fact that the Warsaw Treaty states and the NATO states must, according to this proposal, take joint steps in the field of atomic disarmament that are, on the whole, equivalent in military importance. . . .

The implementation of this initiative, as an effort to arrive at a partial agreement, would smooth the way for broader disarmament agreements and would promote the chief aim of all peoples—the elimination of the threat of atomic war in Europe, and consequently of war in general. It should be said that the proposal was understood in precisely this way by broad public circles and by diverse political circles in the West.

The ruling circles of certain NATO powers, declaring in words their desire to conduct successful negotiations, in actual fact do everything possible to complicate the calling of a summit meeting, if not to rule it out altogether.

For this purpose they advance the trumped-up question of the so-called situation in the countries of Eastern Europe, i.e., a question that in fact does not exist. The conference participants resolutely reject any discussion whatsoever of this question as an intolerable interference in the internal affairs of sovereign states incompatible with international law and the U.N. Charter. . . .

As for the attempts to put the question of German unification on the agenda of a summit conference, such attempts can only be of use to those who oppose the convening of such a conference and who do not wish a successful settlement of this question. . . .

Other states, regardless of the rights they might claim for themselves, are not competent to solve this problem over the heads of the German people and the representatives of their governments, the German Democratic Republic and the Federal German Republic.

The conference participants fully share the view of the Soviet government that a summit meeting should discuss that aspect of the German question for which the four powers are responsible, i.e., the question of a German peace treaty. Enlisting the representatives of both German states in the preparation of a peace treaty—as has been proposed by the Soviet Union—would give the German people clear prospects for the future development of Germany and would serve to unite the efforts of the G.D.R. and the F.G.R. in the matter of restoring the national and state unity of the German people.

The Warsaw Treaty member-states attach great significance to the participation of neutral states in the summit meeting, states that have no military commitments to either of the opposed military alignments and that have demonstrated their dedication to the cause of peace and international cooperation. The conference participants can only express their regret that the U.S.S.R.'s proposal that neutral states participate in the summit conference found no support among the Western powers.

.   .   .   .

Disengagement and NATO*

H. STUART HUGHES (1916-   ) is professor of history at Harvard University and author of *Consciousness and Society* (1958) and *Approach to Peace and Other Essays* (1962). From 1946 to 1948, he was associated with the Department of State. In 1962, campaigning for new American defense and China policies, he was an unsuccessful candidate for the House of Representatives.

. . . .
... The problems of "disengagement" and military alliances in Europe cannot be discussed independently of the political and economic situation in that area. American policy is currently based on assumptions that have long outlived their usefulness and that have acquired a false air of permanence through the power and prestige of three elderly statesmen—Konrad Adenauer, Charles de Gaulle, and Harold Macmillan.

All three of these men at present exert an unshakable authority over their countrymen. But no one of them can go on forever—and in the case of Adenauer the moment of retirement cannot be long postponed. Should one or another leave the scene, there would almost immediately come to the surface a strong current of opposition and criticism that until very recently has been restricted to a small minority. It is significant that the last year has seen widespread questioning of De Gaulle's position and the swelling to a mass movement of the British opposition to Macmillan's military policy. [**303/304**]
. . . .
In brief, De Gaulle and Adenauer and Macmillan have perpetuated into the age of nuclear stalemate an outmoded concept of foreign and military policy, a concept of armed resistance to the Soviet Union based on a coalition of national military forces. At NATO's inception, thirteen years ago, this policy made sense, and both partners in the coalition—the Truman administration and the European governments, which shared a "left-center" ideology—believed in it. Today this is no longer true. From the military standpoint, NATO has become something quite different from what it was at the start. It is no longer a military coalition in the familiar European tradition, provided with sufficient *conventional* ground forces to act as a deterrent to Soviet expansion. It has become little more than a trip wire for "massive retaliation." The United States' decision to supply its European allies with nuclear warheads has robbed NATO of its military *raison d'être*. It has destroyed the earlier concept of an old-fashioned ground army that would make the Soviet Union hesitate to incur the losses and the international opprobrium which overrunning Central and Western Europe would entail, and it has substituted for it a new theory which reduces Europe to the status of an advanced outpost of the United States in the planning for general nuclear war. [**304/306**]
. . . .
If one adds to these political and mili-

* H. Stuart Hughes, from "Disengagement and NATO," *The Liberal Papers*, ed. James Roosevelt (Chicago: Quadrangle Books, 1962), pp. 303-304, 306-311. Copyright © 1962 by James Roosevelt. Reprinted by permission of Doubleday & Company, Inc.

tary considerations the current economic split within the NATO powers between the "inner six" and the "outer seven," one can only conclude that the alliance as originally devised a decade ago is falling apart at the seams. In this crisis of NATO, nationalism and neutralism reinforce each other. The first is largely a conservative tendency, the second is characteristic of the democratic left, but they both in effect work against the NATO alliance. For when a nationalist like De Gaulle exploits his countrymen's nostalgia for past grandeur and concentrates his attention on France's African "mission" and on restoring great power status through an independent atomic capability—when France, which was to have been the key pin of NATO, goes off on a nationalist tangent, then internationally minded Europeans are far less likely to seek their salvation in a military alliance, and far more inclined to trust to disarmament, disengagement, and even neutrality for their future preservation.

Since NATO can scarcely be preserved in its present form, the real question is: Should it be transformed by some new principle or should it be abolished? The first would seem the more prudent—although a change of name might well be in order—since the sudden abolition of NATO might entail a crisis of European confidence. In either case, however, the prime goal should be to keep Europe out of the nuclear race by progressively enlarging a Central European area of military disengagement. The idea of disengagement—of removing the hostile forces of East and of West from direct contact with each other—can be formulated in two different ways. In its more cautious form it proposes merely to forbid the deployment of nuclear weapons in a specified area. In its more thoroughgoing form it suggests that the area in question be neutralized and hence removed from the East-West struggle. The proposal of the latter sort advanced by George F. Kennan in his Reith Lectures over the BBC in 1957 occasioned widespread discussion both in Europe and in this country, where it first [306/307] familiarized the public at large with disengagement possibilities.

This goal can be fully realized only as part of a wider settlement with the Soviet Union. But there are certain things that can be negotiated right away. Among them the most important are the establishment of an initial zone of disengagement and the denial of nuclear weapons to further powers.

The logical place to start negotiation on disengagement is some version of the Rapacki Plan—which has gone through various modifications, but which has usually had as its central feature the nuclear demilitarization of East and West Germany, Poland, and Czechoslovakia. It is far from sure that Khrushchev is currently ready to accept this plan, and it is quite certain that both De Gaulle and Adenauer are against it, but it has great appeal both for Britain and for the Soviet satellites. Above all, the fact that it has been under informal discussion for so long a time has made it appear less threatening than any alternative proposal to both sides in the power struggle. At the very least, an announcement by the American government that it was ready to begin negotiations on this basis would offer two important advantages—it would give evidence that we had serious intentions of reducing military tension in Europe, and it would quite clearly suggest that our policy was no longer tied to the views of our conservative allies.

Moreover, the Rapacki Plan presents a realistic alternative to the "liberation" of East Central Europe about which Republican politicians have talked so much and done so little—witness the failure to give aid to the Hungarian revolution of 1956. On the one hand, its adoption by the United States would offer assurance to the Communist rulers of the Soviet Union and the satellite states that we had abandoned any intention of overthrowing their regimes by subversion or force of arms. At the same time, it would clearly convey to the peoples of East Central Europe that we had not lost interest in their fate—rather, that [307/308] we were substituting for a purely rhetorical notion of "liberation" a more workable policy for relieving direct military pressure on them and thereby for strengthening the liberal tendencies within their borders.

The Rapacki Plan has the final advantage—as the person of its author, the Polish foreign minister, implies—of "disengaging" two of the Soviet satellites with the strongest Western ties. Thus it offers the most coherent proposal that has appeared to date for bridging the gap between the Western and the Soviet spheres. Currently this is no more than a faint hope. But some partial version of the Rapacki Plan might at least run a chance of acceptance on a trial basis. If, for example, the United States and the Soviet Union were to agree on demilitarizing a relatively small but contiguous area including one province of each of the four states in question—say, Bavaria, Saxony, Bohemia, and Silesia—it could be the beginning of a disengagement by stages that would finally include the whole four-nation zone.

The denial of nuclear weapons to fifth or sixth powers—which means preventing Western Germany and Communist China from joining the present "nuclear club"—is absolutely crucial and grows more urgent with each passing month. Since the French bomb test in the Sahara, there have been reports that the Germans have similar plans afoot, and no one knows exactly what nuclear capabilities exist in the Communist camp. One authoritative estimate—that of a committee of the American Academy of Arts and Sciences, published in 1959—suggests that nineteen nations have the technical capability of producing nuclear weapons in the foreseeable future. It should be obvious, then, that on this single matter at least the United States and the Soviet Union have a common interest in closing the nuclear club while there is yet time.

An obvious corollary to such a recommendation is strong opposition to any German plans for nuclear armament. I have already drawn attention to the fact that Adenauer's [308/309] retirement will unquestionably entail changes in his country's foreign policy. These changes might go in either the neutralist or the nationalist direction—with the latter almost certainly including a drive for an independent nuclear capability on the French model. The two policy recommendations I have made both suggest that a neutralist Germany would be far preferable to a nationalist one.

The rearmament of Germany has aroused fears in Eastern Europe that are justified and that extend far beyond Communist opinion. The revival of German nationalist feeling and the return to positions of influence of many of the same individuals and groups that supported Nazi expansion represent a real danger to the peace. A Germany under conservative leadership—once Adenauer's moderating influence was gone—would give rise to widespread anxiety beyond the country's borders. A neutralist or partially demilitarized Germany under Social Democratic leadership would be much more reassuring.

If the United States should advance a serious proposal for disengagement, it would immediately relax tensions aroused by the Berlin issue. More specifically, the Western powers might even go as far as offering diplomatic recognition to East Germany and proposing a United Nations guarantee for Berlin's future status. The guiding principle in these concessions should be a frank recognition of the fact that West Berlin in its present situation is both untenable and an international anomaly. The problem it presents for us is far more human than it is military—that is, we should not be primarily concerned with maintaining an advanced outpost in power politics, but rather with honoring our pledges to two million West Berliners by seeing to it that their lives, their livelihood, and their liberties remain secure.

The final aim, then, in the case of Germany, would be equality of international status for the two German states, which would both eventually be disengaged from military alliances and left free to form some sort of loose federation. [**309/310**] At the start at least, within this federation two contrasting political and economic systems would continue to exist—communism in the East, capitalism in the West. But in the end it would almost certainly be the institutions and practices of West Germany—which would have behind them the bulk of the population and resources of the whole country—that would come to predominate.

So much for immediate goals. How do these proposals leave the long-range situation of NATO and of Europe in general? Here it is important to distinguish between NATO in its strictly military aspect, and the integration of Western Europe on the economic and cultural planes.

From the military standpoint, the logic of the above proposals is a drastic reduction in NATO's scope. A "disengaged" West Germany would cease to be a member. At a subsequent date Italy and Scandinavia might also prefer neutrality. Similarly France might be left to follow its own nationalist course; the policy recommendations I have made obviously imply a loosening of American ties with De Gaulle. Indeed, the logic of such a position might lead to an eventual neutralization of the whole six-nation area. This would leave NATO a truly Atlantic alliance based on the United States, Canada, and Great Britain.

Even within the reduced NATO area a change in armaments policy would be advisable. Should Labour, for example, ever win an election in Britain, the new government might well request the dismantlement of NATO missile or Polaris bases. The United States should be psychologically prepared for this and should begin right now to close down these bases throughout Europe. Currently they are not contributing to the *defense* of the West in any realistic sense; they are simply increasing tension and the danger of an accidental explosion that might bring on general nuclear warfare. Ultimately the defense of Western Europe should be reduced to conventional weapons alone. Kennan's Reith Lectures offer an imaginative suggestion for recasting the Western continental armed forces as [**310/311**] strictly defensive units of a paramilitary or territorial-militia type.

. . . .

Disengagement*

ROBERT E. OSGOOD (1921-), formerly professor of political science at the University of Chicago, is now associated with the Washington Center of Foreign Policy Research of Johns Hopkins University. In 1959, he was NATO visiting professor at Manchester University in England. He is the author of *Ideals and Self-interest in America's Foreign Relations* (1953) and *Limited War: The Challenge to American Strategy* (1957).

1. THE NATURE AND PURPOSE OF DISENGAGEMENT

The history of NATO has been one of mounting difficulties in meeting the requirements of allied security and collaboration in the face of political, economic, and military developments (preeminently, the growth of Soviet nuclear striking power) that were not foreseen at the outset. Necessarily, in a defensive alliance entailing a high level of contributions and integration, the chief instrument by which the members of NATO have sought to merge their particular national interests with the mutual advantages of a collective effort, has been military strategy, broadly conceived. Yet, on the threshold of the missile age, there was cause to doubt that the members of NATO would find a satisfactory solution to the problems of security and collaboration within the complex realm of planning, developing, and declaring military capabilities, deployments, and responses. Consequently, the risks, sacrifices, and perplexities of a joint military effort enhanced the appeal of a more direct resolution of the problems of mutual security by a negotiated accommodation with the Soviet Union, intended to mitigate the political source of strategic difficulties. Like the proposals for nuclear

sharing, the proposed political accommodations were replete with strategic and political implications that directly affected the core of mutual security interests sustaining the alliance.

Hopes for a political amelioration of the sources of tension [308/309] and insecurity in the center of Europe have been focused upon a variety of proposals that are commonly subsumed under the general term "disengagement."[1] Some of these proposals have called for nothing more than arms limitation and control in the center of Europe. In this category the most notable were British Foreign Minister Sir Anthony Eden's suggestion at the Geneva summit conference in July, 1955, of "a demilitarized area between East and West" and Polish Foreign Minister Adam Rapacki's proposals in 1957 and 1958 of a "denuclearized zone," prohibiting the production, stationing, and use of nuclear weapons and reducing conventional forces in Poland, Czechoslovakia, and the two Germanys.* However, the most compre-

---

* Actually, Eden presented two different plans at different times. On January 29, 1954, at the Four-Power Conference of Foreign Ministers in Berlin, he proposed, simply, the reunification of Germany by free and supervised all-German elections. However, the Eden Plan that was repeatedly referred to in Soviet proposals was the one Eden presented at Geneva on July 18, 1955. The part of this threefold plan that got the most attention and came to be identified with the plan as a whole

* Robert E. Osgood, from "Disengagement," *NATO: The Entangling Alliance* (Chicago: University of Chicago Press, 1962), pp. 308-313, 328-330, 346, 407-408. Reprinted with permission of the University of Chicago Press.

hensive proposals have envisaged, in addition to the limitation and control of weapons and forces in a central zone, the withdrawal of foreign troops and the reunification and neutralization of Germany under a mutual security guaranty. The two most in- [309/310] fluential plans of this scope were presented in 1957 by the British Labor party leader Hugh Gaitskell and by George F. Kennan.*

Kennan's proposal, coming at a time when Russia's launching of the Sputniks had made Europe acutely conscious of the hazards of NATO's nuclear dependence and coinciding with a Soviet diplomatic offensive aimed toward "summit" talks, which were designed in part to forestall the placement of American missiles in Europe, caught the fancy of many Europeans. To them, and especially to the British, it seemed like the basis for a political breakthrough in the menacing perplexities of military security. In the course of 1958, however, Russia's renewed intransigence and her patent opposition to the reunification of Germany, together with the coolness of Western governments to a scheme of such far-reaching implications for the strategic and political bases of the security system they had so laboriously created, rendered disengagement a dormant issue.

Premier Khrushchev, confidently proclaiming that the bal- [310/311] ance of power in the world had shifted to the Soviet Union, now concentrated on getting the West to recognize East Germany and withdraw from Berlin. He regarded the only basis of negotiations as Western accession to such stock Soviet demands as a ban on nuclear armaments and tests, the liquidation of all foreign bases in Europe, and a non-aggression pact between the NATO and Warsaw Pact countries. The principal feature of the disengagement proposals that he formally indorsed was Eden's plan to create a demilitarized area and Rapacki's plan to prohibit the stationing and production of atomic weapons in a Central European zone.* Although

* Gaitskell first presented his plan on January 11, 1957, in the Golkin [sic] Lecture at Harvard, which was published in *The Challenge of Coexistence* (Cambridge, Mass.: Harvard University Press, 1957). Here he proposed the reunification of Germany, the withdrawal of foreign troops, and the limitation, inspection, and control of armed forces in Germany, Poland, Czechoslovakia, and Hungary, and, if possible, Rumania and Bulgaria. He speculated that "the Russians might refuse to contemplate the plan without the neutralization on both sides [of Germany] from the start." He opposed the withdrawal of American troops from the Continent. In an article in *Foreign Affairs* in July, 1958, entitled "Disengagement: Why? How?" he presented a modified version of this plan. Gaitskell's plan was almost identical to the plan formulated by his colleague Denis Healey, who largely devised it.

Kennan made his proposal in the Reith lectures at Oxford in November, 1957, and in BBC broadcasts that December. He published it in his book *Russia, the Atom, and the West* (New York: Harper & Bros., 1957), chaps. iii and iv. It included the reunification and neutralization of Germany and the withdrawal of foreign forces from Germany and Eastern Europe, all under guarantees by the great powers. Germany would be under some kind of military restriction (certainly including the prohibition of nuclear weapons), and the European and NATO countries would depend for local defense on "paramilitary" forces "of a territorial-militia type." In his broadcast on December 20 Kennan said he was prepared to see all American forces withdrawn from the Continent and eventually from Britain. In January, 1959, Kennan defended his original proposal and indorsed the Rapacki Plan but said that German security should depend on twelve German divisions instead of on paramilitary forces ("Disengagement Revisited," *Foreign Affairs*, XXXVII [January, 1959], 187-210).

* However, during a television interview with American journalists in June, 1957, Khrushchev, in an expansive mood, also suggested that the United States and other countries withdraw foreign troops from Western Europe, in return for which Russia would withdraw her troops from Eastern Europe (Hinterhoff, *op. cit.*, pp. 204-5).

was the proposal of a demilitarized area between East and West. However, the other parts proposed a supervised limitation of forces and armaments in both Germanys and in the neighboring countries and a mutual security pact to guarantee a united Germany against aggression. Eden said that the whole plan was intended to provide the Soviet Union with reassurances that would make the unification of Germany, free to join NATO, acceptable to the Soviet Union, but Soviet leaders, in their subsequent references to the plan, chose to ignore this aspect.

Rapacki presented his first plan to the United Nations General Assembly on October 2, 1957, and in a memorandum to the powers concerned on February 15, 1958. It proposed an "atom-free zone," to include Poland, Czechoslovakia, and both parts of Germany, in which "nuclear weapons would be neither manufactured nor stockpiled, the equipment and installations designed for their servicing would not be located there, the use of nuclear weapons against the territory of this zone would be prohibited," under a system of ground and aerial control. Rapacki announced the second version of his plan in Warsaw on November 4, 1958. In this he added a reduction of conventional forces in the zone, to go into effect after a first-stage ban on nuclear production and simultaneously with the other denuclearization features.

The complete texts of the two Eden and two Rapacki plans are among the appendixes in Eugène Hinterhoff, *Disengagement* (London: Stevens & Sons, Ltd., 1959).

the British government favored negotiating on such a plan, the United States, supported by Germany and France, curtly rejected it as disrupting NATO's forward strategy without providing any security against violations by powers outside the proposed zone.

The major Soviet goals in Europe continued to be Western recognition of East Germany, the prevention of West German rearmament, the isolation of West Germany from her allies, the sealing-off of the East-West escape route in Berlin, and the removal of the Western presence in Berlin. However, Khrushchev preferred to pursue these goals by inviting a showdown on Berlin and exploiting Western fears of Soviet missile power in order to exacerbate the "contradictions in the capitalist camp" rather than by negotiating comprehensive disengagement schemes, which, by compelling Soviet withdrawal from East Germany, would deprive the Soviet Union of a valuable forward position, jeopardize Soviet control over the East European satellites, and revive the dreaded specter of German expansion eastward.

Thus, suddenly, on November 10, 1958, he demanded an end of the four-power occupation of Berlin and informed the Western governments that they would have to get out of West Berlin and make it a "free city" within six months or else deal with East [311/312] Germany, to which the Soviet Union intended to turn over all her rights in the city. Eventually, through a skilful combination of threats and diplomatic overtures, the Soviet premier first removed President Eisenhower's objections to a summit conference by conceding in the famous Camp David meeting that there would be no time limit on negotiations about Berlin and then succeeded in manipulating an extension of this "slow ultimatum" to get the Western governments, contrary to all their original protestations about the futility of such a vague and unpromising venture, to assemble in Paris in May, 1960, for a four-power conference. Then, when the delegates had assembled in Paris, he dra-

matically withdrew from the conference before it could convene, while bitterly denouncing the flight of the American U-2 espionage plane shot down over Russia.

Yet, despite this rude end to the disengagement ferment stirred up by Kennan's lectures two-and-a-half years before, there could be little doubt that, if Khrushchev so chose, still another Soviet gesture toward a negotiated "relaxation of tensions" would revive Western interest in the project. For disengagement continued to be the most hopeful political means of relieving NATO's military troubles. And disengagement seemed like the only feasible means of resolving the problem of a divided Germany, which could otherwise ignite the spark of a military conflict that even the most complete military preparation might not prevent or extinguish. Therefore, disengagement deserves serious analysis in a study of the strategic problems of NATO because any plan to mitigate the political source of security problems is intrinsically important, because such plans could someday become mutually acceptable, and because, even if they do not, their mere formulation or lack of formulation will affect one of the primary political issues in the cold war: the place of Germany in Europe.

For the purposes of this analysis we can think of disengagement as including any one or all of the following three components: (a) the withdrawal of Soviet and American and other foreign troops from a zone embracing the two Germanys or beyond; (b) arms reduction, limitation, and control in such a [312/313] zone; (c) a political settlement unifying Germany and determining the restrictions, if any, upon her armament and upon her political commitments; (d) some guaranty by the United States, the Soviet Union, and other powers of these three components.

From the West's standpoint the principal value of any scheme of disengagement will lie in alleviating the military and political sources of tensions that jeopardize the maintenance of security by peaceful means. Through disengagement the West may also seek to strengthen its political position and weaken Russia's, just as Russia would certainly hope to advance her political ends against the West. But it is unreasonable to expect either of the two competing nations or blocs of nations to enter knowingly into an agreement that would result in a significant accretion of the relative power of the other. On the other hand, disengagement might reasonably require one or both sides to sacrifice something of immediate security, political advantage, or the immediate reduction of tensions and the risk of war in order to promote the achievement of these goals in the long run. Yet there are clearly stringent limits on the extent to which nations can legitimately sacrifice familiar conditions of military security in the short run—which, after all, may be decisive—for the sake of achieving hypothetical military and political advantages in the future. Accordingly, every disengagement proposal should be assessed in terms of a balance of military and political objectives in the short run and long run. . . . [313/328]

. . . .

. . . If there is a serious danger of a united Germany's severing her ties with the West and joining with the Russians, it lies in the possibility that the division of Germany will lead a desperate and frustrated Federal Republic, unable to get support for her security or for unification from her Western allies, to seek support from Russia.

Nevertheless, an inherently powerful, though formally neutralized, Germany might very well be a disturbing influence in Europe in other ways. It is difficult to imagine such a strong nation in such a crucial geopolitical position placidly playing the non-alignment role of Switzerland or Austria, and it is difficult to imagine the Soviet Union and the United States indefinitely allowing her to play such a role. The question of which way and for what purposes Germany might throw her

weight would create a far more fluid and unstable political balance in Europe than the division of Germany permits. Even the most circumspect German diplomacy might not appease the fears and suspicions of her smaller and weaker neighbors. Only if a unified Germany were to become an integral part of a larger European federation, together with neutral East European states, might she mitigate the unsettling consequences of her neutral status; but the political conditions for such a federation scarcely exist.

On the other hand, the continued division of a resurgent [328/329] Germany could be even more disturbing from the West's standpoint, if, as seems likely, reunification remains a compelling national goal, which the Federal Republic cannot afford to abandon.[10] For, unless the West can convince the Germans that their alliance with NATO is a better assurance of reunification than neutralization and military withdrawal—a proposition that must seem more untenable the longer Germany remains divided—they may conclude some day that the principal obstacle to unity is Germany's membership in NATO, not Soviet imperialism. With a little Soviet encouragement, some future Bonn government might then be tempted to use its economic and military potential (perhaps including a nuclear capability) to bargain directly with Moscow, trading Germany's NATO attachment (and certainly her nuclear arms) for reunification. As Kennan warned, such a bilateral deal, "however innocuous or even constructive in its consequences" it might be, "would set in motion trains of memory, suspicion, and resentment of which only the Communists could be the beneficiaries," if it were made against the wishes of "a Western community which had nailed its flag to the mast of an unconditional capitulation of the Soviet interest in Central and Eastern Europe."[11]

To be sure, in 1961 it was as difficult to foresee conditions under which the Soviet Union would actually grant Germany unification as it was to foresee conditions in which the West German government would accept unification on Soviet terms. But, since Russia was the only country that could grant unification, it would be remarkable if she did not some day, as before the Paris Agreements, use this powerful card in her deck at least to exploit the *prospect* of unification in order to isolate West Germany from the Western community. To offset this danger was one of the best reasons for the NATO powers to formulate and propose a reasonable agreement for German reunification, in order to demonstrate who was to blame for partition. But since such an agreement, to be reasonable, would have to be acceptable not only to the Western powers but also, within some plausible bounds, to the Soviet Union, a proposal of reunification would have to include neutralization (that is, **[329/330]** a prohibition upon Germany's joining NATO or the Warsaw Pact), arms limitation, and military withdrawal.

Of course, even to present such a proposal tentatively without assurance that West Germany approved it would defeat its purpose. In 1961, the Bonn government remained adamantly opposed to any disengagement plan. Hence, her allies could scarcely press this major power to contravene her government's conception of a vital interest merely in order to place the onus of German division on Russia. On the other hand, the Bonn government and her allies could not indefinitely pretend that unification might be obtained by integrating West Germany into the Western community. If reunification through comprehensive disengagement were to be ruled out, West Germany would sooner or later have to accept the fact that the implicit condition of her entanglement in NATO is the suspension of her ambition to unite with East Germany. This would not solve the problem of Berlin, but it would at least impede the Russians from exploiting the division of Berlin and Germany to divide the alliance.

As long as the West Germans know that it is the Russians and not their allies who bear the onus of partition, the security of Western Europe will be served better by the Federal Republic's membership in NATO than by her unification with East Germany under the only terms that Russia might conceivably accept. As long as the West German government is not tempted to make a separate deal with the Russians for unification, the liabilities of a divided Berlin and Germany, from the standpoint of NATO as a whole, are counterbalanced by the advantages of West Germany's integration in NATO and by avoiding the risks of reunification through disengagement.

However, Kennan rightly suggested that more is at stake in the issue of German reunification than the welfare of NATO and *Western* Europe; the welfare of Eastern Europe is also involved, and the interests of the United States are bound up with the state of Europe as a whole. . . . **[330/346]**

. . . .

Only if the Soviet Union, pressed by rising unrest in the satellites and thwarted in her ambitions to consolidate Germany under Communist rule, felt compelled to retrench and stabilize her western front in order to contain a threat from Communist China . . . would she be likely to regard the reunification of Germany under comprehensive disengagement as a profitable bargain. But, short of an improbable diplomatic revolution resulting from some such major reversal in Russia's power position, any mutually acceptable disengagement in the center of Europe is virtually precluded.

Yet even if a diplomatic revolution should lead to comprehensive disengagement, this would not eliminate the Communist threat to Europe or the need for NATO to contain it, as long as the Soviet government continued to be moved by a compulsive image of inevitable Western hostility and by a dynamic drive to destroy the centers of Western power. After all, the West's wartime alliance with the Soviet Union did not eliminate that threat. Disengagement would alter—and, in some ways, aggravate—the conditions of tension and conflict in the center of Europe; it would not terminate the cold war. Therefore, insofar as any kind of disengagement is desirable or feasible, it should be viewed as a complement, not as an alternative, to the strategic requirements of allied security and cohesion. In effect, that means that the external and internal strength of NATO is the prerequisite of acceptable disengagement in a general European settlement, just as it is the prerequisite of acceptable engagement in a divided Europe. [346/407]

. . . .

¹ For a description and analysis of the principal disengagement proposals, see Michael Howard, *Disengagement in Europe* (Baltimore, Md.: Pen-

guin Books, 1958); P. J. D. W., "The Pursuit of Disengagement," *The World Today*, XV (April, 1959), 156-68; Senate Committee on Foreign Relations, Subcommittee on Disarmament, *Handbook on Arms Control and Related Problems in Europe*, 86 Cong., 1 sess.; and, most comprehensive of all, Eugene Hinterhoff, *Disengagement* (London: Stevens & Sons, Ltd., 1959).

. . . .

¹⁰ For a balanced estimate of the strength of West German sentiment for reunification, see Flora Lewis, "The Unstable States of Germany," *Foreign Affairs*, XXXVIII (July, 1960), 588-97, and Gerald Freund, *Germany Between Two Worlds* (Harcourt, Brace & Co., 1961), pp. 94-100. Summing up reunification sentiment, Freund wrote, "Significant forces in the Federal Republic are unenthusiastic about reunification. One finds conflicts of interest, especially [407/408] in the commercial world, which dissipate the power behind reunification efforts. Such conflicts are not of lasting importance and in all sectors of society one finds a keen awareness of the partition problem which, as interest in foreign policy increases, will inevitably arouse a more widespread concern" (*ibid.*, p. 100).

¹¹ Kennan, "Disengagement Revisited," p. 205.

Suggested Topics for Controlled Research

All topics suggested here are for controlled research in this anthology alone. You may select, or your instructor may assign you, a topic from one of the groups of suggested topics; or he may assign you some other topic. Whatever your topic, the length of your paper will depend not only upon it, but upon the material available in this anthology and upon your thoroughness of research and your conciseness in presentation of the results of that research. For each group of topics, a reasonable length is suggested.

A basic group of topics concerns the definitions and the interpretations of "neutralism," "nonalignment," and related terms as they are understood in the developing nations. If you are especially interested in words and their shades of meaning, one project is to classify the meanings attached to "nonalignment," "positive neutrality," "independent policy," and related terms by those who testify for neutralism in this book. This project requires you to show what leaders and nations prefer which terms and why. To begin it, you might investigate why V. K. Krishna Menon rejects the term "neutralist" and what he prefers in its place. A second project is to show how one political ideology of the non-Western world—for example, Arab nationalism as interpreted by Clovis Maqsud—relates to nonalignment. A third project is to examine the cultural and the racial ideas that Janio da Silva Quadros introduces in his discussion of Brazil's new foreign policy in world affairs. A fourth project is to investigate the economic ideas in some selections, for example, in Nehru's address and Madame Bandaranaike's speech. This project should recognize that nonalignment has various

origins and that not all governments of the economically underdeveloped nations have chosen the third path. A fifth project is to investigate the relationship between nonalignment and military security in the new states. The Sato reading is especially relevant to this task. This project should investigate why protagonists of nonalignment reject military alliances for themselves and condemn them for others and show the implications of this policy for the security of the nonaligned. This project should consider that the neutralist ideology may be intended to strengthen the defense system of the neutralist nation. A sixth project is to compare nonalignment in the developing nations with neutralism in the West, in order to clarify differences and also to search for possible common denominators—for instance, horror of war on the part of intellectuals. The length of a paper on a topic in this group might be between 1000 and 2000 words.

A second group of topics concerns the great powers and non-Western neutralism. One project is to study some American viewpoints, examining those of Dulles, Eisenhower, Prouty, and Kennedy, for example—in particular their agreement about the character of nonalignment, their differences over the meaning of nonalignment for the United States in the Cold War, and their insights into the international conduct of the uncommitted nations. Taking only this matter of insight, you might evaluate Senator Prouty's charge that Afro-Asian neutralists have applied a double standard of judgment in world politics. Is he convincing? Based on your reading of the selections in Part One of this anthology, are there extenuating circumstances that might justify "unneutral" neutralism? A second project is to examine Russian views of nonalignment with special attention to the development in Moscow's outlook, beginning with the "two-camp" idea of Leninism. A third project is to trace the changes in Communist China's outlook on nonalignment. The Palmer essay is helpful in this task, comparing it to "More on Nehru's Philosophy in the Light of the Sino-Indian Boundary Question." A fourth project is to compare American and Chinese or Russian and Chinese views of a third way in world affairs. For example, can you detect any differences in principle or emphasis between Moscow and Peking which relate to their ideological differences within the Communist camp? Papers on a topic in this group might run from 1500 to 2500 words.

A third group of topics deals exclusively with disengagement. One project is to examine the proposals in the Healey and Rapacki selections to see what common objectives they may have with respect to Germany and how they might differ in probable outcome, if adopted. A second project is to discuss either the 1958 reply of the United States to the Rapacki proposal or the Osgood analysis of disengagement to see how well either selection evaluates the possible risks and possible virtues of the Polish and Russian approach to disengagement in Central Europe. A third project is to compare the arms reduction plans within disengagement proposals, evaluating and comparing the Chou En-lai, Khrushchev, and Rapacki selections. A fourth project is to investigate the reasons why proposals for nuclear free zones and allied proposals come more readily from Communist than from Western governments. The length of a paper on a topic in this group might be from 1500 to 2500 words.

A fourth group of topics concerns the relationship between neutralism and disengagement. A rereading of the "Introduction" would help you to effectively complete a project here. One project is to examine several writings, for instance, those of Sukarno, Madame Bandaranaike, Kennan, Kremnyev, and Hughes to see if there are common hopes and fears—basic human predispositions apart from politics —that encourage policies of neutralism and disengagement. This project might prove of special interest to those seeking psychological and philosophical clues to the motivations of men and nations. A second project is to consider the argument that the only feasible way to understand any form of neutralism or disengagement is to restrict study to discrete, historical circumstances; one must avoid generalizations about common, underlying forces within and also between these two phenomena. You could debate this thesis with the aid of evidence drawn from throughout this book, or you might stress one case, Japan's, for example, revealed in Nishio, Sato, and Scalapino and Masumi. A third project is to study disengagement and neutralism to see if they are fundamentally responses of the weak—or those who speak for the weak—to the powerful nations which make the crucial decisions governing the political life of the lesser nations. A fourth project is the answer to this question, Can one expect the advocates of forms of disengagement in Europe to also support the nonalignment perspective of many new nations? You might begin by rereading Kennan, Healey, and Khrushchev to grasp some of the ideals and interests which appeal to them, and apply this knowledge to the principles and objectives of nonaligned states, revealed in the "Five Principles of Peaceful Coexistence," the Bandung Conference Communique, and elsewhere. A fifth project is related to the fourth. Would you anticipate that the proponents of nonalignment in the developing countries are in basic agreement with disengagement in Middle Europe? Madame Bandaranaike's address to the Belgrade Conference is useful for this project. The length of a paper on a topic in this group might well run over 2000 words.

There are many other possibilities for productive research projects. Brief papers of about 800 words might describe, without evaluating, Ghana's nonaligned conduct in some international controversies; the reasons for the attraction of Titoism for nonaligned states; or the nature and roots of European neutralism according to Garosci.

Suggested Topics for Library Research

The contents of this book may lead you to find and study other materials to deepen your understanding of neutralism and disengagement.

In making a working bibliography for a library-research paper on any of the topics suggested below, you will find certain bibliographical aids and certain periodicals very useful. First, of course, is the card catalog of your university or college library. Second, are general periodical indexes, among them the *Readers' Guide to Periodical Literature*, the *International Index to Periodicals*, *The New York Times Index*, and *The Official Index* to *The* [London] *Times*. Third, are bibliographies concerned specifically with political science, among them *Public Affairs Information Service*, *Foreign Affairs Bibliography* (in three volumes), and *Publications of the Department of State*. Fourth, are specialized periodicals in which you are likely to find useful articles, among them *Foreign Affairs, American Political Science Review, International Journal, Eastern Economist* (Delhi), *Orbis, Review of International Affairs* (Belgrade), *World Marxist Review, International Affairs* (London), and *World Politics*. This listing is only a sample of the variety and the number of periodicals and reference guides available for library research. All of the periodicals suggested under specific projects should be investigated for the successful completion of these projects.

For each of the projects presented below, a few suggested sources are supplied. These sources are not to be considered exhaustive; they are only offered as a guide and should be supplemented by additional library research. In certain cases you may find equally acceptable sources on which to base the particular project you choose.

A logical topic area for library research is additional testimonies for nonalignment and neutralism. You might criticize, for example, the logic, the style, and the plausibility of the testimonies or you might explore the ideological assumptions, the policy implications, and the historical accuracy of the statements. A mixture of both approaches is possible. One project is to study Yugoslavia's foreign policy since 1948. Among the sources to consult are the Program of the League of Communists of Yugoslavia, adopted by the Seventh Congress of the League in 1958 and published in *Yugoslavia's Way* (New York, 1958), Chapter 3 and Edvard Kardelj, *War and Socialism* (Belgrade, 1960). A second project is to examine continental European neutralism, pursuing some of the ideas and citations in Bartoli, Bundy, and Garosci. A third project is to investigate Canadian neutralism and can be undertaken with the help of James N. Minifie, *Peacemaker or Powdermaker* (Toronto, 1960); James Eayrs, *Northern Approaches* (Toronto, 1961); and newspaper accounts of the Canadian election of 1963. A fourth project is to study India's defense of its nonalignment policy, despite the acceptance of Western military help since the 1962 Sino-Indian crisis. For this project, see, for example, Jawaharlal Nehru, "Changing India," *Foreign Affairs*, XLI (April, 1963), 453-465; 1960-1964 statements by Indian leaders, reprinted in *India News*, issued by the Indian Embassy in Washington and distributed to many libraries; *Indian Affairs Record*; and *Indian Press Digest*. For successful completion of this project, you should refer to the periodicals and general reference guides noted earlier.

A second topic area is found in the rich literature of evaluations dealing with neutralism. One project is to locate comparisons of various kinds of neutralism and then evaluate how well the comparative essays explain neutralism in different political and cultural settings. For this project, see Ernest W. Lefever's essay, "Nehru, Nasser and Nkrumah on Neutralism" in *Neutralism and Nonalignment*, ed. Laurence W. Martin (New York, 1962), pp. 93-121; Chapters 5 and 11 by George Liska in the Martin book; Michael Brecher, "Neutralism," *International Journal*, XVII (Summer, 1962), 224-236; and *New Nations in a Divided World*, ed. Kurt London (New York, 1963). A second project is to analyze the implications of neutralism for specific institutions or countries. For this project, see Chapter 7 by Francis O. Wilcox on the United Nations and Chapter 8 by Arnold Wolfers on United States defense policy, both in *Neutralism and Nonalignment* and Cecil V. Crabb, Jr. "American Diplomatic Tactics and Neutralism," *Political Science Quarterly*, LXXVIII (September, 1963), 418-443. For both the preceding projects, you should investigate the government publications of specific countries. These publications will include statements by heads of government and important political leaders. The impact of nonaligned India on the United Nations can be studied with the help of Ross N. Berkes and Mohinder S. Bedi, *The Diplomacy of India* (Stanford, 1958); and Ernst B. Haas, "Dynamic Environment and Static System," in *The Revolution in World Politics*, ed. Morton A. Kaplan (New York, 1962), Chapter 13. A third project is to investigate the role of nonalignment within the total foreign policy of an uncommitted nation. There are many possibilities here. For the United Arab Republic, see Leonard Binder, "Nasserism" (Chapter 7) and "Egypt's Positive Neutrality" (Chapter 8), both in *The Revolution in World Politics*; and Charles D. Cremeans, *The Arabs and the World* (New York, 1963). For Burma, see U Thant, "A Burmese View of World Tensions," *The Annals*, CCCXVIII (July,

1958), 34-42; and William C. Johnstone, *Burma's Foreign Policy* (Cambridge, 1963). For India, see, among others, Werner Levi, *Free India in Asia* (Minneapolis, 1952); J. C. Kundra, *Indian Foreign Policy: 1947-1954* (Groningen, 1955); Phillips Talbot and S. L. Poplai, *India and America* (New York, 1958); and P. C. Chakravarti, *India's China Policy* (Bloomington, 1962). For Ghana, consult George Padmore, *Pan-Africanism or Communism* (New York, 1956); articles and books by Kwame Nkrumah; John Phillips, *Kwame Nkrumah and the Future of Africa* (New York, 1961); and David E. Apter, *Ghana in Transition* (New York, 1963), pp. 417-421. For Indonesia, see Mohammad Hatta, "Indonesia's Foreign Policy," *Foreign Affairs*, XXXI (April, 1953), 441-452; George McT. Kahin, *The Asian-African Conference* (Ithaca, 1956); Amry Vandenbosch and Richard A. Butwell, *Southeast Asia Among the World Powers* (Lexington, 1958); and articles and books by Sukarno. For this project, consult especially *Asian Survey, Eastern World, Middle East Journal, Asian Recorder, Africa Digest, Journal of Modern African Studies, World Politics*, and government publications of the specific country. A fourth project is to assess the force of neutralism within non-Western nations of the anti-Communist coalition. For Iran, see Lawrence P. Elwell-Sutton, "Nationalism and Neutralism in Iran," *Middle East Journal*, XII (Winter, 1958), 20-32. For Japan, see I. I. Morris, "Japanese Foreign Policy and Neutralism," *International Affairs* (London), XXXVI (April, 1958), 371-382. A fifth project is based on a study of the views of major Communist nations toward the neutrals. Peking's policies are described in A. Doak Barnett, *Communist China and Asia* (New York, 1960) and A. M. Halpern, "The Chinese Communist Line on Neutralism," *The China Quarterly*, No. 5 (January-March, 1961), 90-115. Peking's interpretation of the frontier dispute with India is found in *Documents on the Sino-Indian Boundary Question* (Peking, 1960); *Selected Documents on*

Sino-Indian Relations (Peking, 1962); and *The Sino-Indian Boundary Question*, 2nd ed. (Peking, 1962). For the Russian outlook on neutralism, consult George Ginsburgs, "Neutrality and Neutralism and the Tactics of Soviet Diplomacy," *American Slavic Review*, XIX (December, 1960), 531-560. Additional materials may be found in the *Current Digest of the Soviet Press*, the *Survey of China Mainland Press*, *Problems of Communism*, *Peking Review*, and *World Marxist Review*.

A third topic area is proposals for military or political disengagement. One library project is to compare and contrast two or more proposals. For a proposal made early in the Cold War, consult Arnold Brecht, "The Idea of a Safety Belt," *American Political Science Review*, XLIII (October, 1949), 1001-1009. In 1959, Secretary of State Christian Herter recommended a plan for Germany and Central Europe which represented an advanced position for the West. For his proposal, see the *Department of State Bulletin*, XL (June 1, 1959), 779-781. For critiques of these proposals, see appropriate issues of the periodicals listed at the beginning of this appendix. A famous pacifist supports the Rapacki approach and a disarmed Germany in Bertrand Russell, *Has Man a Future?* (New York, 1962). See also Adam Rapacki, "The Polish Plan For a Nuclear Free Zone Today," *International Affairs* (London), XXXIX (January, 1963), 1-12. Harold Stassen, former disarmament adviser to Eisenhower, has suggested a plan for nuclear free zones reported in *The Christian Science Monitor*, July 22, 1963, p. 1. A second project is to take the Rapacki approach or Kennan's as revealed in *Russia, the Atom, and the West* (New York, 1957) and evaluate it in the light of what Dean Acheson, a vigorous opponent of disengagement says in "The Illusion of Disengagement," *Foreign Affairs*, XXXVI (April, 1958), 371-382. A new version of the Rapacki Plan was presented on March 5, 1964. See also some background works. Among them are Michael Howard, *Disengagement in*

Europe (Baltimore, 1958); Eugene Hinterhoff, *Disengagement* (London, 1959); and Helmut Schmidt, *Defense and Retaliation* (New York, 1962). One interesting project using these sources is to investigate the reasons why disengagement has a special attraction for the socialist parties of Britain and Germany. For example, see Denis Healey, *Neutralism* (London, 1955). Another project, using Schmidt and Acheson, is to study the extent to which disengagement relies on the maintenance of a nuclear stalemate between East and West, a stalemate that creates an atmosphere conducive to the exploration of ideas about ending military confrontation in critical regions with the understanding that these ideas cannot be extended to the umbrella of power itself.

A fifth topic area is the biographies and public papers of leading spokesmen for nonalignment. One project is to write a paper on the qualities of mind and personality which can be detected from the writings of major figures. For Nasser, see *Egypt's Liberation: The Philosophy of the Revolution* (Washington, 1955) and *Nasser's Speeches and Press Interviews* (Cairo, 1958-). A Burmese statesman is studied in Richard Butwell, *U Nu of Burma* (Stanford, 1963). For Nkrumah, see his autobiography *Ghana*, his *I Speak of Freedom*, and *Consciencism*. The autobiography of a Kenyan leader is Tom Mboya, *Freedom and After* (Boston, 1963). In addition, check the particular definitive biographies available. A second project is to study an idea in McGeorge Bundy's essay in this anthology on parallels between American isolationism and European neutralism. Bundy suggests that, after considering the high idealism involved, a hopeful estimate of communism is the result, not the cause of European neutralism of the late forties and early fifties. This project would investigate whether or not there is any evidence for this suggestion in the biographies and public papers of any of the leaders who support neutralism. For example, see Nehru's *Toward Freedom* (New York, 1941); *Glimpses of*

World History (New York, 1942); and *Indian Foreign Policy* (New Delhi, 1961); and Paul F. Power, "Indian Foreign Policy: The Age of Nehru," *The Review of Politics*, XXVI (April, 1964), 257-286. There are numerous biographies of Nehru that will be helpful here.

A sixth topic area is the possible outgrowth of neutralism from, or its close link to, early national history and legal neutrality. One project is to investigate neutralism and American neutrality in the past. Several commentators, among them, John F. Kennedy and Sukarno, have said there is a similarity among all neutral nations, past and present, implying that all new nations have an early, neutral phase. See, for instance, Charles S. Hyneman, *The First American Neutrality* (Urbana, 1934) or Charles Seymour, *American Neutrality* (New Haven, 1935); and the neutrality tradition within the stream of American foreign relations, treated in Alexander DeConde, *A History of American Foreign Policy* (New York, 1963), *passim*. A second project is to study neutralism and legal neutrality at large. See Hans J. Morgenthau, *Dilemmas of Politics* (Chicago, 1958), Chapter 10. Two helpful articles are C. G. Fenwick, "The Legal Aspects of Neutralism," *American Journal of International Law*, LI (January, 1957),

71-74; and Peter Lyon, "Neutrality and the Emergence of the Concept of Neutrality," *The Review of Politics*, XXII (April, 1960), 255-268. A third project is to study the "imposed" neutrality of Austria or Laos as compared with neutralism. See Austria's neutrality law of October 26, 1955, in *Constitutions of Nations*, ed. Amos J. Peaslee, 2nd ed. (The Hague, 1956), p. 147; and the Austrian State Treaty of 1955 in *United States Treaties and Other International Agreements*, VI, pt. 2 (1955), pp. 2369-2535 (TIAS No. 3298). Relevant materials on neutralized Laos are the Declaration and the Protocol on Laos, found in the *Department of State Bulletin*, XLVII (August 13, 1962), 259-263. Study of the neutralization of Laos may lead to a fourth project: investigation of the reasons why President De Gaulle of France has asked for the neutralization of Cambodia and Vietnam, in addition to Laos, and how President Johnson responded to this suggestion. De Gaulle's proposal is reported in *The New York Times*, February 1, 1964, pp. 1, 4. Johnson's provisional response is in the same newspaper, February 2, 1964, p. 62.

The projects and materials outlined here will undoubtedly suggest other topics which will be equally suitable for library research.

Guide to Research

THE IDEA OF RESEARCH

Research is the organized, disciplined search for truth; the aim of all research is to discover the truth about something. That thing may be a historical object like the Stonehenge monuments or a historical event like the Hungarian Revolt or the Battle of Waterloo. It may be a work of literature like Shakespeare's *Julius Cæsar* or Miller's *Death of a Salesman*. It may be a recurring event like the motions of the planets or the circulation of the blood. It may be an experimentally repeatable phenomenon like behavior of rats in a maze or perception apparently unaccounted for by the five senses. Or it may be a political problem like the decision to use the atomic bomb in World War II. Archeology, history, political science, literary criticism and scholarship, astronomy, physiology, and psychology—these are some of the many divisions of research. Indeed, all the sciences—physical, biological, and social—and all other scholarly disciplines share this organized, disciplined search for truth.

The search for truth has often been confused with such aims as confirming prejudice, instilling patriotism, and praising friends and blaming enemies. The attempt to prove the preconceived conclusion *that* one college is superior to another, for example, is not research (though the attempt to discover *whether* one college is so superior is). Research is hostile to prejudice.

General Methods of Research. The best general method of research is first-hand observation. But this method is not always possible and, when it is possible, not always practical.

The best method to begin discovering the truth about something is to observe that thing and the circumstances surrounding it. To discover the truth about *Julius Cæsar* or *Death of a Salesman*, get the play and read it, or go to the theatre and watch a performance. To discover the truth about the planets, observe them through your telescope. To discover the truth about the intelligence of rats, build a maze and run some rats through it.

This first-hand observation is not always possible, however. To discover the truth about the Battle of Waterloo, you can't observe the battle. The best that you or anyone else can do is to observe other persons' observations, the recorded observations of eye-witnesses: diaries, letters, and memoirs, for instance, of soldiers and generals who were in the battle. With more recent historical events—for example, the Hungarian Revolt—you are better off. You can watch films and listen to tape recordings. You may be able to interview people who were there. But these observations are still second-hand; and, on the whole, history can be observed only at second-hand. The sole exception is history that you have been part of. You may have fought in the Hungarian Revolt—though, if you did, you may be prejudiced.

Even when first-hand observation is possible, it is not always practical. You may have a copy of or tickets to *Julius Cæsar* or *Death of a Salesman* but not know enough about the principles of dramatic criticism to interpret the play unaided. You may have a telescope but not know how to use it or, if you do, not know what to make of what you observe through it. You may have some rats but not know how to build a maze or, if you do, not know enough about animal psychology to run your rats through it properly. The best that *you* can do under these circumstances is to supplement whatever first-hand observations you can make with observations of the first-hand observations of other people better-trained or better-equipped than you. Read *Julius Cæsar* or *Death of a Salesman* and also critics' inter-

I

pretations of the play. Observe the planets, if you can, and read treatises on astronomy. Do what you can with your rats, and read reports of experiments with rats. After all, no one can master the special methods and come by the special equipment of all scholarly disciplines. Indeed, few people can do this with more than one discipline, and then not before they're thirty. But all people who want a liberal education should try to discover as much of the truth about as many scholarly disciplines as their abilities and their circumstances permit. Indeed, the achievement of this is what is meant by "a liberal education."

Primary and Secondary Sources. As the foregoing account of the general methods of research suggests, there is, ultimately, only one source of the truth about something—the thing, the event, or the phenomenon itself: the Stonehenge monuments, the Hungarian Revolt, or the Battle of Waterloo; the text of *Julius Cæsar* or *Death of a Salesman;* Robert Oppenheimer's testimony on the use of the atomic bomb against Japan; the motions of the planets or the circulation of blood; extrasensory perceptions or rats running in a maze. Such a source is a *primary* source. And, in historical research, where the thing itself (the Hungarian Revolt or the Battle of Waterloo) cannot be observed at first hand, a report of an eyewitness or a film or a tape recording is also counted as a *primary* source. But any other second-hand source (an interpretation of *Julius Cæsar* or *Death of a Salesman,* a treatise on astronomy, a report of an experiment with rats) is a *secondary* source.

A primary source is, of course, better. But, if a primary source is unavailable to you (if it is a book, perhaps your school library does not have it) or if you are not trained or equipped to use it (you don't know how to run rats through a maze or you have no telescope), then a secondary source must do. In any case, except for the most mature scientists and scholars, a good secondary source is useful and often indispensable.

It is worth noticing that being primary or being secondary is not an intrinsic characteristic of the source itself. It is, rather, a relationship that either exists or does not exist between a given source and a given topic of research. Consequently, a given source may be primary in relation to one given topic but secondary in relation to another. Two examples may serve to make this important point clear. Edward Gibbon's *The Decline and Fall of the Roman Empire* (1776-1788) is a secondary source in relation to the topic of the Roman Empire but a primary source in relation to that of eighteenth-century English prose style or that of eighteenth-century historiography. Samuel Taylor Coleridge's *Lectures on Shakespeare* (1811-1812) is a secondary source in relation to the topic of Shakespeare's plays but a primary source in relation to that of nineteenth-century principles of dramatic criticism or that of Shakespeare's reputation.

It is worth noticing also that a given source may be primary or secondary in relationship to more than one topic. James Joyce's novel *A Portrait of the Artist as a Young Man* is a primary source in relation not only to the topic of the structure of *A Portrait of the Artist as a Young Man* (and dozens of other topics on the novel itself) but also to the topic of use of the stream-of-consciousness technique in twentieth-century fiction.

THE RESEARCH PAPER

A research paper is a paper giving the results of research, the methods by which they were reached, and the sources, primary or secondary, which were used. A research paper attempts to tell the truth about a topic, and also tells how and where this truth was discovered. As we have seen, the sources of a research paper may be either written sources (literary texts and historical documents, for example) or sources of other kinds (experiments, for example). Since a research paper written in school is almost always based upon written (printed) sources, we shall here discuss only that kind. A research paper based upon written sources may be either a library-research paper or a controlled-research paper. A library-research paper is a research paper for which your search for sources is limited to those sources contained in the libraries available to you; a controlled-research paper, to those sources contained in one anthology —to those contained in this volume, for example. Here we shall emphasize the latter kind.

Finding Your Topic. The first step in writing a research paper based upon written sources, whether a library-research or a controlled-research paper, is finding a topic. We say "finding a topic" rather than "choosing a topic" because the process is more like finding a job than choosing a sandwich from a menu. Unless your instructor assigns you a topic, which he may do, you must look for one; and the one you find may not be just what you want but the best one that you can find. But, if you look long and carefully, you may find a topic that so well suits your interests, your capacities, and the time and the space at your disposal that your paper will almost surely be a success.

Finding a topic is the most important single step in writing a research paper, and the things that you should have in mind when looking for a topic are (1) your interests, (2) your capacities, and (3) the time and the space at your disposal. If you are interested in a topic, if you know something about the special methods of research that the topic requires, and if your topic is narrow enough to require no more time than you have for research and no greater development than you can give it in a paper of the length assigned you, then the paper that results will probably be satisfactory. For example, the topic of figures of speech in *Julius Cæsar* may interest you greatly. But, if it does, you must ask yourself whether you know enough about figures of speech to do research on them

and, if you do, whether this topic is narrow enough. Even the topic of metaphors in the play would be too broad for most papers; metaphors in Brutus' soliloquies might be about right. In any case, before you take a topic for a paper, you should do some reading on that topic; otherwise, you won't know whether it is interesting, within your ability to handle, and within the scope of your assigned paper.

Once you think that you've found a topic, take great care in phrasing it. The best phrasing is a question or a series of closely related questions. Better than "The character of Brutus" is "To what extent is Brutus motivated by self-interest and to what extent by the public interest?" The latter is not only more narrow and more precise; it provides you with a criterion of relevance in selecting your sources. At the end of this volume, you will find a list of suggested topics, intended to call your attention to topics that might not occur to you. But these topics are suggestive rather than definitive or precise.

Finding Your Sources. Finding sources for a library-research paper and finding ones for a controlled-research paper, though different in several respects, are alike in certain others. Finding sources in the library requires knowledge of how to use the card catalogue, periodical indexes, special bibliographies, reserve shelves, and encyclopedias. Finding sources in this volume or a similar one does not. But, in either case, you must have a clear idea of what you are looking for; and you must be prepared to put up with a high ratio of looking to finding. In other words, you must have not only criteria of relevance but also a willingness to do a good deal of skimming and a good deal more of careful reading, some of it fruitless.

The basic criterion of relevance you provide by careful phrasing of your topic, a problem discussed in the preceding section. The other criteria you provide by making a preliminary or tentative outline —perhaps in the form of subtopics, perhaps in the form of questions. Such an outline is not to be used for your paper. The outline for your paper will probably be quite different and, in any event, cannot be made until after you find your sources and take your notes. This preliminary outline guides your research and, as we shall see, provides you with the subtopic headings necessary for your note-cards (see "Taking Your Notes," page v).

Making Your Working Bibliography. Once you have found a promising source ("promising" because, though it seems to be relevant, it may turn out not to be) you want to make some record of it so that, once you have completed your search for sources, you can turn back to it, read it, and, if it turns out to be relevant, take notes on it. This record of promising sources is your *working* bibliography. It is so called for two reasons: first, because you work with it as you proceed with your research and the writing of your paper, adding promising sources to it and discarding irrelevant ones; and, second, because this designation distinguishes it from your final bibliography, which appears at the very end of your research paper and contains only sources actually used in the paper. For a controlled-research paper, your working bibliography may be nothing more elaborate than a series of check marks in the table of contents of your research anthology or a list of page numbers. For a library-research paper, however, you need something quite different.

A working bibliography for a library-research paper is a collection of three-by-five cards each representing a promising source and each containing full information about that source. Once you have completed your research, written your paper, and discarded all promising but (as they turned out) irrelevant sources, this bibliography is identical with your final bibliography. Having a separate card for each source enables you to add and to discard sources easily and to sort and arrange them easily in any order you please. Eventually, when this bibliography becomes identical with your final bibliography, you will arrange sources alphabetically by authors' last names. Having full information about each source on its card enables you to turn back to it easily—to locate it in the library without first looking it up again. You find this information in the card catalogue, periodical indexes, or other bibliographical aids; or, when browsing through the shelves or the stacks of the library and coming upon a promising source, you find it in or on the source itself—for example, on the spine and the title page of a book.

If the source is a *book,* you should put the following information on the three-by-five working-bibliography card:

(1) the library call number,
(2) the author's (or authors') full name (or names), last name first for the first author,
(3) the title of the book,
(4) the name of the city of publication,
(5) the name of the publisher (*not* the printer), and
(6) the year of publication (often found on the other side of the title page).

See the example of such a card on the opposite page (note the punctuation carefully).

If the source is a *periodical article,* you should put the following information on the three-by-five working-bibliography card:

(1) the author's (or authors') full name (or names),
(2) the title of the article,
(3) the name of the periodical,
(4) the volume number,
(5) the week, the month, or the season of publication, together with the year, and
(6) the page numbers covered by the article.

See the example of such a card on the opposite page (note the punctuation carefully).

These two forms take care of the two standard cases. For special cases—such things as books with editors or translators as well as authors, books published in several editions or in several volumes, and daily newspapers—see any good handbook of composition.

860.3
J23

Jones, John A., and William C.
Brown. <u>A History of
Serbia</u>. New York: The
Rowland Press, Inc., 1934.

WORKING-BIBLIOGRAPHY CARD FOR A BOOK

Smith, Harold B. "Fishing
in Serbian Waters." <u>Journal
of Balkan Sports</u>, <u>VII</u>
(May, 1936), 26-32.

WORKING-BIBLIOGRAPHY CARD FOR A PERIODICAL ARTICLE

Taking Your Notes. Once you have found sources, entered them in your working bibliography, read them, and found them relevant, taking notes requires your exactly following a standard procedure if your notes are going to be useful to you when you come to write your paper. An extra five minutes given to taking a note correctly can save you a half hour in writing your paper. Here is the standard procedure:

(1) Take all notes on four-by-six cards. Never use notebooks, loose sheets of paper, or backs of old envelopes.

(2) Limit each note to information on a single subtopic of your preliminary outline *and* from a single source. It follows from this that you may have many cards on the same subtopic and many cards from the same source but that you may never have one card on more than one subtopic or from more than one source.

(3) On each card, in addition to the note itself, put

  (a) the appropriate subtopic heading in the upper left-hand corner,

  (b) the name of the source (usually the author's last name will do) in the upper right-hand corner, and

  (c) the page number (or numbers) of that part (or those parts) of the source that you have used in taking your note. If you have used more than one page, indicate your page numbers in such a way that, when you come to write your paper, you can tell what page each part of the note comes from, for you may not use the whole note.

(If you follow these first three rules, you will be able, when you come to outline and to organize your paper, to sort your notes in any way you please—by subtopic, for example—and to arrange them in any order you please. Such flexibility is impossible if you take your notes in a notebook. If you follow the third rule, you will also be able to document your paper—write footnotes, for example—without again referring to the sources themselves.)

(4) In taking the note itself, paraphrase or quote your source or do both; but do only one at a time, and use quotation very sparingly.

Paraphrase and quotation require special care. Anything between paraphrase and quotation is not acceptable to good writers: you either paraphrase or quote, but do nothing in between. To paraphrase a source (or part of a source) is to reproduce it in words and word orders substantially different from the original. When you paraphrase well, you keep the sense of the original but change the language,

retaining some key words, of course, but otherwise using your own words and your own sentence patterns. To quote a source (or part of a source) is to reproduce it exactly. When you quote well, you keep both the sense and the language of the original, retaining its punctuation, its capitalization, its type face (roman or italic), and its spelling (indeed, even its misspelling).

Omissions and additions require special care. If, when quoting, you wish to omit some of the original, you may do so only if the omission does not change the sense of the original (never leave out a "not," for example! *and* if it is indicated by ellipses (three spaced periods: ". . ."). If you wish to add something to the original, you may do so only if the addition does not change the sense of the original (never add a "not"!) *and* it is indicated by square brackets. The most usual additions are explanations ("They [i.e., the people of Paris] were alarmed") and disclaimers of errors in the original, indicated by the Latin *"sic,"* meaning "thus" (Colombis [*sic*] discovered America in 1592 [*sic*]"). You must, of course, carry these ellipses and square brackets from your note-cards to your paper. And, if you type your paper, brackets may be a problem, for most typewriter keyboards do not include them. If your keyboard does not, you may do one of two things—either use the slash ("/") and underlining ("__" and "—") in such a way as to produce a bracket ("⌐" and "⌐") or draw brackets in with a pen. In any event, don't substitute parentheses for brackets.

In your paper, quotations no longer than three or four lines are to be enclosed within a set of quotation marks and run into your text; longer ones are to be set off from the text, without quotation marks, by indention from the left-hand margin and, especially in typewritten copy, by single-spacing. But never use either of these devices unless the language is exactly that of the original.

Your usual treatment of a source should be paraphrase; use quotation only if the